TRAINING YOUR
PET GUINEA PIG

Gerry Bucsis
Barbara Somerville

BARRON'S

Dedication

This book is dedicated to all the guinea pigs that will have better lives because their owners read this book.

Note of Warning

This book deals with the keeping and training of guinea pigs as pets. In working with these animals, you may occasionally sustain scratches or bites. Administer first aid immediately, and seek medical attention if necessary.

Guinea pigs MUST be provided with a large habitat, as cramped living conditions can lead to stress and illness. Supervise your guinea pigs during any out-of-the-cage playtime, and to avoid life-threatening accidents, be particularly careful that your pets do not gnaw on electrical cords, plastic, or small objects. Handle your guinea pigs carefully; they can sustain spinal and other severe injuries if handled incorrectly.

To prevent serious medical problems, it is essential that you provide your guinea pigs with an adequate source of Vitamin C on a daily basis; consult a veterinarian for advice on the correct daily dosage. Guinea pigs can be carriers of serious or even life-threatening diseases that can spread to other guinea pigs, sometimes even to people and other animals. So observe a recommended quarantine period before exposing a new guinea pig to your resident guinea pigs, and always wash your hands thoroughly when handling any ill or quarantined guinea pig. Observe a strict hand-washing protocol after handling any guinea pigs that aren't resident in your home. At the first sign of illness, take your guinea pig to a veterinarian. Also consult your veterinarian for advice on proper nutrition, care, and husbandry for your guinea pigs.

Disclaimer

The information provided in this book is designed to provide helpful information on the keeping, care, husbandry, and training of guinea pigs as pets. Any material, information, text, graphics, illustrations, and/or photos in this book may contain technical inaccuracies, mistakes, errors, omissions, and typographical errors, both in content and presentation. In no event shall the authors or publisher be liable for any errors or omissions with respect to any information contained within this text. Information found in this book should not be relied upon for personal, medical, legal, or financial decisions, and you should consult an appropriate professional for specific advice tailored to your specific situation. The information in this book is provided on an "AS IS" basis without warranties or conditions of any kind, either expressed or implied, including, but not limited to, non-infringement or implied warranties of merchantability or of fitness for a particular purpose. There shall be no liability whatsoever on the part of Barron's Educational Series, Inc., or the authors, for any indirect, punitive, incidental, special, or consequential damages, or any damages whatsoever, arising out of the use of, or inability to use, the information contained within this book.

Acknowledgments

- To our families for their support and understanding.
- To each other: for lots of fun times, laughter, and encouragement. There's never a dull moment when we're writing together!
- To our photography models: Allison, Alexis, and Marzipanda; Sue, Alyssa, Ricky, and Floyd; and, Melanie, Sophie, and Daisy.
- Thanks to Gary for his two-cents worth!
- To the following individuals and companies for their help and cooperation:
  - Bee Line Signs, Welland, ON
  - Jason Casto, Super Pet, Pets International, Inc.
  - Rolf C. Hagen, Inc.
  - Ron Leavens, Pet Valu, Fonthill, ON
- Photos on pages back cover, 31, 34, 36, 40, 54, and 100 from Shutterstock. All other photos are by Gerry Bucsis and Barbara Somerville.
- Products on the following pages are courtesy of Super Pet, Pets International, Inc.: viii, 2, 6, 8, 10, 11, 12, 14, 17, 22, 24, 26, 32, 35, 39, 41, 44, 45, 46, 47, 48, 49, 55, 56, 58, 60, 61, 66, 74, 77, 79, 80, 93, and 96.
- Products on the following pages are courtesy of Rolf. C. Hagen, Inc.: 95
- Products on the following pages are courtesy of Bee Line Signs, Welland, ON: 5, 8, 14, 25, 26, and 50
- The StarMark clicker seen in the photos is used with the consent of Triple Crown Dog Academy, Inc.

All inquiries should be addressed to:
Barron's Educational Series, Inc.
250 Wireless Boulevard
Hauppauge, New York 11788
www.barronseduc.com

Library of Congress Catalog Card No. 2011007731
ISBN: 978-0-7641-4625-1

Library of Congress Cataloging-in-Publication Data
Bucsis, Gerry.
    Training your pet guinea pig/Gerry Bucsis, Barbara Somerville.
        p. cm.
    Includes bibliographical references and index.
    ISBN 978-0-7641-4625-1 (pbk.)
    1. Guinea pigs as pets. 2. Guinea pigs—training.
I. Somerville, Barbara. II. Title.
    SF459.G9B84 2011
    636.935'92—dc22   2011007731

Printed in China
9 8 7 6 5

Contents

Introduction

Are you already a proud guinea pig owner? Or are you thinking of making guinea pigs part of your family? Congratulations! These friendly little animals make wonderful family pets that develop a strong bond with their owners.

Guinea pigs—also known as cavies because of their scientific name *Cavia porcellus*—are ideal pets for today's busy lifestyles. They take short naps throughout the day and night, so matching your schedule with theirs shouldn't be a problem. Unlike hamsters that sleep all day and can get sick or aggressive if disturbed, cavies are ready to play when you are.

As an added bonus, guinea pigs are a lot easier on the pocketbook than most other pets. For starters, they don't cost much. And, if you have any do-it-yourself skills, their housing won't cost much either. You can build a first-rate, super-sized cage with materials that are readily available at local stores or on the Internet. Upkeep costs are very reasonable, too. Food, fresh water, and unlimited hay won't break the bank, and bedding costs can be minimal, depending on what you choose.

If you haven't owned a guinea pig before, here's something to think about. Cavies are much more vocal than other small pets; they have an extensive vocabulary of wheeks, squeals, purrs, coos, gurgles, and chirps. Although many people find these sounds endearing, other people find them annoying. Even if you enjoy the wheeking during the day, it could keep you awake at night, unless you're very careful about cage placement.

A pro or a con, depending on how you look at it, is that guinea pigs live approximately two or three times longer than other small rodents such as hamsters, gerbils, or rats. A cavy is likely to be with you for five to eight years, and maybe even longer. It is important to keep this in mind when considering a cavy as a pet.

Once you've made guinea pigs part of your life, you'll soon realize that they're quite intelligent and easy to train. But why would you even want to train a guinea pig? First, when you're teaching new skills to a cavy, you're challenging it physically and mentally. What a great way to improve your pet's quality of life! Second, training time equals bonding time. During training sessions, you're spending quality time with your guinea pig, and that's never a bad thing!

Chapter One

Preparations Come First

Getting ready for your guinea pig

Are you looking at pet possibilities? Is a guinea pig high on your list? Before making any commitment, stop and think. How much do you really know about guinea pigs? Do you have any idea what they eat and what type of housing they need? Are you familiar with their playtime requirements? And, what do you know about their behavior?

If you're not sure about these guinea pig basics, you have some homework to do. Fortunately, there's plenty of information available. You can read books, check out Internet sites, talk to staff at a pet store, visit local breeders, and contact other owners. The important thing to remember when you're looking for a pet is that impulse buying is "out" and research is "in." Make sure you learn everything you can about any potential pet *before* deciding if it's the right one for you.

So now the research is done and the decision is made...a guinea pig (or two or three) is going to be part of your family! You're probably anxious to dash right out and make that pet purchase ASAP. But wait! There's other shopping to be done first. Have you forgotten that you'll need a cage, accessories, food, bedding, and toys all ready at home before picking out your pal(s)?

A cavy-friendly cage

Guinea pigs spend a lot of time in their cages, but they get stressed if their living quarters are cramped. If you want to have a happy, healthy guinea pig—one that will be a stellar student—it's very important to get the right size cage. What is the right size cage? Think big, big, big! When cage shopping, your motto should be: the bigger, the better.

In the past, the recommended habitat space per guinea pig was

1

To be happy and healthy, guinea pigs need a big cage.

kit, or a homemade habitat, price is probably going to be a factor. A good-sized cage might cost more than you're expecting, so look into all of your options. If you can't afford something suitable, put off your pet purchase until you've saved enough for a cavy-friendly cage.

Commercial cages

If you take a list of the recommended cage sizes along with you to the pet store, you're soon going to realize that it's difficult to find a cage big enough for one cavy, let alone for several. Even if you look at all the possibilities available online, you won't find many suitably sized cages.

There are a few commercially available cages in the 7.5 to 8 square feet (2.3–2.4 sq m) range, approximately 30 × 36 in. (75 × 90 cm) or 24 × 48 in. (60 × 120 cm). But these are about the largest guinea pig cages you'll find on the market right now, though larger sizes might become available in the future.

What if you've already bought a cage and now realize it's too small? You could always keep it as a "quarantine cage" for any of your guinea pigs that get sick. You could also use it as temporary housing for your piggies when cleaning out their new, larger cage, or make it part of an expanded cage system by linking it to a larger living area (see *Multi-level cages and extensions*).

only 2 square feet. This translates into a cage that is about 12 × 24 inches (30 × 60 cm) for one guinea pig. Can you imagine that? That would be like you being cooped up in a small bathroom all of your life! Fortunately, today's standards are much more generous and humane.

The recommended roam-room for a single guinea pig is now a minimum of 7.5 to 8 square feet (2.3–2.4 sq m). Two cavies need at least 10.5 square feet (3.2 sq m), three guinea pigs need a minimum of 13.5 square feet (4.1 sq m), and four piggies need around 16 square feet (4.9 sq m). But remember, these are only the minimum requirements. It's always better to provide the biggest cage you can afford and have space for in your home.

Whether you're looking at a store-bought cage, a cage from a

Build-it-yourself cages

If you're having trouble finding a large enough store-bought cage, don't worry. It doesn't take much skill to make a cage yourself. And you'll be happy to know that some of the very best guinea pig cages are owner-designed and built. Fortunately, you don't have to start completely from scratch when making a do-it-yourself cage; you can make a first-rate cavy habitat by putting together a combination of store-bought items.

The first item you'll need is corrugated plastic, better known as coroplast, which is used to make an easy-clean floor for the cage. Coroplast sheets come in a variety of colors, so you can match the cage to your décor or make it a distinct conversation piece. The second item you'll need is wire-cube shelving, which is used to make the walls of the enclosure. This shelving comes in black, white, and a limited number of colors. With these two products, it's fairly cheap to build what's known as a C&C (cubes and coroplast) cage for your cavies.

The wire-cube shelving is sold under several brand names. It comes in packages containing anywhere from 16 to 40-plus wire-grid panels, along with plastic connectors for joining the panels together. When you go shelf shopping, look for the 14-inch (35 cm) square panels rather than the 15-inch (38 cm) square panels because the spaces in the 15-inch (38 cm) panels are larger, and small-sized guinea pigs could escape through them. Packages of wire-cube shelving are pretty easy to find; department stores, bed-and-bath stores, discount warehouses, and office supply stores all carry them. They're also widely available on the Internet—just google "wire cube shelving." However, if you order from the Internet, the delivery costs could be expensive unless your order qualifies for free shipping.

The coroplast might be harder to find. Your best bet is to look for it in sign shops. You could also look for it in hobby/craft stores or in some home improvement stores. None in stock? Ask if it can be ordered for you.

It's easy to find coroplast sheets on the Internet, but be prepared to pay an arm and a leg for delivery. A sheet large enough to make a suitable cage (4 × 8 feet/1.2 × 2.4 m) is classed as "oversized"

and requires special shipping. You could, however, ask to have a sheet scored (not cut) and folded, so that it would fit into a smaller package for cheaper shipping.

One last item for your shopping list is a bag of small cable ties, lock ties, or zip ties. These ties will be used to connect the wire grids together to form the walls of the cage. The wire-cube shelving does come with plastic connectors, but these connectors are not strong enough on their own to make a sturdy guinea pig habitat.

Once you have your materials on hand, the next step is to assemble the cage.

Assembly time

The easy part of cage construction is erecting the walls. Just stand the grids up, and join them together with the plastic connectors to form a fence-like rectangle. The number of grids you need depends on how large a cage you're planning to make. For example, if you want to make a cage approximately 28 inches (70 cm) wide × 84 inches (210 cm) long, you'll need sixteen grids: two grids for each short side and six grids for each long side. At this point, use the plastic connectors rather than the lock ties to join the grids, because if you change your mind about the size of the cage or the layout, it's easy to pop off the connectors and reconfigure the walls.

If you're going to place the cage on the floor, you can skip this paragraph and go straight to the next one. However, if you're going to place the cage on a desk or a table, you need to buy extra grids to make a wire base for the cage. Why? Sometimes a cage on a table can get knocked or nudged. If it's nudged in such a way that two adjoining sides end up hanging over the table, the whole cage will come crashing down—guinea pigs and all. To prevent this disaster, you need to make a wire bottom for any cage that's going to be placed on a table. To do this, just zip-tie some grids together to make a flat base. Then, put the base on the table, set the grid walls on top of the base, and zip-tie everything together. Picture a big shoe box made out of grid panels to get the idea of what this will look like.

The next step is to make a coroplast tray for the cage. This involves cutting and scoring the coroplast, and forming it into a shallow box shape that will fit inside the wire-grid walls. In order to figure out how large a piece of coroplast you'll need, first measure the inside dimensions of the wire-grid rectangle you've just made, and then add 12 inches (30 cm) to the length and 12 inches (30 cm) to the width. Why add the extra inches? It's because they'll be needed to form a 6-inch (15 cm) side all around the coroplast tray. This mini wall is important because it keeps hay and bedding inside the cage.

Now, mark these measurements onto the coroplast using a felt-tip pen and a ruler. Next, trim the coroplast along the marked lines with a utility knife or sturdy scissors. Then, using your pen and ruler, draw a six-inch (15 cm) border all the way around the trimmed coroplast. Now comes the hard part—you have to score the coroplast all along the lines you've just marked out. Scoring means cutting the plastic partway through with a utility knife or razor blade. Be very careful; you don't want to cut all the way through (see photo).

You'll notice that your marked lines intersect at each corner of the coroplast to form a 6-inch square (15 cm) (see photo). Cut right through one line of each square. Now flip the coroplast over, and fold up the scored parts to form a box. Tape the corners securely with good quality duct tape or vinyl-coated cloth tape. What you've just made is a shallow tray with 6-inch (15 cm) sides. Set the tray inside the wire walls and presto—you have an inexpensive, spacious guinea pig cage! The last step is to reinforce all the adjoining grid sections with zip ties (top, bottom, and center). This gives the walls added strength. Be sure to trim those zip ties so that you and the piggies don't get scratched.

If you have space for an even larger cage—one that will allow you to use the whole sheet of coroplast without trimming off any part of it—stick with six grids for the long walls, but use three grids for the

When scoring the coroplast, be careful not to cut right through it.

short walls. The third grid at each short end will have to overlap the second grid and be secured to it with zip ties.

What about a lid or cover for the cage? Since guinea pigs aren't champion high jumpers, you don't really need to add a lid. But if you have other pets, such as a cat or a dog, you should top the cage with a cover to keep your cavies safe. Two lengths of epoxy-coated wire closet

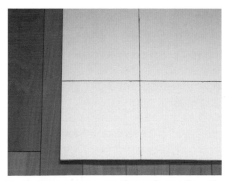

To make a corner, cut through one line of each square.

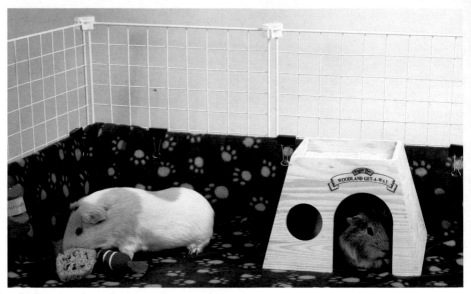

A C&C cage makes the best guinea pig habitat.

shelving will make a fine cover. The length of the cage will determine how long the pieces of shelving need to be. If the shelving overlaps the cage by a few inches, you won't have to bother cutting it. But, if it's longer and needs to be trimmed, use bolt cutters or a hacksaw, and cap the rough edges with plastic end caps. Join the two pieces of shelving together lengthwise with zip ties, and set this homemade lid on top of the cage. If you want to secure the lid to the cage, hook on a few bungee cords.

When you're building a do-it-yourself cage, the easiest type to make is a rectangular one. But if you're really handy, why not browse the Internet or go on YouTube to get ideas and instructions for more elaborate L-shaped or multi-level designs? Let your imagination run wild! For serious do-it-yourselfers, a custom-made guinea pig cage can be a really fun project.

Prepackaged kits

Are you too time-strapped to be getting into cage construction? Or is D-I-Y not your thing? Not a problem! Your cavies can still have the large C&C cage they deserve, but with someone else doing most of the work.

Yes, some enterprising individuals have come up with designs, worked out the measurements, assembled the materials, scored and cut the coroplast, and packaged everything you need into a convenient kit form. All that's left for you is a simple assembly job; just follow the directions enclosed in the kit. How cool is that?

Where can you find one of these kits? Do a Google search for "buy a C&C guinea pig cage," or an eBay search for "guinea pig cages." You'll find everything from the most basic to the most upscale guinea pig housing. If you go the eBay route, be sure to check the "see other items" link on each site that you access. This way, you'll find all the different cage shapes and sizes that a seller offers. Don't forget to check the shipping charges, too!

Multi-level cages and extensions

Which is better for your cavies: a single-level cage or a multi-story cage? What you don't want is the traditional multi-story pet condo, which has several levels, each of them having very limited floor space. The ideal guinea pig cage should have as much floor space as possible. Guinea pigs like to run "piggy laps" around the cage, so the more room they have to run around on the main floor, the better. It is, however, perfectly fine to add a second story as long as you provide an adequate lower floor. But if you go this route, there are some safety issues to keep in mind.

In some C&C cage kits, the second story of the cage is the same size as the first story; in other words, it's a complete floor. But most owners design the second story as a loft that overlooks the first floor. If this is the design you go with, you'll have to make sure the loft is enclosed or has a barrier along the open side so your cavies can't fall over the edge onto the floor below.

How do you design a safe second story? There are lots of ways to do this. Your best plan is to search the Internet or browse YouTube. You'll be amazed at how many innovative designs other enterprising guinea pig owners have come up with. Think you've found a blueprint for the perfect second story? Great! Just make sure it will be sturdy enough and safe enough for your cavies.

Your next concern will be how your cavies are going to get up to the second floor. Gently sloping ramps are the way to go here; guinea pigs won't walk on anything too steep. You can buy ready-made ramps, or you can make them yourself. The most popular ones are constructed from coroplast or from wire grids. If you're using coroplast, you'll need to reinforce it. For example, you could duct-tape a piece of wire grid to the back to make the coroplast ramp sturdier. You should also cover it with a piece of fleece or carpet for better traction.

If you're making a ramp out of a wire grid, use your knee or your foot to bend it into a U-shape; this will provide protective sides for the ramp. You can also bend it into an L-shape. Then, if you place it

Toys and chewies can be hung on the grid wires of C&C cages.

placing a line of small treats up the ramp and onto the second level. Most guinea pigs will be so focused on the food that they'll be up the ramp in no time.

If you have plenty of space, why not give your cavies extra romp room by adding a playroom extension to the cage? For an addition like this, all you need is a cheap kiddie pool made of hard plastic, wire grids connected with zip ties to form a fence around the pool, a section of 4-inch (10 cm) diameter PVC piping to join the pool to the cage, and a few paving bricks for steps at either end of the PVC pipe. Instead of a pool, you could always substitute the smaller cage you were using before you switched to a C&C cage.

Prime location

Any suitably sized guinea pig cage is going to take up quite a bit of floor space in your home, so there will probably be a limited number of places where one will fit. And, for a healthy environment, the cage needs to be out of drafts, away from direct sunlight, and away from heating and cooling vents. Family rooms, living rooms, and dining rooms are usually the best spots. It's not advisable to put the cage in a bathroom or a laundry room because the humidity levels can be too high there.

What about a bedroom? If your teenager is bugging you to let her have Ms. Wheeky as her room-

against an outside cage wall, you will have made a ramp with even higher protective sides. Whatever wire-grid design you choose, be sure to cover the ramp with a piece of low-pile rug or mat. Never let your guinea pigs walk directly on wire because it's very bad for their feet.

You could also be creative and use sisal-covered cat-scratching boards as ramps. These can be attached to the upper floor by drilling holes at the top of the scratching board and using zip ties to secure the ramp to the second story.

Some guinea pigs run up and down ramps just fine; others are more timid and might need encouragement. To train a timid cavy, try mate, should you give her the go-ahead? Probably not. Guinea pigs don't sleep through the night; they tend to take short naps around the clock. They're also very vocal pets, so a light sleeper could have problems adjusting to a guinea pig roommate. There's another point to consider, too. Remember the old saying "out of sight, out of mind"? A guinea pig housed in a bedroom could be unintentionally neglected.

Bedding basics

Before popping your cavies into their new home, you need to cover the bottom of the cage with some sort of flooring or bedding, because the plastic floor of a cage is not guinea pig friendly. It's not soft enough for your pets to walk on or sleep on, and it won't absorb your guinea pigs' urine. So, before going any further, you have some bedding decisions to make.

Unfortunately, where guinea pigs are concerned, bedding basics are *not* so basic! There are lots of choices out there, and it might take some trial and error on your part to find out what works best for you and your piggies.

You shouldn't even consider some of the bedding products that are available. For example, stay away from cedar, pine, sawdust, cat litter, corn cob, straw, and newspaper. Cedar and pine contain phenols that can cause liver and respiratory problems in small ani-

mals. Sawdust and cat litter are too dusty. Corncob bedding and straw get moldy quickly; neither absorbs urine or controls odor well, and some guinea pigs eat corncob bedding. Newspaper used by itself is a very poor choice—it gets wet from urine and stays wet.

So what *should* you use? Wood pulp fiber is one of the most popular choices because it's soft and fluffy—comfy for your cavy to walk on and cozy for it to sleep on. It's also good for absorbency and odor control. However, it's fairly expensive. Paper pellets are a bit cheaper, but your cavy won't find them as comfortable as the fluffy stuff. Hardwood pellets, such as aspen, are another possibility. For a cheaper option, you could look for bulk hardwood stove pellets—just make sure they don't have any chemical additives. Any of these wood pellets are good for absorbency and odor control, but like paper pellets, they're a bit lacking in the comfort department. Hardwood shavings are softer, but they're messier and less absorbent.

Some owners find that they get the best results by using two layers of commercial bedding. For example, they might put aspen pellets on the bottom of the cage for absorbency and top these with a layer of wood pulp fiber or hay for comfort.

Since guinea pigs need large cages, the cost of packaged bedding can really add up over time. Nowadays, lots of guinea pig owners are getting away from packaged pet bedding and are using fabric instead. Non-pilling polyester fleece—the thicker the better—is the fabric of choice because it's soft and wicks away pet urine. Some people buy a piece just large enough to cover the coroplast floor of the cage. Other people buy a piece big enough to go up and over the sides as well. Then, they secure the fleece to the sides with binder clips to keep it in place.

Fleece by itself doesn't make a good fabric floor; you also need a layer of material under the fleece to absorb the wicked-away urine. There are lots of different absorbent materials you can use, such as thick cotton towels, microfiber towels, washable hospital pads, washable or disposable pet/puppy pads, waterproof crib pads, or thick layers of polyester quilt batting. You could also go to a fabric shop and buy some waterproof mattress padding by the yard. You can even layer a couple of different materials for maximum absorbency and odor control. For example, if you put folded towels under the fleece, and washable hospital pads under the towels, your guinea pigs' environment will stay super dry.

Another convenient option is to buy one of the ready-made triple-layered bedspreads that are specially designed to fit the coroplast trays of C&C cages. Or, you can buy one of the fitted fleece sheets made for C&C cages and provide your own absorbent material for underneath the fleece. These colorful bedspreads and sheets can also be custom-made for odd-sized cages.

Although the initial cost of fabric bedding can be fairly high, most of this bedding is washable and reusable, so over time it will be a

A fleece floor is cozy and comfy.

lot cheaper than the throw-away commercial pet bedding. Be sure to wash the fleece three or four times before using it so that it becomes soft and absorbent. When it's cleanup time, shake off or vacuum up the feces and hair, then machine wash the bedding in hot water, using scent-free detergent and a little vinegar, but no fabric softener—fabric softener reduces absorbency. Then tumble dry without dryer sheets. To avoid excessive static, remove the fleece from the dryer while it is still slightly damp, and let it air dry. Here's a handy hint: it's a good idea to buy a larger piece of fabric than you need, because hot water and the hot air of a dryer can sometimes shrink the fleece.

How often will you need to wash the bedding? This depends on how many guinea pigs you have and how sensitive your nose is!

A hidey house is a must

In the wild, guinea pigs have many predators, and their only defense is to run away and hide. Domestic guinea pigs share this built-in fear of predators, so they need a hidey house or two in their cage where they can hole up and feel safe. Cavies also use a hidey house when they want to feel relaxed or stress-free, or when they want to be alone. For the ins and outs of hideaways, see Chapter 9.

A vet for your pet

Guinea pigs don't need yearly vaccinations, but if you think this means they never need to see a veterinarian, think again. Like other pets, cavies should have a yearly examination so that any potential problems can be caught early and treated.

Don't procrastinate when it comes to finding a vet. Since emergencies can happen in the blink of an eye, you should have a veterinarian lined up from day one. Call the pet clinics in your area and find out which ones take guinea pig patients. This is important because not all vets have experience in treating cavies.

As soon as you find a veterinarian, start putting aside a little money every month into a "vet fund." This way, you'll always have money on hand for any medical emergencies that crop up.

Chapter Two

Good Nutrition Is Important for Lifelong Learning

Healthy body, healthy mind

For training purposes, you want your guinea pigs to be in tip-top condition—lively, alert, and raring to go! The best way to ensure this is by providing them with a well-balanced and nutritious diet.

Some guinea pig pellets are more nutritious than others. Do your research!

One thing is for sure…guinea pigs *love* to eat. And eat. And eat. And eat. But they can also be picky eaters and will often turn up their noses at something unfamiliar. So, it's a good idea to introduce them to a variety of good foods at an early age. This way, they won't develop poor eating habits.

Since guinea pigs are strict vegetarians (herbivores), meat and dairy products shouldn't be on their menu. Instead, your pet's daily diet should consist of guinea pig pellets and hay for breakfast, lunch, dinner, and snacks, along with a varied selection of vegetables and fruits.

Nutrition basics

Commercial guinea pig pellets should be the main staple of your cavies' diet, and they should be freely available to your pets at all times. But not all pellets are created equal. What you want are high-quality pellets that are free of dyes and additives. Avoid pellet mixtures that include seeds, nuts, and dried fruits because your pets will pick out these yummy bits instead of eating the pellets. Also, those high-fat and high-sugar ingredients can cause health problems for your cavies. Stay away, too, from brands that contain sweeteners or have corn or corn by-products as one of the main ingredients. And, never substitute rabbit pellets if you run out of guinea pig pellets, as they don't contain the vitamin C that is absolutely essential for cavies.

Young cavies and pregnant cavies should be given alfalfa-based pellets, which are higher in calcium and protein; adult guinea pigs thrive best on timothy hay–based pellets. Whatever pellets you're buying, make sure they're fresh. This is because the vitamin C that's vital to guinea pig health (see next section) loses its potency quickly. Pellets have a shelf life of about 90 days after being manufactured, so always check the "best before" date on the package, and use up all the pellets by that date. However, pellets that have *stabilized* vitamin C as an ingredient last a lot longer…anywhere from 12 to 24 months. Whichever pellets you buy, store them in a cool, dry cupboard because vitamin C degrades when exposed to light.

Pellets can be served in heavy ceramic bowls or in J-feeders. The problem with bowls is that guinea pigs like to sit in them and are perfectly happy to use their food bowl as a toilet bowl. Yuck! Then they'll

refuse to eat the soiled food. So, if you have a bowl-sitter, get a J-feeder. What if one of your cavies keeps nudging the others away from the food? You'll have to get an additional bowl or J-feeder so no little piggy goes hungry.

The other staple of a guinea pig's diet is fresh hay. A cavy must have hay on a daily basis, and it should be available 24/7. Hay is an important part of your pet's diet for three reasons. First, it provides good nutrition. Second, it provides roughage that aids digestion. Third, it gives your pet something to chomp and chew on, and this prevents your cavy's teeth from becoming overgrown.

There are lots of different types of hay, but the most readily available are timothy and alfalfa. Timothy hay is best for adult guinea pigs,

Hay racks are handy, but not for young or small guinea pigs; they can get their heads stuck.

A vital vitamin

Guinea pigs need vitamin C to survive. Unfortunately, their bodies don't manufacture it, so they have to get it in other ways. The first way is through a well-balanced diet. Guinea pig pellets fortified with vitamin C are good for starters, but pellets alone don't provide enough vitamin C on a daily basis. So, you'll have to supplement them with a variety of fresh foods. Cavy-friendly foods that are rich in vitamin C include bell peppers (especially red and orange ones), kale, mustard greens, parsley, guava, kiwis, and strawberries. Broccoli, brussels sprouts, cauliflower, and cabbage are also rich in vitamin C, but these cruciferous vegetables can cause bloating and gas, so offer them in small amounts only once or twice a week, or as occasional treats.

The second way to ensure that your pets are getting enough vitamin C is to add a supplement to their diet. The easiest way to do this is to buy made-for-guinea-pig vitamin C tablets and follow the directions. Liquid vitamin C is also available; some brands are given by mouth, while others are added to water. Don't buy the kind that is added to drinking water, because some guinea pigs don't like the taste and will absolutely refuse to drink the water. Another possibility is to buy made-for-people vitamin C liquid, powder, or chewable tablets. But if you go this route, you'll need to get guidance from your veterinarian

while alfalfa—with its higher protein, calcium, and carbohydrate levels—is best for pregnant, nursing, and young cavies. And how do you serve up the hay? The most obvious answer is to buy a hay rack or wheel and set it up in the cage. Or, you could fill an empty tissue box with hay.

Cavies are crazy about hay. For them, it's not just food; a hay pile is also a place to play and a place to sleep. So, some owners designate the second level of their cavy's cage as a hay loft, while other owners design the habitat to include a "hay playground" that is separate from the main part of the cage. Still others cover the whole cage floor with hay. Whichever way you go, always use fresh hay, and change it often so that it doesn't have a chance to get smelly and moldy.

about the proper dosage for your cavies.

Given the importance of vitamin C in your cavy's diet, why not use fruits and veggies that have high levels of this vital vitamin as training rewards? You can't go wrong with these treats…they're cheap, readily available, and nutritious.

Vegetables and fruits

Now it's time to open the refrigerator door and see what fruits and vegetables you can put on your guinea pig's menu. From the vegetable bin, you could offer carrots; celery leaves/stalks (cut into small pieces and strings removed); cucumbers; green, leafy lettuce such as arugula, bib, Boston, endive, escarole, radicchio, and romaine; spinach; tomatoes (remove the toxic green stem and leaves); and zucchini.

Do you have an herb garden in your backyard? You could pick a few sprigs of fresh basil, chicory, cilantro, coriander, dill weed, or thyme to add to your guinea pig's salad. And, if you have dandelion leaves or clover growing in your lawn, and they haven't been treated with chemicals, toss some of those into the salad, too.

For dessert, stick to fruits such as apples, bananas, blueberries, grapefruit, seedless grapes, honeydew melon, kiwis, pears, seedless orange

segments, strawberries, tangerines, and seedless watermelon. Although cavies love fruit, you should ration it carefully because of its high sugar content. The fresh food portion of your pet's diet should consist mainly of vegetables.

Not only is it important to give your cavies more vegetables than fruits, it's also important to keep the portions small. And fresh food should be served at room temperature because guinea pigs don't like

Vegetables and fruits should be part of a guinea pig's daily diet.

cold food. Always wash fruits and vegetables thoroughly, and remove any leftovers from the cage promptly, before they have a chance to spoil.

The recommended serving of vegetables (including a little fruit) for cavies is approximately one cup per cavy, per day. It's fortunate that piggies like their veggies, because these are what you're going to use as training treats. It's amazing what your pets will do for a nibble of carrot or a sprig of parsley!

Stay away from...

There are some foods you should never give to your guinea pigs, and others that you should give very sparingly. On the never-pass-their-lips list should be meat, meat products, dairy products, chocolate, peanut butter, cooked/fried foods, and baked goods. Why? Cavies are strict herbivores; their digestive systems are not designed to process these foods. And, if you're thinking of sharing your chips or pretzels, think again. People snacks are bad news for piggies, and the same is true for high-sugar/high-fat pet treats like seed sticks and yogurt drops. Your best bet is to stick with veggies and a little bit of fruit. But even here you have to be careful. Never feed dried beans or peas, hot peppers, iceberg lettuce, nuts, potatoes, rhubarb, or any seeds (including sunflower seeds and green pepper seeds). On the small-amounts-only-please list should be broccoli, Brus-

sels sprouts, cabbage, and cauli-flower. These veggies can cause gas and make your piggy uncomfortable, so offer them only in very small pieces a couple of times a week. If your cavy becomes "gassy," don't offer them at all. Guinea pigs love carrots, but this doesn't mean they can wolf down as many as they'd like! Don't offer more than one small carrot, or a portion of a carrot per guinea pig, per day.

On the Internet, you'll find all sorts of conflicting information about what, and what not, to feed your guinea pig. For example, some guinea pig experts recommend that cavies should have a trace-mineral salt block in their cage. They maintain that mineral blocks can help cavies avoid nutritional deficiencies and possible medical problems. Other experts, however, advise against the use of trace-mineral salt blocks. They maintain that blocks can actually cause some guinea pig health problems. This conflicting advice can be very confusing. So, if you have any concerns about what to give your guinea pigs, check with a veterinarian who specializes in small animals.

H$_2$O

In addition to pellets and hay, fresh water should be available to your cavies at all times. If the water in your area is high in chlorine or minerals, you should provide filtered, spring, or bottled water instead.

Water can be served in a heavy ceramic bowl, but some guinea pigs like to play and/or sit in their water bowls, and the water can become fouled with bedding, feces, or urine. So, if you go with a bowl, you'll need to change the water several times a day.

A sipper bottle is a more hygienic option. Look for one with a non-chewable metal tube, and be sure to check it daily in case it gets plugged up. To prevent bacteria buildup, give it a good scrub with a bottle brush several times a week.

Dietary changes

Guinea pigs have sensitive digestive systems and can have difficulty adjusting to a change in food and/or water. But what if the pellets your cavies have been eating are discontinued? Or, what if you want to switch your pets to a more nutritious food? The best advice is to make the change gradually. Begin by substituting one-quarter of the current brand of pellets with the new brand. Then after a week, go to equal amounts of old and new pellets. In another week, the mix should be three-quarters new to one-quarter old. And in week four, you can switch over totally to the new brand. During the changeover, you'll need to monitor your guinea pigs on a daily basis to make sure that they are, in fact, eating and staying healthy.

If you move to a new town where the water has a different mineral or

Water stays clean in a sipper bottle.

chemical composition, your guinea pigs could have problems with diarrhea. What's more, if they don't like the taste of the new water, they might flat-out refuse to drink it. To avoid problems like this, why not switch them gradually to a brand of bottled water that's available both where you live now and where you're moving to? Then, after you've been in your new home for a while, you can slowly switch your cavies over to the local water.

Changes in your pets' diet or water supply are not something you should take lightly. But, if you plan well ahead and keep a close eye on your pets, they should be able to make the transition without suffering from any health problems.

Chapter Three
Choosing Your Trainees

Which little piggies?

The great moment has arrived! Now that you've built the cage, made it comfy, and stocked up on the right types of foods, it's time to go guinea pig shopping! Remember, guinea pigs are not a short-term commitment. They will be part of your family for anywhere from five to eight years, so you'll want to give some careful thought to your choices.

Where to buy

Although most owners buy their cavies at a pet shop, this certainly isn't the only option. In the last few years, the Internet has opened a whole new way of finding the perfect pet. With just a few clicks of the mouse, you can get onto free local classifieds sites, link to the "pets" category, and do a search for "guinea pigs." There are sure to be several hopefuls needing good homes. The Internet is also a great way to find your nearest small animal shelter or rescue center, where there are often piggies waiting for adoption.

With another few clicks, you can bring up listings of cavy associations and breeders in your state or province. The advantage of buying from a reputable breeder is that you can tap into their experience to help you make your choice.

An only cavy is a lonely cavy

In the wild, guinea pigs band together in small herds. They are very sociable animals who live

Look for buddies that have already bonded.

together, forage together, sleep together, and communicate with one another. Cavies thrive on companionship, so if you keep a single guinea pig as a pet, its life will be pretty lonesome. Maybe you think that you're going to be your cavy's best buddy. But think again. With today's busy lifestyles, how many hours a day can you spend with your pet? Probably not enough. The fact is, if you want to be a responsible cavy owner, you should really plan on having two or more guinea pigs. This way, when you can't be around, the cavies can keep each other company.

However, just like people, not all guinea pigs hit it off. So how can you be sure that the cavies you buy will get along together? The easiest way to get compatible guinea pigs is to purchase a same-sex pair or group that has already bonded. These could be cavies that have been matched up at a shelter or by

a breeder, or they could be cavies from the same litter in a pet store. How many guinea pigs should you buy? Some experts recommend that groupings of three to five guinea pigs work best, but you'll have to decide how many you have room for, how many you can afford, and how many you're willing to clean up after.

If you already own a single guinea pig and now realize that it needs a buddy or two—or if you have a small group of cavies and want to add to it—you'll find lots of information about introducing strangers in Chapter 5.

Breeds of guinea pigs

Unlike dog breeds, which are distinguished by body type, size, and temperament, guinea pig breeds are determined solely by coat type. At the moment, there are thirteen

breeds of guinea pigs recognized by the American Cavy Breeders Association, and sixteen breeds recognized in Canada. Each of these breeds also has several different color varieties. Then there are the rare breeds like Skinny Pigs, Baldwins, Swiss Teddies, and Ridgebacks. And, of course, the Heinz-57 mixed breeds.

But for training purposes, it's not what you see on the outside that counts. It doesn't matter if you choose a long-haired or short-haired cavy, a silkie or a satin; there's virtually no difference temperament-wise between the breeds. It's the disposition of the *individual* guinea pig that you have to consider when selecting a good trainee.

Male or female?

Male or female? Which sex is easier to train? Some experienced guinea pig owners feel that boars are more active and curious—great qualities for trainees. Other owners feel that sows are more docile and people-friendly—also good traits for trainees. The fact is, there's no real consensus; what you read about males on one website, you're just as likely to read about females on another site. So, in the end, the gender of a guinea pig isn't the issue when it comes to training. What *does* matter is the personality of the individual cavy, and how well it is socialized.

Young or old?

Are you torn between a baby guinea pig (pup) on one hand and an adult adoptee on the other? Will it make any differences for training purposes? As with any pet, it's usually easier to start training at an early age. After all, a young animal is eager to learn and hasn't had time to develop bad habits. However, this doesn't mean that you can't teach an old guinea pig new tricks! It might take a little more time and patience on your part, but you do have one ace up your sleeve—guinea pigs love food and will do just about anything to get some.

Remember, training isn't just about the end result. It's about keeping your guinea pigs mentally stimulated and physically active. It's also a good way to bond with your cavies and to have fun together. So whether you opt for a new baby or an older adoptee, training is always worthwhile.

Pick of the litter

So now it's crunch time—time to pick out your own best buddies. But faced with a cage full of guinea pig hopefuls, how can you tell which ones to take home? Rule #1: Look for healthy piggies—ones with bright eyes, glossy coats, no bald spots, no overgrown teeth, and no discharge from eyes, ears, nose, or anus. Rule #2: Look for alert, active cavies—ones that are outgoing,

Breeds Recognized by the Ontario Cavy Club

Abyssinian
Satin Abyssinian
Boucle (Alpaca)
Coronet
Satin Crested
White Crested
Merino
Peruvian
Satin Peruvian
Silkie
Satin Silkie
Smooth Coat or American
Satin Smooth Coat
Satin Teddy
Teddy
Texel

curious, and people-friendly. Usually these will be the ones that are snooping around the cage rather than cowering in a corner.

Many guinea pigs are more active in the morning and evening, so these are good times to make your choices. But if you can manage it,

it's a good idea to visit your piggy possibilities several times; if you only visit once, it might be siesta time for some of the cavies, and obviously they won't have the desire to get up and go when they're sleeping.

When picking out guinea pigs (or any pet), the most important thing is: *never buy on impulse*. Take your time. Be choosy. After all, these critters will be your companions for many years to come.

Word of Warning: Guinea pigs can become sexually active by the time they're three to four weeks old,

so males and females should be housed in separate cages as soon as they're weaned. Unfortunately, not everyone selling guinea pigs knows how to tell the sex of a young pup, and many guinea pig owners end up with more pets than they paid for. To avoid surprise litters, check with a knowledgeable breeder or veterinarian, or do some Internet research and learn how to tell the sexes apart yourself. This way, when you're looking at a group of guinea pigs, you'll know if the sexes have been properly segregated.

Chapter Four
Training Your Cavies to Trust You

Stress-free homecoming

Now that you've picked out the perfect piggies, you'll you want to make the trip from the breeder, shelter, or pet shop to your home as stress-free as possible. How do you do this?

First of all, take along a suitable pet carrier, preferably one that has a seat belt slot. Although some people use a cardboard box, this isn't a great idea because it's not a safe way to transport a pet. Think about it. If you have to stop the car suddenly, the cardboard box could fly off the seat. Even if a friend or family member is holding the box, there's no saying he/she could hold on to it in an emergency.

Make the carrier comfy with a sleep sack and some hay. It also helps to put in a handful or two of bedding from their previous cage because the familiar scent makes the move less stressful. If the ride home is short, you won't have to worry about providing water. If the ride is a bit longer, why not put a slice or two of cucumber in the carrier? Cucumber, with its high water content, will keep your cavy from getting thirsty. On a really long trip, you'll need to stop every so often and offer your cavy a drink from a bowl or a sipper bottle. Just make sure to take out the water container before you start driving again so water doesn't spill or drip and get everything soaked.

On the way home, keep the noise level in the car down: no loud music, no bickering over which kid sits next to the new pet(s), no honking the horn. Instead, talk softly and keep the atmosphere calm. Moving to a new home is stressful for any pet; your job is to make the move as painless as possible.

Settling in

As soon as you reach home, gently place your new cavies into their new cage. Now comes the hard part—leave them alone! They need a few days to settle in and become familiar with this strange environ-

ment. So don't invite all your friends over to take a peek, don't keep taking the guinea pigs in and out of the cage, and don't have a TV or loud music blaring. The cavies need a calm environment if they're to have a smooth adjustment to their new home.

For the first few days, all you need to do is give them fresh food and water. You should also sit by their cage and talk to them softly. Otherwise, just leave them to explore the cage at their own pace.

Connecting with your cavies

The very first step in training your guinea pigs is to train them to get along with you and the rest of your family members. Your aim is to have cavies that are well socialized and not afraid of you.

Some guinea pigs are born fearless or have been socialized before you get them. These confident cavies will come running right over to you if you offer them a tasty treat. Others guinea pigs are not so bold. They'll run away or freeze if you get too close. These timid piggies will need to be taught to like you.

What's the best way to do this? Start by sitting near the cage and talking to the guinea pigs as often as you can. This way, they get used to your presence, your scent, and the sound of your voice. When chatting to your cavies, never loom over the cage like a predator waiting to nab them! Always sit down low so they don't see you as a threat.

The next step is to put your hand slowly into the cage, and hold out a tasty treat, such as a sprig of parsley or a piece of carrot. Don't wiggle the treat in front of your cavy's nose. Instead, keep your hand still, and wait for your pet to come to you. This might take some time if you have a very timid cavy. But be patient! Remember, you're building trust. The whole idea behind offering treats is that your cavy will come to associate you with good things and will be happy to see you.

Once a guinea pig is comfortable taking treats from your hand, you can offer the food with one hand and stroke your guinea pig with the other. This gets your pet accustomed to your touch, as well as to your scent. Some cavies might be a bit skittish at first and might run away when you touch them. But persevere. It helps to know that cavies can be particular about where they're touched. Some prefer having their heads stroked, while others prefer having their backs rubbed. Be sure to stroke in the direction of hair growth, not against it. Guinea pigs don't like to have their fur ruffled.

You should connect like this with each guinea pig several times a day. The more often you interact with your pets, the faster they'll learn to trust you.

Handling how-to

After your guinea pigs get used to your touch, the next step is to pick them up and hold them. But before you do this, here are some facts you need to know. Many guinea pigs are afraid of being picked up. They feel exposed and vulnerable as soon as their four feet leave the ground. For this reason, you have to be patient with your piggy and approach the handling process slowly.

Something else you need to know is that guinea pigs may look well-built and chunky, but their body structure is actually quite fragile. So you have to be careful how you hold them. No squeezing, please. If you hold them too tightly, you

First step in bonding—offer a veggie treat.

Get your
guinea pig
used to your
touch; pet it
in its cage.

feel confident about being held, it's best to sit on the floor for handling sessions. Have a towel handy to put on your lap; you'll need it to prevent any urine or feces from soiling your clothing. For even better protection, you could invest in a waterproof guinea pig lap pad or lap mat; these can be purchased online.

Now for the first handling session. Start with the cavy that seems most people-friendly. Scoop it up gently, cradling its bottom with one hand and supporting its chest with the other hand. Remember, some guinea pigs don't like to be picked up and may try to nip. But if you're careful to splay your hand over its chest and up under its chin, there's less of a chance of getting nipped. Once you've got a hold of the cavy, support it against your chest and keep it there while you sit down. For the first handling session, you can either continue to hold the cavy against your chest while you talk to it, or you can lower it onto your lap if it seems calm enough. Whatever you do, don't flip it onto its back or hold it in your arms like a doll— guinea pigs do *not* like to be on their backs.

Some cavies don't mind being held. Others start fidgeting and squirming as they try to get away. Sometimes fidgeting just means that your guinea pig needs a bathroom break, so put it back into the cage and then pick it up again a few minutes later. If your pet is still squirmy, hold on to it firmly until it settles down, before putting it back into the

could unintentionally hurt or injure them. But guinea pigs are also quite squirmy and tend to jump if startled. Although you can't hold them too tightly, you have to keep a firm grip on them to prevent them from falling and breaking a bone or from getting a more serious injury. It's a delicate balance!

Here's another point to keep in mind. You should never approach a guinea pig from behind. Cavies are instinctively afraid of predators and get very nervous if anything swoops down on them from the rear. They may even bite in fear. To avoid this, talk to them as you move toward the cage, and make sure they see you coming before you pick them up.

Until you feel confident about holding your cavies, and your cavies cage. Why? If you put a cavy back into its cage the minute it squirms, it quickly learns that squirming gets it what it wants. If you hold onto it for a short time until it becomes calm, it learns that being held is not something to be afraid of.

Make the first handling session a short one—no more than a few minutes. Frequent, short sessions are better than infrequent, long ones. Most guinea pigs don't like being held for too long, and anyway, you have other cavies in the cage waiting for their turn! The whole idea is get each cavy accustomed to you, and to being held, a little at a time.

When it's time to return a cavy to the cage, be careful! Guinea pigs often struggle and try to jump out of their owners' hands as they're being lowered back into the cage. To prevent accidents, you have to teach your pet not to wriggle or jump. How do you do this? If your cavy starts squirming as you're lowering it toward the cage floor, hold it just above the floor until it stops struggling. Then when it's calm, lower it completely until all four feet are touching the ground. Some cavies will start struggling again as soon as they feel their feet hit the floor. If this happens, hold on to them a little longer until they settle down. This whole process teaches your piggy that struggling and squirming won't get it anywhere; only calm behavior will get results. This is a very necessary lesson for a guinea pig to learn, because a squirming cavy can easily be dropped and injured.

Grooming builds trust

Another way to build trust with your cavies is to spend time grooming them. Long-haired guinea pigs need to be brushed daily to prevent their hair from becoming tangled and matted. But even short-haired guinea pigs need grooming to get rid of loose hair and any debris that's caught in their fur. So why not make the grooming sessions bonding sessions?

Put your cavy on your lap, and give it a little treat. Then while it's munching away, brush it with a soft-bristled brush. Always start at your

Brushing your pet is a great way to bond with it.

Don't brush your pet's fur in the wrong direction. Always brush from head to rear.

pet's head, and brush toward its rump. Most guinea pigs like being brushed, and you'll probably be rewarded with some contented purring.

Family fun

Don't hog all the guinea pig fun for yourself! Let other family members in on the action. Just remember that when you're training your cavies to get along with other people in the family, you have to take the introductions a step at a time and not rush your piggies.

When it comes to younger family members, tweens and teens are perfectly capable of handling and looking after cavies. But young children need adult supervision because it's difficult for a young child to control a squirmy cavy, and squirmy cavies can easily be dropped or injured. Also, little kids have a tendency to squeeze their pets hard, as if they were furry toys. This, too, can result

in the cavy being injured. To avoid accidents, a safe way to encourage young children to bond with the family piggies is for an adult to hold each cavy, and let the kids pet or brush it and offer it treats.

No nipping, please

Guinea pigs are gentle critters, known for their good nature and sweet disposition. They don't often bite, but when they do, there's usually an explanation for it. Do you have a little nipper on your hands? Then you'll have to do some detective work to figure out what's causing the biting behavior.

The most common reason for a guinea pig to nip or bite is that it's afraid. Remember, in the wild, guinea pigs are prey for other animals, so their fear factor is well developed. If you grab a cavy from behind, chase it, corner it, or loom over it, its instinctive fear might take over, and you could be nipped or bitten.

Another reason why a cavy might nip or bite is that it doesn't like how it's being handled. For example, some cavies don't like being lifted or held, some don't like having their hair rubbed in the wrong direction, and others don't like having their ears or rear-ends petted. What if your guinea pig nips while it's sitting on your lap? It could just want to get down, or it could need to relieve itself.

Guinea pigs have a great sense of smell, so if you've been making a salad for supper, here's a handy hint. Wash your hands before handling your cavies. Otherwise, they will smell the veggies on your fingers and might nip in hopes of getting a taste.

Like puppies, young cavies sometimes go through a nippy stage. Be patient! The nipping should pass as the youngsters get older. You'll have to be patient, too, if you've adopted a guinea pig that's been maltreated in the past. With time, and lots of kind handling, it will slowly learn that not all humans are bad.

Sometimes a cavy will bite if it's bored, and sometimes it will bite in frustration if its cage is too small, too hot, or too crowded. A large, well-ventilated cage furnished with lots of toys should take care of this problem. Plenty of out-of-the-cage playtime should help, too.

If you're doing everything right, and your guinea pig is still nipping or biting, perhaps it has health issues that are causing it to have sensitive skin. Take It to a veterinarian and have it checked for mites or other skin problems. Has your pet been given a clean bill of health? Then maybe you've just got a guinea pig with attitude! When handling a cavy with attitude, try spraying your hands with a bitter pet spray before picking it up.

Whatever you do, never shout, scold, or discipline a nippy cavy; it won't understand. What you need to do is figure out what's causing the problem, and then take steps to fix it.

Bonding takes time

During the bonding process, it's important to realize that some outgoing piggies bond very quickly with their new families, but other more timid guinea pigs take quite a bit longer to trust their owners. A lot depends on the individual personalities of the guinea pigs and how much time you're willing to spend socializing them. Not all of your guinea pigs will learn to love you in the first week, so be patient! Time spent socializing your cavies is time well spent because you'll end up with well-adjusted, well-socialized guinea pigs that are good candidates for training.

Chapter Five

Fostering Friendship: Guinea Pig Introductions

Time for another cavy?

Did you buy a single guinea pig without knowing that it would be much happier with a companion? Or have you owned a pair of cavies for a while, and now one has died? Or, have you just seen an ad, "Guinea Pig Needs a New Home," and would like to place this rescue cavy with your own little herd? Before making the commitment, you need to realize that a newcomer is not always accepted by a resident cavy or cavies. But take heart! If you read through this chapter, you'll find out that there are quite a few steps you can take to make the introductions go smoothly. First, however, you'll need to know which groupings of cavies work, and which don't.

Which groupings work?

In the wild, the natural grouping is one dominant boar along with several sows. All male offspring are chased to the outskirts of the group at sexual maturity and eventually leave to establish their own herds. The female offspring either stay with the family group or leave to join another herd.

But this "natural" grouping isn't going to work at your house—pretty soon you'd have more little piggies than you could count! So what will work? There are several possibilities.

As you read in Chapter 3, the easiest way to go, especially for new guinea pig owners, is to buy a same-sex pair or group that has already bonded. You should be able to find such a grouping at a reputable breeder's, a shelter, or a pet shop. Remember, *same-sex* is the key here—you won't have any worries about unwanted babies or risks associated with neutering/spaying.

If you have a choice between a group of males or a group of females, which should you pick? Does it make any difference? Some owners have a preference for females; they think that sows are quieter and less likely to squabble. Other owners have a preference for males; they think that boars are more active and people-friendly. But the fact of the matter is, you're just as likely to find quiet, sociable males and active, people-friendly females. So, the bottom line is, that the personality of the individual guinea pig is what's important, not its gender.

The next question is: how many boars or sows can live together peaceably? There's no magic number here. Again, it's a matter of the individual personalities and how well they hit it off. Usually, several sows can be housed together without too many hassles, though they may scuffle a bit until they sort out the pecking order. Occasionally, however, a really dominant sow may have to be housed only with sub-missive females to prevent fights from breaking out.

With males, this dominance issue can be even more of a problem. Put two assertive males together, and you'll have battling boars for sure. However, this doesn't mean that boars can't be housed together. A dominant boar will usually get along fine with a submissive male or two, or with one or two younger, smaller males. Some owners even keep four or five boars together. The key to success here is to have a large enough cage, and to provide several bowls, bottles, and hideaways so that the boars don't have to compete with one another for food, water, and a place to sleep. Be aware, however, that the scent of a female will quickly upset the apple cart and turn a friendly group of males into an aggressive group in no time. So, if you choose to keep boars, don't house any sows in the same area.

Now and again, cage mates that have been getting along perfectly well for months suddenly start harassing each other. What gives? This mostly happens when young guinea pigs become adolescents and either start jockeying for the "top piggy" spot or start fighting over territory. Once these issues are sorted out, the fighting frequently stops. But occasionally, peaceful relations can't be re-established; in this case, you might have to partition the existing cage or house the rivals in separate cages.

Same-sex groups are the norm, but they're not the only possibility. Another potential grouping is one (and only one) neutered male with one or more females. This combination closely mimics the family grouping that is found in the wild. However, any neutering carries some risk to a cavy, so before going this route, do your research and discuss the pros and cons of neutering with your veterinarian.

Quarantine comes first

When you bring home a new guinea pig, it's tempting just to plunk it right into the cage with your resident pig or piggies. But wait! This is a very bad idea. What if the new cavy has undetected health problems? What if it starts scratching (mites) or sneezing (respiratory problems)? Some medical problems are easily overlooked; others take a few days to show up. So to be on the safe side, you need to quarantine a newbie for two or three weeks. Otherwise, you take the chance of infecting the rest of your herd.

Quarantine means keeping the new guinea pig in a separate cage, in a separate room. But fortunately, because the quarantine cage is temporary housing, it doesn't need to be as large as the permanent cage. However, please don't keep the new cavy in a small travel cage. There needs to be enough room for it to stretch its legs and move around.

Quarantine also means being especially vigilant about good hygiene. Always wash your hands thoroughly before and after handling the newcomer—yes, every single time! And, if there are any signs of health problems, get that guinea pig to a veterinarian ASAP.

Socializing sessions

Now that quarantine is over, it's time for the first face-to-face meeting. Hmmm…will the introductions go smoothly, or will the cavies start brawling? It's time to find out!

Your first big decision is: where will the introductions take place? Cavies are territorial, so you can't just take a strange cavy and plop it into the resident cavies' cage. The newcomer would be at an immediate disadvantage; it would be seen as an unwelcome intruder, and the other cavies would likely gang up on it.

A better plan is to set up the introductions on neutral territory. You need to pick a spot where none of the guinea pigs has played before and left its scent. This could be a bathroom, a hallway, or a mud room. Or, you could partition off a section of the kitchen. Another possibility is to set up a pet playpen on the laundry room floor or outside on the grass, under a shady tree. You could even resort to a bathtub or a sofa. Whatever area you pick, make sure that's it's fairly spacious so that the guinea pigs are able to get away from one other.

Start by spreading out clean towels or blankets on the floor. Then put down a few piles of hay and several little piles of fresh veggies. Guinea pigs are easily distracted by food, and they're more likely to bond when tasty tidbits are part of the introduction process. A few brand-new toys are a good idea, too (no prior piggy scent). But forget tunnels, tubes, and hidey-homes; these can encourage the sort of territorial behavior that leads to guinea pig fights.

Before bringing in the piggies, round up some extra towels, a pair of heavy work gloves or well-padded oven mitts, and a dustpan. You need to keep these items handy in case the cavies really go at one another and you have to separate them.

When everything is ready, go get the guinea pigs. It's important to put them all into the area at the same time so that none of them has a chance to mark the area with their scent before the rest arrive. (You might need an extra pair of helping hands here.)

Be prepared for conflict

Now sit back, watch carefully, and let the guinea pigs do their own thing. If you're lucky, your cavies will hit it off right away—they'll touch noses, share food, and snuggle together.

It's more likely, however, that your piggies will do a bit of scrapping to establish dominance. Don't be surprised if they chase one another, sniff rear ends, mount each other, and chatter their teeth. They might also fluff out their hair to make themselves look bigger and badder. And you'll probably see some of them swaying from side to side on stiff legs, while rumbling away like a motor boat. All of this is normal behavior and shouldn't worry you.

Introducing two cavy strangers isn't always easy.

bite anything in reach. Now toss towels over the cavies to separate them, or place the dustpan between them as a barrier and use it to push them apart. Then scoop them up, and return them to their separate cages.

Same-scent strategies

If your guinea pigs don't get along when you introduce them on neutral ground, here's an alternative approach to try. In fact, some owners follow this route as their standard procedure.

First, spread out some nice, clean, fluffy towels on the floor of a warm bathroom. Then, spread a flannel baby blanket on the bottom of the bathtub (to prevent the cavies from slipping), and run about three-quarters of an inch of lukewarm water into the tub. Next, put all the guinea pigs into the water together, and soap them up with some mild guinea pig, kitten, or ferret shampoo. Be careful! Don't get any soap in their eyes. Once the cavies are squeaky clean, rinse them off well, using a plastic cup. Then plop them onto those soft towels, and rub and fluff until the piggies are dry. To dry them off completely, you'll probably need extra towels, or you could use a hair dryer at the lowest setting. Just don't get the dryer too close—you don't want your cavies to be hurt by the heat.

In fact, even more aggressive behavior is still considered normal. So don't be alarmed if the little gladiators start nipping at one another and grabbing mouthfuls of fur. They might also start making threatening noises, such as hissing or huffing. And, if they start yawning, don't be fooled—they're not getting tired; they're baring their big teeth at each other. Your natural instinct might be to call a halt to the session, but if you do, you're only postponing the inevitable dominance faceoff. The pecking order *must* be resolved, or the new guinea pig will never fit in.

You should, however, step in if the cavies go on the attack. How will you know they're in attack mode? If they rise up on their hind legs in a challenging posture, or if they lunge furiously at one another, or if they bite hard and draw blood, then it's time to separate them. Put those gloves on—battling guinea pigs will

Now that they've had a bath, and they all smell the same, give those clean little critters some time to run around the bathroom. Put a clean blanket on the floor, along with some hay, veggies, and brand new toys (see *Socializing sessions*). Then watch and see if this session goes any better than the last one. If the sparring is within acceptable limits this time around, the cavies are ready to go into the same cage. However, before rounding them up, you'll have to get the cage ready. This is a big job! In fact, it's such a big job that you should probably get someone else to do it while you're concentrating on the guinea pig introductions.

Don't have a helper? Then you'll have to do things a little differently. You'll need to give the cage a major cleaning *before* the big bath. This means you'll need to "store" your little herd of cage mates somewhere safe (such as a pet playpen or an enclosed shower) while you do the cage cleaning. You won't have to worry about the newbie, of course, because it's safe in the quarantine cage.

A clean cage for a fresh start

For a fresh start, the cage has to be scrubbed completely from top to bottom before you can put the clean cavies in together—every trace of guinea pig smell has to be removed.

And that's not all. Every single thing in the cage has to be cleaned, too. The aim here is to make the cage another neutral area.

To rid the cage of guinea pig scents, take everything out of it, then wash the floor and the wire grids thoroughly with either a 50/50 solution of vinegar and water, or with a pet odor-control cleaning product. Rinse well. Everything in the cage—bottles, bowls, hutches, toys—needs to be scrubbed well or put into the dishwasher. Fleece and sleep sacks should go into the washing machine. After the cage has been cleaned and reassembled, put in fresh fleece or bedding, fresh food and water, and fresh

A few brand-new toys can help make socializing sessions successful.

hay. Every cleaned item should be put in a different spot from where it was before. And, it's a good idea to introduce some new toys, too. The game plan is to make the cage seem new and different to every single guinea pig.

Neighbors, not roommates

If you follow all of the instructions above and out-and-out battles are still an issue, then it's doubtful if these particular cavies will ever get along together. So now what do you do? You might have to house the combatants separately in adjacent cages, or at least erect a grid divider within a large C&C cage. This way, they can see each other, smell each other, and wheek at

each other, but they won't be able to pounce on each other.

Another possibility, if you have a group of cavies, is to split the group into two, and try different matchups until you come up with two compatible groups. Again, these groups will have to be housed in separate cages, or they'll have to live on different sides of a grid in the same large C&C cage.

Guinea pigs and other pets

In the wild, guinea pigs have many predators. But did you realize that there could be predators lurking in your house as well? Dogs, cats, and ferrets are just some of the animals that could potentially harm your guinea pigs. And although you'll see websites where guinea pig owners report how well their cavies get along with their other pets, it's always best to err on the side of caution.

And here's something else to think about. Even if your other pets are showing no inclination to attack your cavies, their very presence or scent could be stressing the piggies big-time. Not a good thing for training! For training purposes, you want a calm, focused cavy. So, if you have other animals in the house, it's best to keep them well away from the guinea pigs.

Chapter Six

Learning Guinea Pig Language

Guinea pig sounds: a translation guide

One of the things owners find most endearing about guinea pigs is that they can talk. Okay, maybe they don't talk exactly, but they can certainly communicate! Have you ever heard your cavy wheek, chirp, chutter, or rumble? Then you know it has many different ways to express itself.

By learning what your guinea pigs are trying to tell you, you'll know if the time is right for training, or if it would be better to wait until later.

Wheeking

Wheeking is the sound that most people associate with guinea pigs. And what are your cavies trying to tell you with that distinctive "wheek wheek"? Sometimes they're just saying: "Hello, there! Good to see you." But usually they're saying: "We want food! We want food! We want food!" Expect to hear wheeking when you come home from work (excited to see you), when you walk near their cage (expecting food), when you open the refrigerator door (veggies are coming), or when you rustle the hay bag (yum, yum). You might also hear a higher-pitched wheek when one cavy is looking for another.

There's also a softer-sounding wheek that guinea pigs sometimes use when they're hanging out together. This sort of conversational wheeking means that the herd is happy.

Chutting

Chutter, chutter, chutter...mutter, mutter, mutter. This is the familiar sound that guinea pigs make when loafing around the cage, socializing with one another, and figuring out what to do next. Again, this is a sound that equals contentment.

Cooing

Cooing is a comforting sound that mother guinea pigs use to reassure their pups. It's also a sound that adult cavies use to reassure one

another that everything is okay. And if a guinea pig coos at you, you're in luck! It means that the cavy is happy to be with you, and accepts you as part of the herd.

Purring or chortling

When a cat purrs, everyone knows it's content. But did you know that guinea pigs purr, too, and for the same reason? So when you're holding your piggy and are petting and stroking it, don't be surprised to hear a gentle purring noise. Guinea pigs also make this contented sound when they're grooming one another, or when they're getting a treat. Expect lots of purring during training

sessions; the petting and treats are almost guaranteed to start it up.

Chirping

Chirping is a fairly rare sound, and many cavy owners will never hear it. But if you do hear it, you can't mistake it—it sounds exactly like a bird chirping. Often a chirping guinea pig will raise its head up to cheep; sometimes it will even look as if it's in a trance. And, frequently, the other piggies in the cage stop what they're doing, stand still, and listen.

Why do guinea pigs chirp? There are lots of different opinions, but no one knows for sure. Some owners say that their cavies chirp when startled. Other owners report that sows sometimes chirp prior to giving birth. Still other owners insist that their guinea pigs pipe up just for the heck of it.

Do you have a furry chirper? If so, don't disturb it mid-song. Its attention certainly won't be focused on training.

Rumbling

A rumble is a bit like a purr but is deeper and more vibrating. Think of a boat's motor—that's what it sounds like. Rumbling is often heard as part of the mating ritual. Both males and females do it. But strange to say, cavies also rumble when they're warning other guinea pigs: "Keep away! Get out of my space!"

Sometimes a guinea pig might rumble at you; for example, if you're petting it and it wants you to stop.

Teeth chattering

Teeth chattering is just that—a rapid clacking of teeth. It's a very distinctive warning sound, frequently used when dominance issues are being worked out. A little bit of teeth chattering usually indicates that a guinea pig is angry, afraid, or upset. If it's chattering at another cavy, it's telling it to keep away. If it's chattering at you, it wants you to keep away. This is your cue to forget any training plans for the moment, and put your piggy back in its cage.

Aggressive teeth chattering is much more serious; it's usually a sign that one cavy is about to attack another. Don't wait for the attack to happen! Grab a towel or dustpan and separate the piggies immediately.

Hissing

Hissing, sometimes referred to as huffing, puffing, or snorting, sounds a bit like a forceful breath of air. Like teeth chattering, it means that your cavy is mad—really mad—and not in the mood for training.

Whining

Whining is a guinea pig's way of complaining and letting another guinea pig (or its owner) know that it doesn't want to be disturbed. This kind of grumbling isn't something to worry about. It doesn't mean that your cavy is getting ready to start a fight—it is just feeling annoyed and bothered.

Shrieking

Shrieking or screaming is not something you want to hear. It's a sound that indicates distress, alarm, pain, or injury. Take this piercing squeal as a cry for help, and go check it out immediately.

An audio guide

Are you having difficulty distinguishing one guinea pig sound from another? Don't worry; help is just a click away! You can hear the various vocalizations on guinea pig websites or on YouTube. Then, once you're clued in to what your cavies are saying, you'll know when the moment is right for training and when it's not.

Chapter Seven
Decoding Body Language

Gauging your guinea pig's mood

Not only is it important to pay attention to the sounds your guinea pigs make, you should also pay attention to their body language. By watching how your cavies move, act, and interact, you can gauge whether they are happy, content, fearful, miserable, or mad. Then you'll know if they're in the mood for training, or if you should wait until later.

Pop-corning

Pop-corning is when your cavy is springing up into the air, bounc-ing around the cage, and generally looking joyful. Piggies popcorn when they're happy, perhaps because you've just walked into the room, or perhaps because you've rustled a treat bag. Whatever the reason for it, whenever you see pop-corning, it's a sign that your cavy is in a very good mood.

Running laps

One very good reason for providing your cavies with a large habitat is that they love to do quick sprints around their cage. This spontaneous racing around is commonly referred to as running laps. And, like pop-corning, piggy laps are a sign that all is well with your cavies' world.

Sniffing and/or touching noses

Guinea pigs rely a lot on their sense of smell. You'll frequently see them sniffing their buddies (at either end), or sniffing around their cage

By paying close attention to your cavy's body language, you can tell its mood.

and its contents. This is completely normal behavior; it's how cavies get to know each other and how they check out their environment.

Cavies also sniff one another and touch noses as a way of saying "Hi there! How's it going?" Don't be surprised to find yourself given the sniff and touch treatment, too. It's your cavies' way of treating you like one of the gang.

Nudging and head tossing

Nudging means "Get out of my space" or "Leave me alone." It's common to see guinea pigs bumping one another out of the way at the food bowl, or nosing one another out of a sleep house. You might even get a nudge or two as well. For example, if you're petting your cavy and it's had enough, it might nudge you with its nose or toss its head and try to push your hand out of the way. Take the hint! Leave the petting for later.

Freezing

Have you ever seen a guinea pig going about its business and then suddenly standing completely still, not moving a muscle or blinking an eye? This is called freezing, and it's what cavies do when they're startled or when they feel threatened. For example, a guinea pig might freeze when it hears a loud noise (a door slamming), or it might freeze when it's frightened (a dog bounding up to its cage). Cavies will often stand still like this until they feel the danger is past.

If your cavies are freezing a lot, monitor them carefully until you know what's stressing them out. Then take steps to fix the problem. After all, you don't want your pets being fearful all the time.

Fleeing and stampeding

Another way that guinea pigs react to stress or danger is to run away and hide. A new pet might behave this way until it gets used to you. If a group of guinea pigs is startled, they stampede. In other words, they all run off in different directions. This is a herd behavior, meant to confound a predator; when a herd splits up like this, a predator can't chase them all.

Squirming

Sometimes when you're holding a cavy, it will squirm because it wants to get down to go to the bathroom. Other times it will squirm because it's had enough of being held. When a cavy squirms, it means "I want down!" So take the hint.

Rumble-strutting

There's no mistaking rumble-strutting. This is when a guinea pig sways it's hips, rocks from side to side on stiff legs, and makes a deep rumbling noise. Sometimes it's part of the mating ritual; sometimes it's a display of dominance. This is all normal behavior. But if the rumble-strutting takes a more aggressive turn—perhaps accompanied by teeth chattering—this is your cue to separate the strutting pigs before fighting breaks out.

Reading the signs

This quick guide to guinea pig body language should be a big help when you're trying to figure out if your cavies are in the right frame of mind for learning. If they're looking content, or if they're running laps around the cage or pop-corning, this is a good time for training. If they're squirming, head tossing, or rumble-strutting, wait until they're in a more upbeat mood before launching into any lessons.

Chapter Eight
A Need to Gnaw

Chomping and chewing

Although you won't see your guinea pig flashing those pearly whites too often, those twenty teeth are there alright, and what's more, they're constantly growing. Because cavy teeth never stop growing, you have to make sure that your guinea pigs have plenty of the right stuff to chomp and chew on. And what is the right stuff? Hay, hay, and more hay...as well as vegetables and hard guinea pig pellets. As cavies chew these foods, they grind them between their teeth, and it's this grinding action that keeps the teeth from becoming overgrown. Or, to put it another way, guinea pigs need to gnaw for tooth control.

Management vs. training

The fact is, however, no matter how much hay or how many veggies you provide, your cavies are going to chew on other things as well. You can't train a guinea pig not to gnaw, so instead, you'll have to train yourself to manage their gnawing.

This means providing owner-approved chewies and devising strategies for keeping your cavies away from dangerous items such as electric cords and expensive items like your antique blanket box.

Owner-approved chewies

Not all guinea pigs like to gnaw on the same things, so your best plan is to offer a variety of "gnawables" that your cavies can chew on safely. There are lots of products available in pet stores or on the Internet that might tempt your champion chewers. Alfalfa cubes and timothy hay cubes are good for starters. There are also hard treats in the shape of citrus slices that not only promote healthy chewing but also provide cavies with some of the vitamin C they need. You can also find lots of wood chews in all different shapes and sizes. Look for the ones made specifically for guinea pigs. Some

Cavies need to gnaw. Give them owner-approved chewies.

with accessories that can be safely chewed on. Wooden hideaways and hutches are good choices, as are willow balls, tunnels, and twig bundles. The same goes for grassy huts, mats, beds, and balls. Surprisingly, hanging bird toys—the wooden ones—appeal to many cavies, too.

Always keep a supply of favorite chew toys on hand, because you'll need to replace the gnawed ones every so often when grunge or safety becomes a factor—or when they disappear!

Short on cash, but big on initiative? Cardboard tubes, such as paper towel or toilet paper tubes, make great chew toys—and they're free! Recycle them to your guinea pig rather than your recycle bin. But before you give them to your cavies, be sure to cut them through from end to end; you don't want little guinea pig heads getting stuck.

Other free cavy favorites are tree branches and twigs. If you don't have any in your own backyard, ask a friend or neighbor for some. But be careful! You can't give your guinea pig anything that has been sprayed with pesticides or herbicides. Be aware, too, that not every tree species is safe. What's on the okay list? Look for apple, ash, aspen, beech, mulberry, pear, and willow. If there is an orchard in your area, you could ask the farmer for some pruned branches from pear or apple trees. Again, be sure to ask for pesticide-free branches. Maybe you'll be lucky and find an organic orchard near your house!

rodent and rabbit chewies are fine, too, but always check the label to make sure they're recommended for guinea pigs. Don't be upset if your guinea pigs won't touch these commercial chewies; some cavies like them, while others don't.

Guinea pigs don't only gnaw on chewies, however; they sharpen their teeth on some of their cage accessories as well. For this reason, it's best to furnish their cage

What's on the toxic list? Stay away from cedar, oak, redwood, walnut, or fruit trees, where the fruit has a pit (e.g., cherry, apricot, plum, peach). For any other type of tree, you'll need to do your own research or check with your veterinarian.

What not to give

Your backyard might be a good place to find pieces of wood for your cavies to gnaw on, but what about your workshop? If you have scraps of wood left over from your latest D-I-Y project, is it okay to give those to your guinea pigs? The short answer is no. You can't be sure that the wood from a lumber yard hasn't been treated with, or exposed to, chemicals.

You might think that a tough piece of rawhide would be the ideal thing to keep your guinea pigs' teeth trimmed. But think again. Cavies are strict herbivores and should never have meat products on their menu. Rawhide is dried animal skin, so it's a definite cavy no-no. The same goes for other dog chews. You should pass these up, too, and stick with products made for guinea pigs. Again, some rabbit and rodent chewies are fine, but be sure to check the label to see if they're recommended for guinea pigs. What about seed gnaw sticks? These hard sticks usually contain honey and are high in sugar and fat—not a healthy choice for guinea pigs.

Lesson plans for lessening the damage

Guinea pigs don't come pre-programmed to know what's safe, or okay, for them to chew, and what's not. Since you can't teach them this valuable information, it's up to you to protect your guinea pigs and provide them with a safe environment, both inside and outside the cage.

This means furnishing their cage with non-toxic wood and ceramic items, rather than with non-digestible plastic accessories (unless, of course, your cavies don't chew plastic). It also means pet-proofing their out-of-the-cage play area so that

there's nothing dangerous or valuable in the vicinity. For information on how to do this, see Chapter 10.

Some guinea pigs develop the habit of gnawing on their cage wires. You can't very well move the cage walls out of the way, so what can you do instead? You could try coating the wires with a strong, bitter gel to prevent the chewing. But, more often than not, biting cage bars is actually a symptom of another problem. What you really need to do is track down the root of the problem, and take steps to fix it.

For example, is your cavy bored? Then add more or new toys to the cage, or give the guinea pig some extra out-of-the-cage playtime. Is it by itself? Then get it a companion or two. Is the cage too small? Then provide a bigger habitat.

Hair chewing

Have you ever noticed that one of your cavies has had a recent haircut? And a pretty good one at that? The fact is, sometimes guinea pigs chew each others' hair, and occasionally, they even chew their own hair. This hair chewing, known as *barbering*, is a bit of a mystery. Some people think cavies do it out of stress or boredom; others think it's a dominance issue. But no one knows for sure.

Unfortunately, you can't train a cavy to stop this obsessive behavior. So what can you do? You could try misting the barbered piggies with a bitter spray made for pets—stay well away from the eye area—though this doesn't always work. You could improve the piggies' living conditions (see previous section). But again, there are no guarantees that this will solve the problem. You could also move the barber to a separate cage. But why bother—unless, of course, any of your guinea pigs are suffering physically, or you're planning to enter them in a cavy show.

If one of your cavies is self-barbering, take it to the veterinarian and have it checked for mites or skin problems.

This guinea pig is enjoying some wood chews.

Chapter Nine

Challenge Your Cavy's IQ—Set Up a Stimulating Cage

Keeping your cavies on their toes

The majority of cavies spend a great deal of time in their cages. So, if you want to be good to your guinea pigs, you should provide them with a large cage (see Chapter 1), and make that cage into a stimulating environment. This is one of the best things you can do to improve your pets' quality of life. A stimulating environment keeps them from being bored and fosters their curiosity. This in turn makes them better candidates for training.

Hideaways

The most important piece of cage furniture is some sort of hideaway where a cavy can go when it needs to feel safe and secure. Even if you sometimes find all your cavies squeezed together into one favorite hidey-hole, there should be a separate hiding place for each cavy in the cage, because a lack of private

space can be a major cause of tension in the group.

Fortunately, you'll have no trouble finding suitable hideaways. If you're looking for something to buy, wooden houses, grassy hutches and balls, flexible log tunnels, and rigid cardboard tunnels are all excellent choices. Hard-plastic igloos and ferret tunnels are other good choices, as long as your guinea pigs don't chew plastic. If you do an Internet search for "guinea pig curtains,"

you'll find an easy-to-assemble fabric hideaway made from fleecy material and a wire-cage grid. Or, you can go to the hardware store and buy some sections of smooth PVC pipe, 6 to 8 inches (15–20 cm) in diameter.

For cheaper options, you could use terra-cotta flower pots turned on their sides, or inexpensive plastic veggie bins turned upside down. And, if you have any grids left over from building a C&C cage, you could bend them into a U-shape and slip them into material sleeves. For no-cost options, you could use paper bags or large tissue boxes, or you could turn a shoe box upside down and cut an entryway in one side.

Tents and hammocks

Other possibilities for guinea pig hangouts are tents and hammocks. You can buy a nylon tent that is made for guinea pigs that comes with removable fleecy flooring. Or, you can pick up a tent that is made for ferrets. Need something fast? You could tie a piece of string to two adjacent cage walls, then take a section of newspaper, fold it in half, and hang it over the string to make an instant tent. A folded piece of sturdy cardboard makes a good tent, too.

Many guinea pigs like fabric hammocks, but with these, you have to be careful. You can't hang them up high off the floor in case your piggies fall out. In fact, where hammocks are concerned, think low, as in really close to the ground so that entrances and exits will be safe and easy. Hammocks, either store-bought or homemade, can be hung in a corner of the cage by attaching them to the wire walls.

Sleep sacks and cavy cozies

Many cavies like to crawl into sleep sacks or take a snooze on cavy cozies. These colorful sleeping bags and beds are comfy, washable, and durable. If you can't find something made specifically for guinea pigs, look for something made for ferrets.

Needing a fun project for a rainy afternoon? Sleep sacks are cheap and easy to make. Just take a piece of thick, cozy fleece, fold it over, stitch up two sides, and there you have it!

Bricks, stones, and rocks

Flat river rocks, bricks, and large stones might seem like unlikely objects to put in a cavy cage. But think about it. Every time your cavies climb onto a flat stone, it's as if they're doing step-ups at the gym. Up, down, up, down, up, down—they can get quite an aerobic work-out in a day!

And what's more, walking across the hard, rough surface of a flat brick, rock, or stone is a good way for guinea pigs to keep their toenails trimmed. To encourage walking on stones, why not put one under the water bottle and another under the hay rack so that your cavies have to walk on them to get water or food?

Hanging toys and treats

Hanging up a variety of cage toys will give your cavies a whole extra range of activities to focus on. As a bonus, they'll be getting some stretching exercise as they reach up to play with the toys.

There are lots of hanging toys on pet store shelves that are suitable

for guinea pigs. Look for strings of wooden chewies that can be clipped to the cage wires, or special metal skewers that attach to the cage grids. You can buy replacement chewies for the skewers, or you can raid the vegetable bin in your fridge and stack the skewers with veggies. Another neat product is a wire ball that can be stuffed with a variety of greens, veggies, or hay. You'll also find chewies that look like a

Pet-safe loofah chewies can be hung on the cage wires or used as floor toys.

sliced-up loofah. Try tying some of these onto the wires at different levels. Another novel toy is a stainless-steel bird mirror—no plastic frames or chains, please. For added fun, look for a metal mirror with a bell attached.

When you're picking out hanging toys, stay away from any that have plastic parts, tiny bells, or loops. Cavies can chew off and swallow little pieces of plastic; they can choke on a small bell; and they can get their heads stuck in a smaller loop than you might think.

Here's something easy and cheap you can do to brighten up your guinea pig's life. Stretch a long shoe or skate lace or a piece of clothesline from one side of the cage to the other, and secure each end to the cage wires. Now clip bunches of parsley or romaine lettuce leaves onto the line with mini binder clips. When your piggies start pulling on the parsley, be sure to have your camera ready to record the fun!

Stuffed toys

Some guinea pigs play with stuffed toys. They like to use them as pillows, snuggle up to them, and drag them around the cage. This is perfectly fine as long as the toy doesn't come with feathers, button eyes, a pom-pom nose, or anything else that can be chewed off. The stuffing can be a problem, too. If a cavy chews a toy open and tries to eat the stuffing, you'll have to remove that toy. Or, you could make it cavy-friendly by taking out the original stuffing and replacing it with hay or bedding. Too much work? Then replace the toy with a sock pillow. It's easy to make one yourself by stuffing a small sock with hay, and tying or sewing the open end shut.

Rearranging the furniture

One good, no-cost way to keep your cavies on their toes is to rearrange their cage furniture from time to time. This is like giving your guinea pigs a brand new cage, because they have to figure out the cage layout all over again. However, some cavies don't tolerate change; it can stress them out and make them sick. So if your pets show any signs of stress after you've moved things around, put everything back the way it was.

Another plan for stimulating your guinea pigs' curiosity is to take out a couple of the familiar cage toys and replace them with new ones. But don't throw out the old ones (unless they're badly gnawed). Store them in a cabinet, then return them to the cage a few months later. As far as your cavies are concerned, they'll seem like brand-new toys.

Hide-and-seek

In the wild, guinea pigs don't get their food served to them in a bowl! They have to search for it themselves. So why not give your piggies a chance to mimic this foraging behavior? You can do this by hid-

ing chunks of carrot and other small veggie pieces throughout the cage; your pets will have fun tracking them down. You can also stuff a grassy ball with hay, bury a slice of cucumber in the center, or hide a wedge of zucchini in a tunnel. Then sit back and watch the fun; all guinea pigs love treasure hunts.

Of course, it's up to you to keep track of the veggies and remove any uneaten ones before they spoil.

Chapter Ten
Out-of-the-Cage Playtime

Exercise is a must

With their short legs and stocky bodies, guinea pigs have a plump, cuddly appearance that is instantly appealing. However, it doesn't take much for cavies to cross the line from pleasingly plump to overweight or obese. So don't let your pets become couch potato piggies—get them out of that cage, and start them on an exercise program! Not only will exercise keep

them healthy, fit, and trim—it will also give their brain a workout and greatly improve their quality of life.

Picking a play area

Even if your guinea pigs have a large cage, out-of-the-cage playtime will give them a lot more run room and will let them see more of the "world." Unfortunately, you can't just open the cage door, holler "Playtime!" and leave your cavies to their own devices. This would be a recipe for disaster. You'd have cavies scampering all over your house or apartment, peeing and pooping as they went, testing their teeth on your furniture, chewing electric cords, and getting into all sorts of unsafe situations.

So think very carefully when picking your pets' play place. What you're looking for is a room or hallway that can be blocked off from the rest of your living space and made safe for your guinea pigs. A bathroom or hallway can be a good choice, since these spaces are rel-

Without exercise, a guinea pig can become obese.

atively free of furniture and often contain a handy cupboard or closet where guinea pig paraphernalia can be stored. A kitchen can be a good choice, too, as long as you keep all household cleaners out of reach and block off any spaces between cupboards and appliances with cardboard and duct tape.

Living rooms, family rooms, and bedrooms are generally not the best places for cavies to play in. Just think of the disasters waiting to happen. There's furniture to be gnawed, plants to be nibbled, carpets to be soiled, and cords to be chewed. So unless you're going to be very diligent about cavy-proofing, it's better to choose a more sparsely furnished area.

Flooring considerations

When you're trying to decide where to have the guinea pig playground, here's something to keep in mind: cleanup will be easier if you choose an area with a washable floor. This way, to keep things sanitary, all you have to do is pick up the feces and give the floor a quick mop after each playtime. However, not all washable floors are stain-proof and odor-proof. For example, urine can seep between the boards of hardwood flooring.

And that's not the only problem. Even if you're happy that your cavies are running around on a washable floor, they probably won't be. Most cavies don't like walking on tile or linoleum because their feet slip on smooth flooring. For better traction, it's best to cover hard flooring with a washable blanket or with several washable, rubber-backed mats. You could even top these with a layer of newspaper. Then when playtime is over, just roll up the newspaper, feces and all, and put it in the garbage.

Many guinea pig owners allow their cavies to run free on carpeted areas in their homes. Just go on YouTube and check out the videos. But before *you* go this route, here's something to think about. If your pets are running around peeing and pooping at will, it won't be long before your carpet is stained and smelly. What's the answer? The best plan is to set up a pet playpen (see *A guinea pig playpen*).

Safety first: guinea pig proofing

Before letting your pets loose in the play area, you have to make it safe for them. So, pick up any small items that could be choked on or swallowed. Put plants and plastic bags well out of reach. Shut all cupboard doors, and keep all electric, computer, telephone, and window blind cords out of reach as well. Then look around. Are there any small spaces that your piggies could wiggle their way into, such as

Wooden baseboards are a favorite target, especially where a corner sticks out into the room. A jutting corner gives your cavy a convenient place to bite into the wood. How can you protect those corners? You could use double-sided tape to attach a ninety-degree section of vinyl baseboard over the existing wooden baseboard. Or, you could try smearing the baseboards with a bitter gel. This stuff encourages many guinea pigs to keep their teeth to themselves.

What if you've found the perfect space for guinea pig playtime, but unfortunately, grandma's fancy antique dresser is sitting in the corner? Not a problem! Just fence off the dresser with wire grids, ziplocked together. You could even use the same type of wire-grid fencing to block off part of a room so that your piggies are kept out.

the gaps between cupboards and appliances? If so, block them off. And see to it that dogs, cats, ferrets, parrots or other pets are all in another room so they can't bother the guinea pigs.

Okay. You've made the play place safe *for* your pets, now it's time to make it safe *from* your pets. Gnawing is the number-one problem here. Guinea pigs are champion chewers and will chomp on just about anything. To keep the chomping in check, your best bet is to remove anything gnawable, and protect what's left. For example, if your guinea pigs are playing in the kitchen, you could remove the kitchen chairs; then slip the wooden table legs into sections of PVC pipe—not a fashionable look, maybe, but a functional solution.

Setup...keep it simple

Once you've picked the play spot, gather together a few toys to make it into a fun playground. Remember, you'll have to pick everything up again at the end of playtime, so keep the setup simple. A tunnel, a grass ball, some chew toys, a bowl of water, and some handfuls of hay will be fine.

And don't forget a hideaway or two. These are a must! Even during playtime, guinea pigs need a place where they can hide and feel safe.

Supervised play

During out-of-the-cage playtime, the main playground rule is: supervise, supervise, supervise. After all, cavies are curious critters; you never know what they'll get into. It's also possible that you might have overlooked something when you did the cavy proofing. Or, what if you drop something on the floor? You might not notice it, but you can bet your cavy will!

Watch your step

When you look at a cavy's short legs and chunky body, you'd never think that it could be quick on its feet. But believe it or not, a guinea pig can break into a sprint at a moment's notice and dart around the play area like a medal-winning runner. Just think of the chaos when several cavies are running around at the same time! You'll have to be very careful not to step on them.

The best way to prevent accidents is to shuffle along when walking in the play area. If you don't lift your feet off the ground, then there's no chance you'll step on a cavy.

Floor time

Some confident cavies can leave the security of their cage and go straight into a new playground with no problem at all. They'll explore the whole area, run piggy laps, and start playing with the toys. Other more timid cavies will do a "piggy freeze," or head for the nearest hutch and hole up.

How do you help a scaredy cat adjust to new surroundings? Whatever you do, don't start pushing or poking the frightened cavy. And if it's gone into a hutch, don't grab the hutch away and leave the poor thing exposed—you'll just frighten it even more. Instead, just leave it alone. Over time, it will get used to the new area and will feel at home there.

You can help the process along by offering little treats to the timid cavy in its hideaway so that it associates the new playground with good things. Then, take the process a step further by luring it out of its hiding place with a tasty tidbit and some encouraging words.

Guinea pigs need to feel secure. Put a hideaway in any play area.

plastic drop cloth or shower curtain, top it with a cheap fleece blanket or two, unroll the playpen, stand it up, overlap the ends, and secure them with the Velcro strap that's provided. Add some toys, tunnels, water bowls, and hay, and you're ready to go—no cavy proofing, no gnawed furniture, no stained floors. When playtime is over, remove the toys, roll up the playpen, clean the blankets and plastic, and store everything away.

Another possibility is to make a pen out of wire-shelving grids, the kind used for C&C cages. If you join the sections together with heavy-duty twist ties or lock ties, you'll be able to fold up the pen, accordion-style, for easy storage. Don't connect the sections too tightly, though, or you'll have difficulty folding them up.

A guinea pig playpen

What can you do if you don't have any area in your home that's suitable for a cavy playground? The answer is simple—set up a pet playpen. What sort of playpen? The answer to this question is not quite so simple. Many of the wire playpens for small pets on the market are smaller than a good-sized C&C cage. You could join two or three wire pens together to make one large pen, but that might be expensive. Or, you could opt for a flexible plastic playpen (google: plastic "wall" pet playpen). These easy-to-use enclosures are a breeze to set up. Just lay down a heavy-duty

Outdoor play

A guinea pig playpen also comes in handy for outdoor exercise. Most guinea pigs enjoy a breath of fresh air, so why not set up a playpen in a shady area, and give them a mini-vacation?

Choose a good day for outside adventures—not too hot, not too cold. If you're setting up the playpen on grass, make sure that the grass is dry and weed-free, and that it hasn't been sprayed with chemicals or contaminated by other animals. If you're setting up on a deck or patio, lay a blanket down first so the cavies will have something comfy under foot. Put a hutch, a water bowl, some hay, and one or two toys in the pen. Pop in the cavies, then supervise, supervise, supervise.

With outside playtime, supervision is a must. After all, the neighbor's cat could come calling, a hawk could swoop down, or a shady spot could become a sunny spot and bake the poor piggies. If you're concerned about predatory birds or animals, cover the playpen with chicken wire, or drape a sheet over the top of the pen and secure it with clothespins.

Of course, if your cavies are outside on grass, they'll eat the grass, and this can give them diarrhea if they haven't eaten grass before. To avoid this, start with short playtimes, maybe five minutes at a time, and gradually work up to longer playtimes. This will give your cavy's digestive system time to adjust.

Use the same strategy if you have any timid guinea pigs that aren't enjoying the great outdoors. Get them used to outdoor playtime a little at a time. What happens if one of your cavies doesn't seem to be comfortable outside after a few trial sessions? Don't force the issue. Stick to indoor exercise for any nervous Nelly or timid Thomas.

If your guinea pig plays on grass, make sure the grass has not been sprayed with chemicals.

Chapter Eleven

Learning Through Play

Fun and games with your guinea pigs

Think how bored you would be if you had to sit around in a small room all day with nothing at all to do. Wouldn't you go stir crazy? Well, what's true for you is also true for your cavies. They can get bored, too, if they're confined to a small space with nothing to keep them busy. So take a hard look at the life you're providing for your guinea pigs. Are you letting them languish day after day, or are you providing them with interesting and stimulating activities?

Guinea pigs that have plenty of activities to occupy their time become confident and outgoing. They develop a healthy curiosity and are willing to try new things—good traits for training! Not only that, playtime encourages the group to socialize and work out any dominance issues.

The good news is, you don't have to spend tons of money for your guinea pigs to have tons of fun!

Tunnel fun

Tunnels are a cavy favorite. They come in a variety of different materials such as cardboard, grass, hay, willow, and plastic. You can also find fabric tunnels with peek-a-boo holes. Why not connect several of these tunnels together end to end, or connect them at the peek-a-boo holes to make a maze? Hard-plastic ferret tunnels are suitable for guinea pigs, and they're easy to find. Or, you could buy a few sections of 4–6-inch (10–15-cm) diameter PVC pipe at a building supply store. Add

some elbows and T-connectors, and you can make a really elaborate tube system. Are your cavies plastic munchers? Then opt for tunnels made of natural material like willow or hay.

Feeling creative? Link tunnels to hutches or igloos, and watch your guinea pigs scoot from one to the other. Or take shoe boxes and tissue boxes, cut holes in the ends, and connect them with duct tape to form a network of tunnels.

Antics with paper and cardboard

For really cheap fun, paper and cardboard are hard to beat. Grab some paper bags, toss them into the play area, and watch the guinea pigs

scurry from one to the other. Or take a sheet of newspaper and crinkle it up. Presto—a paper ball! It you don't want your cavies playing with newspaper, use blank computer paper instead.

Tissue boxes and oatmeal containers stuffed with hay are fun for your guinea pigs to rummage in. The same goes for empty toilet paper rolls or paper towel rolls. You can stuff these with hay and put the odd veggie treat inside. Just be sure to slice the tube lengthwise first to prevent stuck piggies.

Toss toys

Guinea pigs like to toss small toys around, so keep a supply of sisal carrots and sisal corn on hand. Some bunny toss toys are also okay

for cavies, as are some small baby rattles and rings of baby keys. Plastic spoons are a possibility, too, as long as you're on hand to supervise. Are you good with a needle and thread? A baby sock stuffed with hay and sewn shut makes a great toss toy.

For something a little different, buy a small-animal bounce-back toy. Although these toys can't be tossed around, some guinea pigs enjoy nudging them and making them sway back and forth.

Baked pine cones

Here's a novel idea for a guinea pig toss toy. Gather some short, stubby pine cones with fully opened seed scales; they should come from trees that have never been sprayed. Arrange them on a double layer of foil or on a disposable cookie sheet; otherwise, the sap will drip onto your oven or ruin your favorite cookie sheet. Now bake them in a 200°F (93°C) oven for half an hour to steril-

ize them. Cool them completely and give them to your cavies to play with.

Balls

A guinea pig playground won't be complete without a ball or two (or three or four) for your cavies to push around. Paper balls, ping-pong balls, willow balls, and vine balls are all good choices. Wooden chew balls are good, too, but if you buy the kind with a nut in the center, supervise your guinea pigs when they're playing with it, and don't let them get at the nut—cavies can choke on shell fragments.

Digging for treasure

In the cage and out, cavies get a kick out of scavenging for treasures. All you need to do is hide a few little treats—under hay, in tunnels, or behind water bowls. This is one game that won't need any prompting on your part!

Stay away from...

Just because a toy is marketed for guinea pigs doesn't mean that it's safe for them. Exercise wheels and large exercise balls are examples. You might think that these toys will give your pets a great workout. In fact, they can injure guinea pigs because cavies don't have flexible backs like other small rodents.

Chapter Twelve

Training Technique #1—Lure-Reward Training

Luring with food

Now that your guinea pigs have settled in and feel comfortable with you, it's time to step up the training. There are all sorts of things you can teach your cavies, and there are different techniques for training them. The simplest technique is known as lure-reward training. It involves a four-step process:

1. You give your guinea pig a verbal cue, such as "Circle!"

2. You entice your guinea pig to perform the desired behavior by luring it with a treat.

3. Your guinea pig performs the behavior.

4. You reward it with the treat.

Why does this simple technique work? It's because guinea pigs will do almost anything for food! Of course, it's got to be the right food. The trick is to find treats that your guinea pigs go crazy over, and that could be something different for each cavy.

Picking the treats

Always stick with healthy treats like cilantro, carrots, romaine or leaf lettuce, parsley, bell peppers, blueberries, or cantaloupe. Once you have the treats lined up, the next thing is to dice them into very small pieces. There are two reasons for this. One—it's never a good idea to over-feed your cavy, and two— it's important to give your cavy a reward that it can eat quickly so that its attention stays focused on the

training rather than on the munching. Make sure to chop the treats into small pieces *before* the training sessions start, because you're going to be doling out several treats in quick succession. Short on time? You could hold out a chunk of vegetable to your cavy, and let it take one bite at a time as a reward.

Remember—a cavy shouldn't have more than one cup of vegetables/fruit per day and shouldn't have too much of any one fruit or vegetable at a time (see Chapter 2). So, offer a variety of treats, and vary the rewards from training session to training session.

Treats on the "no-no" list

Treat food does not mean *junk food*. Don't give your guinea pigs anything sugary, fatty, gooey, or salty. And pass on the snack food, the people food, the processed food, and the packaged treats. In other words, provide nutritious foods only, please.

Turning in a circle

It's a good idea to start lure-reward training in the play area (see Chapter 10), but don't start the training sessions until your cavies feel at home there. Before getting down to business, let them run around for a while to burn off their excess energy. Then pick out one trainee, and put the other cavies back in the cage so

they won't distract your piggy pupil or fight over the treats. When you own several guinea pigs, teaching one pet at a time is the way to go.

Now put the toys away so that your pet isn't distracted and can focus on training rather than playing. Leave a hutch out, though, to give your cavy a feeling of security.

For starters, it's best to train your cavies to do something easy, like turning in a circle. Here's how it's done. Hold a baby carrot in front of your cavy's nose. Let it have a good sniff and then a tiny taste—not a huge mouthful, just a nibble! After the bite is swallowed, put the carrot in front of your pet's nose again and say "Circle!" Now, using the carrot as a lure, lead your cavy around in a small, tight circle. When your guinea pig has completed the circle, give it another nibble of carrot as a reward, and heap on the praise.

Practice a few more times, but don't make your cavy dizzy! Remember, cavies have a short attention span, so it's always better to have frequent, brief training sessions rather than one long session. Before you know it, your cavy will be turning in a circle whenever you give the command, and will no longer need to be lured with the carrot.

Most cavies catch on pretty quickly. But if one of your pets is a slow learner, you'll have to teach it the behavior in stages. With this method, you reward your guinea pig with a nibble of carrot after you've led it a quarter of the way through the circle. Then reward it

Entice your guinea pig with a tasty carrot.

when it gets halfway through, and again when it gets three-quarters of the way through. Finally, give it a nice *big* bite of carrot when it has completed the circle. Breaking the behavior into smaller stages like this makes the learning process more manageable for some cavies.

No matter what you're training your guinea pigs to do, repetition is a key factor in ingraining the behavior. By getting your pets to do something over and over again, you help them to connect the command with the behavior you're teaching.

Random rewards

While your cavy is learning a behavior, it's important to hand out a reward each and every time it performs successfully. However, once your guinea pig has become a circle-turning pro, you can cut back on the treats a bit. Instead of dishing out a goody every single time your guinea pig turns around on com-

mand, give it a treat every second or third time. This is known as an *intermittent reward*, and research shows that, once a behavior is learned, intermittent rewards do a better job of reinforcing the behavior than giving a reward every single time.

What happens if a cavy starts ignoring your commands? Go back to rewarding that cavy every time it performs successfully.

A positive experience

Always make the training sessions a positive experience. Learning should be fun, so never yell at or get upset with your guinea pigs; they won't understand anyway. And if you find yourself getting frustrated because one of your cavies isn't catching on fast enough (not all piggies are created equal), stop the session and try again later. It's always better to quit while you're ahead!

Chapter Thirteen

Training Technique #2—Clicker Training

What is clicker training?

Click-treat, click-treat, click-treat! Have you heard about clicker training (CT), the successful pet-training technique that pet owners everywhere are raving about? Over recent years, CT has become one of the most popular techniques for training pets and other animals. How does it work? Clicker training uses positive reinforcement to teach animals specific behaviors. In other words, the animal gets a reward for behaving in a certain way and is then motivated to repeat the behavior for additional rewards. For your guinea pig, the positive reinforcement is going to be food, food, food. The clicker will be used to signal the fact that your pet has done exactly what you want, which will result in an immediate food reward for your cavy.

Why has this training method become so popular? There are several reasons. For starters, the technique is simple, it's easily learned, and it *works*. What's more, a clicker always sounds the same, no matter who's doing the clicking. Best of all, there's no punishment involved, so it's always a positive experience for your pet—and for you!

You might have seen clickers in the dog section of a pet store and wondered what they were. Or, maybe you've seen CT demonstrated with dogs on television. What you probably don't know, however, is that this training method is highly effective when teaching behaviors to a wide variety of animals. Ferrets, rabbits, cats, rats, monkeys, horses, birds, and dolphins all respond to the sound of a clicker. So why not give clicker training a try with your guinea pig? You've got nothing to lose but the cost of the clicker!

The clicker and the treats

You don't need much to get started—just a clicker and a supply of your cavy's favorite treats. A clicker is a small, handheld device that makes a clicking sound when you press it. You shouldn't have any difficulty finding one; they're widely available in pet stores and on the Internet, and you can buy one for a few dollars. In fact, it's a good idea to buy a couple at the same time in case you misplace one and can't find it when you need it. Just be sure to buy the same brand so the sound will be consistent.

Some clickers come with a wrist strap, some come with a finger strap, and some of them have a hole so they can be attached to a key ring. Some have a loud click, while others have a softer sound. For a guinea pig, what's needed is a clicker that's loud enough to be heard clearly, but not so loud that it scares your piggy. If your cavy seems afraid of the clicker, look for one with a quieter "click" sound. Or, you might be able to modify the one you have. If you wrap it with electrical tape, taking care to avoid the button, you should be able to muffle the sound. On the Internet, some people recommend using a ballpoint pen as a clicker. But, if you go this route, you can't use a ballpoint pen for anything else (like writing) because your cavies will get confused and think you're clicking for them.

What about treats? Again, stick with vegetables and fruits (see Chapter 12), and dice them into small pieces. Or, you might find it more convenient to hold out a sprig of parsley or a baby carrot and let your cavies take a bite as a reward.

"Charging" the clicker

As with lure-reward training, you should always teach clicker training to one guinea pig at a time. Take your first pupil to the play area, and leave the other guinea pigs in the cage. Ideally, the caged cavies shouldn't be able to hear the clicker, or they'll be looking for rewards, too!

Now for the first step—there's not much to it, but it is an important step. Sit down on the floor close to your pet; have some treats in one hand and the clicker in the other. Press the clicker once, and give your pet a treat right away. Then, continue to click-treat, click-treat, click-treat. That's all there is to the first step, which is known as *charging* or *loading* the clicker. What does loading the clicker accomplish? It teaches your pet that a click equals a treat. The precise timing is important. As soon as you click, give that cavy a single treat. Immediately!

Charging the clicker is simple—click-treat, click-treat.

At this stage, you're not actually teaching your pet any specific behavior. What you *are* doing is teaching it to associate the sound of the clicker with a reward. You do this by click-treating five to ten times in quick succession. Keep the treats tiny—a single leaf of parsley, a sliver of strawberry, a bit of bell pepper, a bite-sized chunk of carrot—something that can be gobbled down quickly by your pet. Next, vary the intervals between the clicks. Ten seconds—click. Five seconds—click. Three seconds—click. Seven seconds—click. This random clicking reinforces the connection between the sound and the treat.

Now the game plan is to repeat the loading of the clicker several times a day over the next day or two (or three or four) until your guinea pig is consistently making the association between the click and the reward. How will you be able to tell that your pet understands the connection? If it gets excited and starts wheeking whenever you bring out the clicker, or if it comes running over to you looking for a treat, then you can be pretty sure your cavy has received the message.

Once your pet has made the connection between the click and the reward, you can start teaching it some actual behaviors.

Capturing a behavior

In clicker training, there are four different ways to get a particular behavior you want from your pet. These are capturing, luring, modeling, and shaping. In this section, you'll learn about capturing a behavior. *Capturing* means catching your pet in the act of doing whatever you want it to do, and then marking that behavior with a click. For example, if your guinea pig is already running through tunnels in the play area (see Chapter 11), you shouldn't have any difficulty teaching it to run through a tunnel on command. Here's how.

Sit down in the play area, armed with your clicker and treats, and watch carefully. Whenever you see your cavy entering a tunnel, get ready to click! Don't click-treat, though, until your pet is actually

Use clicker training to teach your cavy to run through a tunnel. A piece of parsley works as a food lure.

coming out of the tunnel; just peering out of the exit or twitching that little nose doesn't count. Why not? Because what you're teaching your piggy is that *exiting* the tunnel is what gets him/her the reward.

Now wait until your cavy exits the tunnel again—click-treat. And again—click-treat. And again—click-treat. That's enough for this session. Training sessions should always be kept short because small animals have a limited attention span. It's always better to fit in several short sessions per day rather than one marathon session.

Keep practicing the same way over the next several days until the lightbulb goes on, and your cavy starts scurrying through the tunnel without prompting, in hopes of a reward.

Luring and modeling for results

Is your guinea pig showing no interest whatsoever in exploring the tunnels you've so thoughtfully provided? Have you sat there for a week already, and your cavy hasn't even sniffed at a tunnel? If this is the case, then how are you ever going to capture the behavior? Looks like you'll have to try something else instead if you're going to move things along.

Your next approach could be to *lure* your pet through the tunnel with a treat. With a short tube, you can just hold a treat in your hand, put your hand into the tube, and lure your pet this way. With a longer tunnel, you might have to tie a carrot to the end of a string and lure your pet by pulling on the string. No cheating! Don't let your pupil grab a bite.

As with capturing, you must wait until your little trainee emerges from the tube before clicking and treating. Now lure your cavy through the tube several more times, clicking and treating every time it pops out. Several practice sessions a day should soon have your guinea pig sprinting through that tunnel.

You might be wondering why you should even bother with a clicker if you can train your cavy with a food lure. One reason is that when you use a clicker, it's easier to pinpoint the precise behavior that your cavy is being rewarded for. Another reason is that the clicker has a unique sound that your pet hears only during training sessions (unlike your voice), and this sound conditions your cavy to think: "I've done what you wanted, and now I'm going to get a reward!"

Another way of encouraging your guinea pig to run through a tunnel is by *modeling*. No, this doesn't mean that you have to sprint through the tunnel yourself to show your guinea pig what to do! What it means is that you model your guinea pig's behavior by placing your pet at the opening of the tunnel, and giving it a gentle nudge in the right direction. As soon as the piggy comes out the other end, click, treat, and repeat.

Make a hoop free-standing by attaching it to a heavy bookend.

at a time—clicking and treating each step of the way. When you teach your cavy this way, it masters the behavior in small stages until, eventually, it reaches a final goal. In this section, the final goal will be hopping through a hoop.

First, though, you'll need a hoop. Your best bet here is an embroidery hoop. You can find them in any craft store or in the hobby section of a large discount store. Made of wood or plastic, they come in a whole range of sizes to accommodate piggies that are large or small.

When teaching hoop-hopping, some owners hold the hoop in one hand and manage the clicker and treats with the other. Other owners find it easier to have one hand on the clicker, and one hand free for dispensing the treats. Unfortunately, this doesn't leave a hand for holding the hoop! How can you get around this problem? You'll need to figure out a way to secure the hoop so you don't have to hold it. If your cavy exercises in a pet playpen with wire sides, the hoop can be attached to the wires with a couple of twist ties, lock ties, or zip ties. Attach the ties in such a way that the bottom of the hoop rests on the floor. If your cavy's play area isn't surrounded by a wire enclosure, you'll have to make the hoop freestanding by duct-taping it to a heavy coffee mug or bookend. The point here is to make the hoop both freestanding and sturdy—you don't want your guinea pig knocking over the hoop while leaping through it.

Many animal behavior specialists don't consider luring and modeling the best ways of getting behaviors from a pet, because luring relies on bribery, and modeling relies on your physical input. But these techniques can be very useful if your pet isn't cooperating or isn't giving you anything behavior-wise that you can work with.

Shaping, step-by-step

Shaping is an excellent clicker training method because it makes the animal think for itself, which ingrains the desired behavior better. It also allows an owner to teach more complicated behaviors. How does it work? You shape a behavior by teaching it to your pet one step

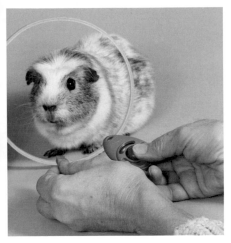
Click-treat when your guinea pig gets close to the hoop.

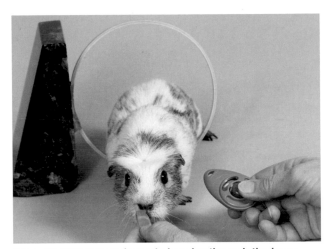
Click-treat as your guinea pig is going through the hoop.

To get started with the shaping, wait patiently until your guinea pig happens to walk close to the hoop, within about 6 to 8 inches (15–20 cm). Click-treat. This reward is just for being near the hoop. Then repeat this clicking and rewarding every time your pet comes this close to the hoop. Next, click-treat only when your piggy gets a bit closer— maybe within 4 to 6 inches (10–15 cm). Again, give a reward several times for coming within this distance of the hoop. After that, wait until your cavy is just 2 to 3 inches (5–7.5 cm) away before you click-treat, and repeat, repeat, repeat. See how your piggy is getting closer and closer to the hoop? Now, wait until your trainee is right beside the hoop before click-treating.

Then, be patient. Wait until those four little paws walk right through the hoop. Again, click-treat, and repeat several times.

So far, using a step-by-step process, you've trained your cavy to *walk* through the hoop. The next step is to teach it how to *hop* through it.

Begin by raising the hoop a quarter of an inch off the ground. Your cavy will hardly notice the difference, because it will still be able

Click-treat when your guinea pig has gone through the hoop.

to walk over the hoop. Click and reward for every successful walk-over. Then, once your pet is consistently clearing the hoop at this height, raise the hoop a little higher. Click-treat, and repeat. Then lift the hoop even higher. Click-treat and repeat. Before long, that little piggy will graduate from walking over the hoop to jumping through it.

Just remember, however, that cavies have short legs and aren't built for hurdling. So for safety's sake, never raise the hoop higher than 1 inch (2.5 cm) off the ground. And, if your cavy isn't comfortable jumping this high, don't force the issue. After all, your pet will still look cute, even if it's jumping only half an inch off the ground.

Shaping might seem like a slow process, but it's well worth the effort because it really works. Some guinea pigs master the sequence of steps pretty quickly; others take a bit longer to catch on. But regardless of how fast your cavy learns, the process can be fun for both of you!

Adding a cue or command

Whether you've used capturing, luring, modeling, or shaping to get a specific behavior from your guinea pig, you have to wait until your pet is reliably performing that behavior before going on to the next step in clicker training, which is adding a command—known in CT as the *cue*.

It might seem odd to wait this long before adding the command, but that's how it's done in clicker training. You ingrain the behavior first by clicking, treating, and repeating. Then, when your pet is doing exactly what you want, you add the cue. The reason for doing things this way is that you want the command to be linked only to the final, perfected behavior. For example, in shaping hoop-hopping, you want your guinea pig to know that "Hop!" is linked only to the final step of hopping through the hoop, and not to any of the intermediate steps, such as walking up to the hoop or walking through it.

Adding the cue is a process. Let's take hoop-hopping again as an example. When your guinea pig has learned to be a good hoop-hopper, call out the command "Hop!" or "Jump!" (or whatever other single word command seems good to you) while your pet is *in the act* of jumping. The moment it has cleared the hoop, click and treat. Practice this a while. The next step is to call out the cue just *before* your piggy jumps. Then click and treat once it's cleared the hoop. Again, practice this over and over. Your goal is to get to the stage where, whenever you call out "Hop," your guinea pig jumps through the hoop.

An important point to keep in mind when giving the cue is to give it only once. If you repeat the cue, your cavy will think that "Hop, hop!" is the command, and it won't spring into action until you've said "Hop!" twice.

Unrequested repeat performances

Some animals are pretty smart. As soon as they realize that a particular behavior nets them a treat, they start performing that behavior over and over again, without being cued, in hopes of getting a reward. Many pet owners find this unprompted behavior quite cute at first, but over time it can become really annoying. You can't prevent unsolicited behavior from starting, but you can stop it. How? Reward only cued behavior— no command, no reward.

Phasing out the clicker

Do you continue using the clicker once your guinea pig is running through a tunnel or hopping through a hoop on cue? The short answer is no. Once your pet has learned a behavior and can repeat it at your command, it's time to stop using the clicker to mark *that* behavior and start using it to teach your pet something else. In clicker training, the clicker is reserved for teaching new behaviors, or for reacquainting your pet with a skill that it has already learned but has managed to forget.

And what about the rewards? Do you phase these out, too? Not if you want your pet to keep performing! Even when you've stopped using the clicker for training a particular behavior, you still have to keep up the treats because if you don't, your pet will stop cooperating. However, as you learned in the lure-reward chapter, intermittent rewards often reinforce a behavior better than regular rewards. So instead of handing out a treat every time your pet performs on cue, give the rewards on a more random basis.

Clicking for success

So now your little piggy is a tunnel-running, hoop-hopping pro. But there's no need to stop there. Why not use CT to teach your pet a

Don't let your guinea pig call the shots! Reward only the behavior you ask for.

whole range of tricks and behaviors? Check out the next few chapters to read about the amazing things that guinea pigs can learn. And, if you're a fan of clicker training, you can teach all of these behaviors by using the same basic CT method:

1. Get your pet to perform a desired behavior by catching it in the act, luring it with a treat, giving it a little "help," or shaping its behavior step-by-step.

2. Mark the behavior with a click so your pet knows it has done what you want.

3. The very moment you click, reward with a treat.

4. Add the cue when your pet is consistently performing the desired behavior.

Has this short introduction to clicker training motivated you to explore the method further? Unfortunately, not a lot has been written about using clicker training for small animals. However, there are plenty of books and websites that explain

DOs and DON'Ts of clicker training

- DO practice on the floor in the play area.
- DO reward immediately after every click.
- DO speak nicely to your pet.
- DO keep training sessions short.
- DO keep training sessions fun.
- DO train one cavy at a time; trying to train two together can be confusing for the guinea pigs.
- DO clear the area of other pets.

- DON'T start a training session after your cavy's just eaten a meal.
- DON'T scold or punish; clicker training is positive training.
- DON'T click the clicker in your pet's face.
- DON'T click more than once to mark a behavior.
- DON'T yell out your cues.
- DON'T keep repeating the cue word when you give a command; once is enough.
- DON'T use the clicker for anything else.

how to use clicker training for dogs, cats, birds, and other animals. It's easy to take the CT techniques in those books and websites and adapt them for cavies. And, if you'd like to see how other owners have clicker-trained their guinea pigs, why not search the Internet for videos? They're fun to watch, and you'll pick up lots of training tips.

Chapter Fourteen

Coming When Called

Coming on command

Most pet owners understand the importance of training a dog to come when called, but it might not be so obvious why you'd want to teach that skill to a guinea pig. But think about it. If your guinea pigs are in a large cage (as they should be), how are you going to get them out for playtime without chasing them around the cage or frightening them by swooping down from above? Or, when playtime is over, how are you going to catch your cavies to put them back in the cage? The answer is simple: teach them to come when called, and save yourself and your cavies a lot of hassle.

There's more than one way of getting your guinea pigs to run up to you on command. Lure-reward training and clicker training both work well; use whichever technique you prefer.

Luring and rewarding

When you're training your guinea pig to come on command, it's best to teach this behavior in the play area, and it's best to sit down so that you're not towering over your pet. Get comfortable, and have the treats handy. A carrot or a slice of apple makes a good treat for this lesson because your cavy can take little bites as rewards.

Now it's time to get down to business. Start by sitting a few inches away from your pet. Hold out a slice of apple—close enough for your guinea pig to smell the treat but not close enough to bite it. Give a one-word verbal cue, such as "Come!" Then, entice your guinea pig to come toward you by luring it with the apple. When it gets right up to you, reward it with a nibble.

Since guinea pigs are such food hogs, most of them will be more than happy to follow a food lure. If yours doesn't, perhaps it's not hungry; try again later. Or perhaps you have the wrong treat; offer something tastier. Or, perhaps you're the problem. You may have yanked the lure too quickly, so try again, but slowly and steadily this time.

Once your trainee has got the hang of following the lure, repeat the whole process several more times to help ingrain the behavior. That's enough for the first training session. You will, however, have to repeat this process daily, preferably several times a day, until your cavy is coming to you consistently. Then, it's time to start increasing the distance your guinea pig has to cover. You began by luring your pet a few inches. Now try luring it a few more inches, and then a few more inches, until your guinea pig is covering a few feet to get to you. Over time and with practice, your cavy will no longer need to be lured at all but will come trotting over to you whenever you say "Come!"

Some owners whistle or clap for their cavies.

Using an alternative cue

Instead of using a verbal cue, some people prefer to use a sound cue. For example, instead of saying "Come," they ring a bell for their cavy or whistle for it. Use whatever works best for you, but always use the same cue. You'll just confuse your cavy if you whistle for it sometimes and call for it at other time. Also, think carefully about the sound you choose—you can't pick a sound that you already use for something else. After all, you don't want your cavy waiting hopefully for a treat when you're actually whistling for the dog!

Clicking for your cavy

Were you inspired by what you read in the chapter on clicker training? Then you might want to review that chapter and use this training method when teaching your guinea pig to come when called. Remember, in clicker training, there are four different ways of getting a behavior from an animal. These are capturing, luring, modeling, and shaping. If you plan on *capturing* the behavior, you'll have to wait until your cavy comes right up to you. Only then do you click and reward. After that, you'll have to do some more waiting until your pet gets close to you again. With friendly guinea pigs you shouldn't have to wait too long, because they'll probably come over to you quite frequently. But, if you have a piggy that's not quite so people-friendly, you could be waiting forever to capture this behavior.

Not willing to wait? A quicker way to get results is to *lure* your pet toward you. As in the *luring and rewarding* section, use a food treat to entice your pet to come over to you. However, in clicker training, there are a couple of differences from strict lure-reward training. One difference is that in clicker training, you mark each successful completion of the behavior (coming up to you) with a click before giving the reward. Another difference is that you don't add the cue ("Come") until your guinea pig has mastered the behavior, whereas in lure-reward training, the cue comes first.

Another way to encourage your guinea pig to come when called is to *model* its behavior. This means giving your trainee a little helping hand by guiding it gently toward you. Then, when it reaches you, click and reward.

Shaping is another technique used in clicker training. You shape a behavior by teaching it to your pet one step at a time—clicking and treating each step of the way. How does this work when coaching your cavy to come when called? First, sit down on the floor with the

clicker and treats. Now, whenever your guinea pig makes a move in your direction, click and treat. And repeat, repeat, repeat. Then wait until your cavy comes a bit closer before clicking and treating—then a little closer, and a little closer, until finally, your guinea pig is coming right up to you. Here's an important point to keep in mind. When your piggy is coming to within a foot of you, don't click when it's 2 feet (.67 m) away. That would be backsliding! Remember, there's a plan to the clicking. The goal is to get your guinea pig to come closer and closer to you a few inches at a time, until eventually your pet is being rewarded for coming right up to you.

Don't forget—whether you're capturing, luring, modeling, or shaping your pet's behavior, in clicker training you always add the cue after your pet has mastered the behavior.

Keep practicing

Whatever training method you're using, it's important to practice on a regular basis. After all, it's repetition that ingrains the behavior. But don't overdo the practicing. Frequent, short sessions get better results than long, drawn-out sessions. And, the bottom line is that training sessions should be fun!

Chapter Fifteen
Litter Training

Fact or fiction?

As every cavy owner knows, guinea pigs are absolute pros in the peeing and pooping department. Here are the facts. Adult cavies urinate every twenty minutes or so, and babies go even more frequently. And, because guinea pigs eat a huge amount of roughage, they tend to leave a little trail of poop pellets wherever they go. This is why many owners refer to their pets as "poop machines" or "poop factories."

Although you can't stop the production line, it is possible to train some cavies to go to the bathroom in specific areas of the cage and playground. How is this done? By training your pets to use a litter box or litter area.

Unfortunately, this is not as easy as it sounds. Cavies are not cats. They don't have the same inborn litter-box savvy and rarely learn to use a litter box 100 percent of the time. So what can you expect? This really depends on the individual guinea pig. Some cavies learn to use a litter box, or a specified litter area, most of the time; others cavies are suc-

cessful some of the time; and still others never catch on at all.

It's also the case that even when guinea pigs learn to urinate in the box, they don't always poop there. There's a reason for this. Guinea pigs defecate very frequently, so you can't expect them to head back to the box for every single poop deposit. They'd never get out of the box! Fortunately, stray poop pellets are easy to pick up, and cleanup is fairly simple. Just get out a whisk broom and dustpan for any fleecy flooring, and use a plastic spoon and cup to pick up feces in regular pet bedding.

It's not the easiest job to litter-train a guinea pig—or two, or three. It will take a fair bit of time and effort on your part. However, if you're patient and have realistic expectations, you might be surprised at what your pets can achieve.

Coprophagy

One fact you need to know before getting started on litter training is that guinea pigs eat some of their own feces. Yep, this might sound (and look) pretty gross to you, but it's perfectly normal for cavies. The practice is called coprophagy, a word that means "eating feces." Cavies produce two different types of feces: the regular, harder waste pellets and, the smaller, softer, edible pellets. These softer pellets contain recycled nutrients that weren't extracted from a guinea pig's food on its first pass through the digestive system. The vitamins and minerals the pellets contain are necessary for a guinea pig's health and well-being, so never try to stop your pets from eating their own feces; you'd be compromising their health.

Picking a suitable litter box

Guinea pigs have very short legs, so it's important to provide a litter box with a low entryway. After all, if your cavies can't get into the box, they certainly won't use it! Most cat boxes and rabbit pans are too high for guinea pigs, so you can cross these off your list. Ferret litter boxes, on the other hand, are usually suitable for cavies because they have low entranceways to accommodate short ferret legs. If you're shopping on the Internet, realize that photos can be deceiving; what looks like a low entryway in a photo might actually be too high for your guinea pigs.

Another possibility is to make your own cavy litter box. This is

A guinea pig litter box needs a low entranceway.

where your imagination and do-it-yourself skills come in handy! The very simplest homemade litter box is not a box at all; it's just a paper bag turned on its side, with several layers of newspapers or paper towels laid inside, and a little hay stashed at the back. With a paper bag, guinea

Use a paper bag and hay for a cheap, disposable litter box.

pigs have the privacy they like, and you have the easiest possible cleanup. Just toss and replace the bag, or recycle it if pet-waste recycling is available in your area.

For a sturdier, more durable litter box, you could buy a rigid-plastic dish pan and make an opening in it. Do this by either cutting off one corner of the pan, or by cutting out a low doorway in one of the short ends of the pan. This job is easier if you cut the plastic with a high-speed rotary tool, but a hacksaw will work too. Smooth off the cut edges of the doorway with sandpaper so your cavies won't get scratched on any rough edges.

An even better idea is to use a rigid-plastic storage box with a lid.

Cut out and sand an entryway as described for the dish pan, then replace the lid. This D-I-Y litter box makes an excellent guinea pig bathroom because most cavies prefer to do their business in private, and in a dark corner. Of course, if you make the dishpan litter box, you could always make it more private by draping a towel over the top and securing the towel with binder clips.

Do you have you some coroplast left over from making the cage? Or, are you the type of fashion-conscious cavy owner who would like to have the litter pan color-coordinated with the cage? Then you could make a shallow coroplast pan or a higher, lidded coroplast box for your guinea pigs.

If you're not too great at do-it-yourself projects, you could always buy a ready-made coroplast pan from the Internet. Just google "washable coroplast litter box," and you'll find a link to a site where you can buy a ready-to-assemble coroplast box, complete with a triple-layered, washable litter liner. This liner is like a slipcover; it goes right over the whole tray box so there are no exposed plastic edges for your guinea pigs to chew. As an optional extra, you can buy a grid and curtain accessory that turns the litter box into a private bathroom.

Litter choices

Now that you've bought or made a litter box or two, you'll have to decide what you're going to put in them. There are lots of litter choices out there, but not all of them are suitable for guinea pigs. For example, you should never buy clay cat litter. It's dusty and can cause your pet to have respiratory problems. Never use cedar or pine shavings because these shavings contain phenols, which are chemical compounds that can also cause respiratory problems in small animals. What about kiln-dried cedar or pine? The jury is still out concerning the safety of these products for small animals, so check with your veterinarian before opting for either of these types of litter.

Aspen pellets have good absorption and odor control.

Remember, guinea pigs are herbivores, so grain-based or grass-based litters are not the best choice. These litters can easily be mistaken for food pellets, and you certainly don't want your cavies filling up on litter pellets rather than guinea pig pellets! Some owners use corncob litter, but again, guinea pigs sometimes eat this litter, and if they do, they can develop intestinal problems.

Newspaper and paper towels are readily available and cheap, so many people use these in the litter box and top them with a layer of hay. But if you're going to go this route, you'll have to clean out the litter box frequently because once the paper gets wet, it's likely to stay wet. Also, many cavies like to play with paper, and some of them develop the annoying habit of dragging the newspaper out of the box.

So what are good litter choices for cavies? Hardwood shavings and pellets (like aspen) get good reviews, as do paper pellets and wood-pulp small-animal litter. Another product that's growing in popularity is biodegradable hemp litter. It's a good idea to top any of these litters with a soft layer of hay. This encourages the guinea pigs to go into the box because they can eat the hay as they're going about their business. Of course, the hay will get wet and will have to be changed every day.

If your guinea pigs aren't going into the box at all, perhaps the smell or the texture of the litter is not to their liking. Try another litter. And how about hanging a hay rack or treat ball right next to the box? This will encourage your guinea pigs to get down to business because they can snack on the job.

Tip: hang a treat ball next to the litter box.

private corner of the cage—so that's where the litter box should go. It's always better to put the pan where your guinea pigs want it, rather than where you think it should go.

To encourage your pets to use the litter box, prime it with some pee and poop. First, place some fecal pellets in the pan. Then, if you're using small-pet bedding in the cage, put some urine-soaked bedding into the box. Or, if you're using fleece as cage flooring, blot up some urine with a couple of small pieces of paper towel and add these to the box. For added encouragement, put some hay or some pieces of carrot at the back of the box.

Whenever you see your cavies performing in the litter box, give them lots of praise and a tasty treat. In fact, it's not a bad idea to give them a treat just for going into the box! This way, they'll associate the litter pan with good things and will be more likely to make repeat visits.

Whatever kind of box you pick, and whatever type of litter you put in it, you'll have to keep the facilities clean, clean, clean. Replace the litter on a regular basis, and at the same time, give the box a good wash with scent-free soap, rinsing it well. Another tip is to have two identical boxes so that when one is being washed, the other one can be in use.

Cage training

The first step in litter training is to monitor your guinea pigs' activities carefully, so that you can figure out which corner of the cage they're using for their bathroom breaks. Cavies tend to urinate in the same spot—usually in the darkest, most

Training in the play area

Whatever type of litter box you've provided in the cage, it's a good idea to provide that same type in the play area. This way, your guinea pigs will know what the box is for and hopefully, they'll use it in both places.

As with cage training, the first step in play-place training is to keep an eye on your cavies and see where they prefer to go to the bathroom…usually in the darkest, most out-of-the-way spot. That's where to put the litter box.

Now, as with cage training, prime the box with some feces and urine-soaked bedding or paper towel. Add some hay to encourage visits, and be ready with tasty treats for rewards.

Chances are, if your guinea pigs are using the litter box in their cage, they'll catch on in the play area, too. But what if one of your gang decides to use a different bathroom spot? Save yourself the gray hair by providing an extra box.

Potty station

As an alternative to a litter box in the play area, some owners have had good success with setting up a "potty station" for their guinea pigs' floor time. To set up a potty station, you'll need either a washable, waterproof hospital pad or a low-pile, rubber-backed, washable bathroom rug. (You might even need a couple of pads or rugs side-by-side if you have several cavies.) Lay the pad or rug in the area of the play place where your cavies are going potty. Top it with a thick layer of newspaper, then add some fecal pellets and wet bedding. What you've just put together is a litter area. Since a litter area is much larger and less confining than a litter box, your cavies have a better chance of "going" in the right spot.

It helps to add a water bowl, a few small piles of hay, and a hutch to the potty station. This way, the station becomes the central hub of your pets' play place. And, since guinea pigs tend to relieve themselves near their food and water, they're likely to use the area as their bathroom.

Cleanup of the potty station is simple. Just toss and replace the paper daily, and machine wash the rug or pad when necessary.

Accidents will happen!

It might take some trial and error to work out the right combination of box, litter, and location. And getting this right is still no guarantee of complete success. Remember guinea pigs are not cats—they're not going to hit that litter box 100 percent of the time. And, even if your pets get the hang of urinating in the box, they might not always poop there.

The best way to approach litter training is with patience and praise. Never scold or get mad at your guinea pigs for missing the box; they won't have a clue what the problem is, and all you'll do is frighten them. What you should be aiming for is to keep litter training stress-free. How do you do this? Reinforce the good behavior with praise and treats, and clean up any accidents without complaint.

Chapter Sixteen
Teaching Tricks

Make life interesting

There's more to teaching tricks than making your guinea pigs look cute. Training your cavies is a way to stimulate them mentally and keep them active physically. Another big plus is that training time strengthens the bond between you and your pets. What's more, it's fun!

Which training method to use?

You're already familiar with two basic methods of training guinea pigs: lure-reward training and clicker training. So which one are you going to use for teaching tricks to your cavies? It's really up to you. Some pet owners swear by clicker training; others prefer the lure-reward method. Still others make use of both methods. For example, they might use lure-reward training to teach turning in circles, and clicker training for jumping through a hoop. There's no right or wrong here. Go

with whatever works best for you and your pets.

In this chapter, you'll find step-by-step instructions for teaching your cavies a variety of tricks. Some of the tricks will be taught using the lure-reward method; others use the clicker training method. But feel free to adapt the instructions to whichever technique you feel most comfortable with. And, if you can't remember the ins and outs of each method, you might want to go back and review the lure-reward and clicker training chapters before getting started.

Touching a target stick

This trick involves teaching your guinea pig to touch a ball at the end of a stick. So, the first thing you need to do is either buy or make a target stick. You'll find a variety of target sticks for training dogs and cats in pet stores or on the Internet. Most of these are retractable, and some even have a clicker in the handle. This is a handy feature

By taking things step-by-step, your guinea pig will go from looking at the stick . . .

because you don't have to juggle both a stick and a clicker. Feeling innovative (or cheap)? You could make your own target stick by jamming a sponge ball onto the end of a stick, a wooden skewer, a skinny dowel, or a long pencil.

Now you're going to use the clicker to shape your guinea pig's behavior—in this case, to touch the target stick. So sit down in the play area, and hold the ball of the target stick 2 to 4 inches (5–10 cm) in front of your guinea pig's face. Every time your cavy even *looks* at the stick, click and treat. Next, keeping the stick in the same position, wait until your pet makes a move toward it. Again, click, treat, and repeat. Then wait until your piggy actually touches the stick before clicking and treating. Take note: your cavy has to be reliably touching the stick before you can take this training any further.

. . . to touching the stick.

Click-treat and repeat—a guinea pig can learn to follow a target stick.

What comes next? You continue shaping your guinea pig's behavior so that your pet learns to touch the target stick when you hold it in a variety of different positions. For example, you could try holding the stick above your piggy's nose. As soon as your pet actually reaches up and touches the target, click and treat. Then repeat, repeat, repeat until your pet is consistently touching the stick every time you hold it up at this height. Then try holding the stick to the left side of your cavy. When your trainee finally has the hang of this, move the stick over to the right side. Remember, every new position needs to be mastered before you move on to the next one.

Now it's time to increase the distance between your cavy and the stick. So hold the stick further away from your cavy's nose, perhaps 6 to 8 inches (15–20 cm), and wait until your cavy walks over and touches it. Click, treat, and repeat at this distance. Once your pet is a pro at 6 inches (15 cm), increase the distance to 12 inches (30 cm); click, treat, and repeat.

Mission accomplished? Not quite. Don't forget, you still have to add the cue. As soon as your guinea pig is consistently touching the target stick, add the word "Touch." But remember, adding the cue is a process. In target stick training, first call out "Touch" when your piggy's nose is right on the target (repeat, repeat). Then, change your timing, and say "Touch" immediately before your piggy touches the target (repeat, repeat). Then, change your timing again, and call out the cue as your cavy is moving toward the target (repeat, repeat). What you're doing here is teaching your guinea pig to connect the command to the action. Your eventual goal is to get to the point where your guinea pig will come right up to the target and touch it whenever you say "Touch." At this stage, you phase out the clicker for this behavior, and start using it to teach something new.

If you need to refresh your memory about the process of adding the cue and phasing out the clicker, refer back to Chapter 13 for detailed instructions.

Follow me!

Now that your cavy is touching a target stick on command, it's time to make that stick a moving target. To do this, hold the stick right in front of your cavy's nose. But don't let your pet touch it! Instead, start pulling the stick toward yourself. Your piggy will almost certainly follow it because the little genius already knows that touching the target results in a treat. After you've pulled the stick back about 8 inches, let your trainee touch the target, then click and treat. And repeat, repeat, repeat. Then increase the distance a bit at a time, clicking, treating, and repeating, each step of the way. Before long, your guinea pig will be following the stick across the room! Then, it's time to add the "Follow" cue.

A guinea pig scampering after a target stick looks cute, but the cuteness factor is not all that's involved here. There are also useful reasons for teaching this behavior! For example, you can use the stick to lead your cavy back to its cage after playtime. Or, if your cavy somehow gets under the sofa, just extend the

stick, call out "Follow," and your pet will come scooting out in no time. As an added plus, you can use the target stick to teach your pet other tricks like hopping through a hoop or running through a tunnel. Just get your cavy to follow the moving stick.

Stand up and beg

Most guinea pigs look pretty cute when they stand up on their hind legs and beg. And, it's a simple trick to teach them with the lure-reward method. All you need is a little patience and a supply of veggie treats.

The first step is to hold a treat, like a parsley sprig, in front of your piggy's nose. Sniff, sniff! Now that you've got your pet's attention, give the command "Stand" or use a hand signal to indicate *up*. At the same time, start raising the parsley. If you have an agile guinea pig, you might be able to lure it into a standing position at the very first try. If not, you'll have to teach this trick in stages. Here's how.

Dangle the parsley in front of your cavy's nose so that it gets a good whiff. Say the word "Stand," and slowly lift up the parsley. When your cavy stretches its head to follow the veggie lure, let it grab a nibble. Repeat this a few times. The next stage is to say "Stand" again, and raise that parsley sprig a little bit higher so that your cavy has to reach up further to get a bite. As before, repeat several times. Then,

Head up . . .

. . . all the way up!

. . . half-way up . . .

it's just a matter of raising the sprig a bit higher and a bit higher until eventually, your piggy is standing on its hind legs to get at the parsley.

Practice and repetition is what ingrains the behavior and what gets your guinea pig to connect the command with the standing up. How long will this take? It depends a lot on the individual guinea pig. Some little Einsteins can learn to stand on command pretty quickly; others need lots of repetition before they realize that "Stand" means "get up on those hind legs." Still others will follow the lure but will just look at you blankly when you give the command "Stand."

A word of caution here: not all cavies are physically capable of standing up on their hind legs. Older or obese guinea pigs, or guinea pigs that are ill or have had injuries, might not be strong enough to perform this trick. Never push any guinea pig beyond its abilities! Training should be fun and safe.

Rolling a ball

Before you can teach your cavy to roll a ball, you need to buy one. What's suitable? A regular tennis ball, a pet tennis ball, a small-animal treat ball, a hard-plastic dog ball, a kid's PVC ball, or a ping-pong ball will all work. It doesn't matter whether the ball is big or small, as long as it's lightweight enough for your guinea pig to push around, and sturdy enough so your pet can't chew bits off and swallow them.

After you've picked out a ball, pick out one of your guinea pigs and pop both ball and piggy into the play area. Now sit back and watch. Your cavy might be curious (especially if you rub the ball with a piece of cucumber or parsley) and might nudge the ball along with its nose. If so, you're in luck! You've captured the behavior, so click and treat. Then wait and repeat; wait and repeat.

If you're not so lucky, you'll have to shape the behavior. Is your piggy looking at the ball? Click and treat. Is it making a move toward the ball? Click and treat. Is it giving the ball

a little nudge? Click and treat. Is it pushing the ball along? Click and treat. Is it pushing it even further? Click and treat. Get the idea? You're shaping your pet's behavior a little at a time, by a process of repetition and reward. Now it's just a matter of

adding a cue, and getting in a lot of practice.

Ringing a bell

If you check out guinea pig videos on the Internet, you'll probably find some clips of cavies ringing bells. Pretty cute, huh? Well, your cavies could do this, too. All you'll need is a bell and a handful of delicious veggie treats.

You don't need to attach the bell to the cage wires—you can hold it instead.

When you go to the pet store for a bell, it's a good idea to visit the bird aisle first. Here, you'll find a variety of small, metal parrot and budgie bells that are perfect for piggies. But before you whip out your wallet, give all the bells a good shake. What you're looking for is something with a nice, soft tone, because anything too harsh or loud can scare a guinea pig. Most bird bells are attached to a chain, either metal or plastic. Avoid the plastic ones unless they're guaranteed chew-proof.

When you get home, clip the chain onto the cage wire so that the bell is hanging at your cavy's nose level. Next, rub the bell with a freshly cut slice of cucumber or a parsley sprig. This gives the bell a tantalizing aroma that will whet your piggy's curiosity. Now, park your cavy right next to the bell and say "Ring." At this point, the smell of veggie on the bell should pique your pet's interest and encourage it to nose at the bell. As soon as your cavy touches it, dish out a veggie treat, and keep treating for every touch.

Has your cavy made the bell ring with all this touching? The minute your trainee manages this feat, heap on the praise and hand out extra treats. After that, reward your cavy only when it actually rings the bell . . . touching is no longer enough.

Keep repeating the ring-and-reward process until you're certain that your piggy understands what "Ring" means. Before you know it, your pet will impress all of your fam-

Use a target stick . . .

ily and friends with its bell-ringing skill.

The Guinea Pig Olympics

Do you have some athletic guinea pigs on your hands? Why not set up a mini obstacle course and train your mini athletes to sprint around it? This is a great way to encourage your guinea pigs to get the exercise they need.

You can make a colorful and challenging course with half a dozen brightly colored mini traffic cones to use as weave poles, a section of ferret tunnels, and a small barbell-shaped hand weight. The mini cones can be found on the Internet or in toy stores. For a more contemporary, industrial look, you could use a few unopened soda cans for weave poles, a flat brick as a mini balance beam, and a piece of black PVC piping for a tunnel. Or, you can use your own imagination to dream up other

. . . to teach your guinea pig . . .

. . . to go through an obstacle course.

obstacles. But remember, whatever you come up with, your guinea pigs' safety has to be your number one concern—avoid using items that are sharp, wobbly, or too high.

After you've put the course together, grab a tasty guinea pig treat, and plop a cavy at the start line. You can also grab your target stick if you've taught your cavy to follow one. Now what you're going to do is lure your piggy through the course one section at a time. For example, when you're teaching your guinea pig to weave through the cones or soda cans, give the command "Race," and then lure your pet around the first two cones. Give it a treat, and repeat the two-cone training several times. Then say "Race," and lure your pet around three cones; treat and repeat. When your cavy has learned to weave its way through all the cans or cones, the next step is to lure it from the start line, in and out of the cones, and then through the tunnel. Treat

and repeat; treat and repeat. Now, lure your piggy from the start of the course, around the cones, through the tunnel, and over the hand-weight hurdle. Again, treat and repeat. The training is complete when you can give the command "Race," and your guinea pig sprints around the whole course without needing to be lured. Don't forget to reward that clever piggy with a treat!

Some small animals respond better to obstacle-course training if you start them off with the final obstacle in the course and then work back to the start, one obstacle at a time. For example, in a course that consists of cone weaving (first obstacle), a tunnel (second obstacle), and a hurdle (third obstacle), have your pet master the hurdle first. Then teach it how to run through the tunnel, and lastly, how to weave through the cones.

Here's something to keep in mind: an obstacle course involves multi-task training, so it will take

Guinea pig basketball: pick up a ball . . .

multiple practice sessions before your guinea pig masters the whole course. But the training is entertaining for both of you, isn't it?

More tricks for treats

So now you've taught your guinea pigs to ring bells, roll balls, and sprint around obstacle courses...but don't stop there! There are lots of other tricks you can try! For example, piggies look really cute when they learn to give high-fives with one paw, or wave with both paws. And, have you thought about training a cavy to flip a jar lid or pick up a small wicker basket with its teeth? You can even teach a guinea pig to play a version of basketball. How? Coach it to pick up a small cat lattice ball with its

teeth, and then place the ball into a shallow bowl.

When you're teaching tricks, use whatever method works best for you. After all, it's not the method that's important. What *is* important is that your pets have a more active and interesting life.

. . . drop it in the bowl.

Chapter Seventeen
Lessons in Leash Walking

Leash walking a guinea pig?

Everyone knows that dogs need to be walked, but have you ever thought about leash walking your cavies? Hmmm…weird or what? But think about it. Why wouldn't your piggies enjoy a whiff of fresh air? To make this happen, you just have to be safety-conscious and use your common sense.

Choosing a harness and leash

Choosing a harness and leash is pretty easy—buy a set made for guinea pigs. Never, never, never use a collar instead of a harness. To start with, a guinea pig can easily escape from a collar, and a collar can also choke your cavy. So with guinea pigs, a well-fitting harness is the only way to go.

Harnesses come in a variety of types and sizes. To find one that's just right, take your cavy to the store for a fitting. What you're looking for is a harness that's snug but not too tight. Then, clip on a leash and you're ready to go.

Getting your cavy accustomed to the harness

Before setting a foot out the door, you should practice leash walking indoors. There are two reasons for this—you need to get your guinea pig accustomed to its new gear, and you need to make sure that your pet can't escape from the harness.

Putting a harness on a cavy might not be the easiest thing you've ever done. Some piggies tolerate it, no problem; others don't want anything to do with it. If your cavy is a wiggler, be careful because guinea pigs are easily injured. Try distracting your pet with a treat—while your cavy's concentrating on munching, you can be concentrating on fitting its harness. Remember, guinea pigs have small bodies but lots of fur,

A harness and leash for outdoor strolls.

so fit the harness to the body rather than to the fur.

Got the harness on? Now take some practice strolls around the house. You have to make sure that your guinea pig has no problems walking in its new harness, and that your pet can't wriggle out of the harness. Do not skip this step!

The great outdoors

After some practice runs inside, it's time to venture outside. Many guinea pigs will never get beyond the backyard or the patio...they're just too nervous of noise or new situations. And that's just fine! But some guinea pigs enjoy short strolls around the neighborhood. However, always keep a watchful eye on your pet, and never push it past its toler-

ance level. If your cavy keeps backing up or freezing in place, or if it's showing any obvious signs of distress, gently scoop it up and take it right back inside. Does this mean the end of outdoor leash walking? Not necessarily. Over time, a nervous piggy can often be desensitized to outdoor sights and sounds by taking it on frequent, short walks.

On the other hand, if your guinea pig is really frightened, forget the outdoor walks. It's better to have a happy indoor piggy, rather than a miserable outdoor one.

Outdoor rules

If you're going to be taking your cavy out and about, here are a few rules to follow. In the summer, avoid

Check the fit—a harness should be snug, but not too tight.

taking walks on hot days. Remember, your guinea pig is wearing a fur coat—unless your guinea pig's a skinny pig, of course! But hairless or not, cavies don't tolerate heat, so limit your summer strolls to mild days rather than hot ones. In winter, too, strolls should be limited to mild days. You might enjoy the cold and the snow, but your guinea pigs certainly won't.

Anytime you've got your guinea pigs out on grass, make absolutely sure that the grass is free of pesticides and herbicides. These chemicals can be lethal to small, furry animals. Not sure if your neighbor's grass is sprayed? If there are any doubts in your mind, find somewhere else for your guinea pigs to graze.

During your outdoor adventures, always be on the lookout for other animals. Even animals on a leash can be a threat, because some owners aren't too good at controlling their pets. So always be on the safe side. If you see another animal approaching, scoop up your pet, and walk off in the other direction.

Chapter Eighteen

Guinea Pig Travel Plans

The stay-at-home guinea pig

Many guinea pigs get stressed out in unfamiliar surroundings; they prefer to spend their lives chilling out at home. So, when vacation time rolls around, it's generally best to leave your cavies at home with a responsible friend, relative, neighbor, or pet sitter to take care of them. If you go this route, be sure to write down specific instructions for feeding and cleanup. And, in case there's a medical emergency while you're gone, you should always leave your veterinarian's phone number in a prominent place, as well as a contact number for yourself.

Is your guinea pig a home-lover?

What if you can't find a suitable sitter? You might have to board your pets instead. In that case, try to find a boarding facility that specializes in small animals, or one that can house your cavies in a separate area—well away from barking dogs or yowling cats.

Here's another pet-sitting possibility. If there's a guinea pig club in your area, you might be able to set up a reciprocal pet-sitting arrangement with a member who lives close to you.

Short trips

Sometimes, however, you won't have any option; your cavies will have to leave the house. For example, you might have to take them to a vet appointment. Or, you might

A pet-carrier is convenient for short trips.

have to drive them to a local guinea pig show. After all, they won't win any ribbons sitting at home!

When you're traveling with your cavies, the first step is to buy a suitable travel carrier. For a short trip, you don't need a huge carrier, but you do need one that's large enough for your guinea pig to move around in. Look for one that can be secured in place with a seat belt. This way, if you have to stop suddenly, the cage won't fly off the seat and become a dangerous missile.

Before using the carrier in your car, it's a good idea to get your cavies accustomed to it. If you place it in their play area, and put in some hay and a cozy sleep sack, they'll be encouraged to check it out.

Even on a short trip, your guinea pigs could get thirsty. So, take along some water, or toss some cucumber slices into their carrier. Cucumbers, with their high moisture content, can quench a cavy's thirst.

When transporting your pets in a vehicle, always pay close attention to the temperature. On cold days, warm up the car before putting in the carrier. On hot days, crank up the air conditioner, and use a window shade made especially for vehicles. These shades block out the sunlight and heat but don't obstruct the driver's view.

Longer journeys

If you're moving into a new house, or going to a cavy show in another state, the car ride could be a long one. So do your pets a favor—invest in a large pet carrier or a commercial guinea pig cage so that your piggies have some roam room. Stock the carrier with all the comforts of home, such as food, hay, cozy bedding, and a chew toy or two. Provide some cucumber slices or pieces of juicy fruit so they don't get thirsty. But don't put in a water bottle—it could jiggle around and leak. Even worse, your cavies could crack a tooth on the sipper if the car hits a bump while they're drinking. With no sipper bottle in the carrier, you'll have to make frequent stops to offer your cavies a drink. These breaks will also give you a chance to check on your guinea pigs.

Air travel

Most cavies will never be near an airport. But what if you're moving from the east cost to the west coast and are planning to travel by air? Can you take your guinea pigs with you?

You won't know until you contact the airlines that fly to your destination and ask the following questions:
• Are guinea pigs allowed to travel in the cabin in a carrier?
• Are you allowed to have more than one guinea pig in a carrier?
• What are the specifications for an airline-approved carrier?
• For air travel, does a guinea pig need a veterinary health certificate or any other documentation?
• What is the cost?

Guinea pigs should always fly with you in the passenger cabin of the airplane. Never arrange for your cavies to travel in the pet cargo section; it would be too nerve-wracking for them, and there would be too many factors beyond your control (e.g., noise, unsafe handling, tarmac temperature, etc.).

Make all of your plans well in advance, and get all of the information in writing. This way, you won't run into any hassles when you show up at the check-in counter.

For additional tips on traveling with pets, surf the Internet or search pet forums for the latest info.

Chapter Nineteen
A Lifetime of Learning

Ongoing interaction

So now you've learned the basics of training your guinea pigs. But don't stop there! Make training time part of your pets' daily playtime. If you keep up the practice, your cavies won't backslide and forget everything you've taught them. Not only that, you can build on what they've learned already, and teach them new and more complicated behaviors.

Guinea pigs are individuals

Not all guinea pigs are created equal. Some are quite bright and catch on quickly, while others are a little more intellectually challenged. But that's okay! No matter where your piggies are on the IQ scale, they all deserve a chance to reach their potential. Just don't be too rigid when it comes to training. Use whatever approach works, keeping each piggy's individual abilities in mind. Remember, training is supposed to be fun—not guinea pig boot camp!

A two-way reward

Training has benefits for both you and your pets. *You* get to spend quality time with your guinea pigs; you also have the satisfaction of knowing that you're improving their quality of life. *Your piggies* have a more challenging and stimulating existence; their brains and bodies get a good workout with every training session. As a bonus, time spent training equals time spent bonding.

So, whatever way you look at it, when you spend time training, you and your piggies all end up winners!

Information

Useful web sites

www.guinealynx.info
www.cavyspirit.com
www.guineapigcages.com
www.guineapigzone.com

Literature

Guinea Pigs, Popular Pet Series
Bowtie Press, Inc.
Magabook

Critters Magazine
Bowtie Press, Inc.
An annual magazine, which includes informational articles on guinea pigs.

Cavy associations

American Cavy Breeders Association
www.acbaonline.com

American Rabbit Breeders
   Association
arba.net

National Cavy Club
www.nationalcavyclub.co.uk

Index

The
Cure
for
Crushes

The
Cure
for
Crushes

(and other deadly plagues)

KAREN RIVERS

POLESTAR
An Imprint of Raincoast Books

Raincoast Books acknowledges the ongoing financial support of the
Government of Canada through The Canada Council for the Arts and
the Book Publishing Industry Development Program (BPIDP); and the
Government of British Columbia through the BC Arts Council.

Editor: Lynn Henry
Typesetting: Teresa Bubela

CANADIAN CATALOGUING IN PUBLICATION DATA

Rivers, Karen, 1970-
   The cure for crushes : and other deadly plagues / Karen Rivers.

ISBN 1-55192-779-9
   I. Title.
PS8585.I8778C87 2005   jC813'.54   C2004-906984-5

LIBRARY OF CONGRESS CONTROL NUMBER: 2005921632

Raincoast Books   In the United States:
9050 Shaughnessy Street   Publishers Group West
Vancouver, British Columbia   1700 Fourth Street
Canada, V6P 6E5   Berkeley, California
www.raincoast.com   94710

At Raincoast Books we are committed to protecting the environment and to
the responsible use of natural resources. We are acting on this commitment
by working with suppliers and printers to phase out our use of paper produced
from ancient forests. This book is one step towards that goal. It is printed on
100% ancient-forest-free paper (40% post-consumer recycled), processed chlorine-
and acid-free, and supplied by New Leaf paper. It is printed with vegetable-based
inks. For further information, visit our website at www.raincoast.com. We are
working with Markets Initiative (www.oldgrowthfree.com) on this project.

Printed in Canada by Webcom Ltd.
10 9 8 7 6 5 4 3 2 1

For everyone who has ever energetically maintained an inappropriate crush for completely unknown reasons and pretended (even to yourself) not to be doing it. Stop crushing! And start living your life! I insist. It will all work out for the best, I promise.

CONTENTS

crush

n 1: leather that has had its grain pattern accentuated [syn: crushed leather] 2: a dense crowd of people [syn: jam, press] 3: temporary love of an adolescent [syn: puppy love, calf love, infatuation] 4: the act of crushing [syn: crunch, compaction] v 1: come down on; "The government oppresses political activists" [syn: oppress, suppress] 2: to compress with violence, out of natural shape or condition; "crush an aluminum can"; "squeeze a lemon" [syn: squash, squelch, mash, squeeze] 3: come out better in a competition, race, or conflict; "Agassi beat Becker in tennis championship"; "We beat the competition"; "Harvard defeated Yale in the last football game" [syn: beat, beat out, trounce, vanquish] 4: break into small pieces; "The car crushed the toy" 5: crush or bruise; "jam a toe" [syn: jam] 6: make ineffective; "Martin Luther King tried to break down racial discrimination" [syn: break down] 7: become injured, broken, or distorted by pressure; "The plastic bottle crushed against the wall."

— WORDNET ® 1.6

crusha·ble adj.
crusher n.
crush'proof (-proof) adj.

Synonyms: crush, mash, pulp, smash, squash
These verbs mean to press forcefully so as to reduce to a pulpy mass

— THE AMERICAN HERITAGE ® DICTIONARY OF THE ENGLISH LANGUAGE, FOURTH EDITION

JANUARY

TGYML (The Greatest Year of My Life), cont'd.

Dear Junior,

So, hi. I'm back!

I missed you, even though it's only been a couple of weeks. You look good. Just kidding! You look the same as always: like a laptop. I wish there was a way to pick off that stupid Ben Affleck sticker, but there isn't. De nada.

Anyway, it's been a busy time. Christmas. School holidays. The having-a-boyfriend thing (more on this later!). Meeting my mom (she's a nun — how can this even be true?). Dad's court case.

But now school's back and everything's back to normal. Well, sort of normal.

Nope, not really normal at all.

Okay, it's gone awry.

A bit.

Okay, a lot.

It's just ... well, let me summarize.

Summary of The Greatest Year of My Life, so far, up to this point:
1. Have become active member in Student Council (aka Hell).

Note to Self: Find out if it is too late to quit Student Council as all activities relating to the words "pep" and "rally" hurt my head. Not to mention "prom," "graduation" or the dreaded word: "theme." Student Council President Bruce Bartelson has, in the course of only *four days* since returning to school from Christmas vacation, mentioned "prom" 87 times. I think that he waits for me in the hall so he can say, "Hi Haley, blah blah blah PROM blah blah blah." This is making me anxious.

Further Note to Self: Try to recall how and why I volunteered to be on the Every Dance of the Year, Not to Mention Prom Committee. I'm not a joiner! I'm not even a participator! How did it happen? How?
    Argh.

2. Have almost finished English, Math, Science and Auto Mechanics (elective for first semester) and must start studying for February final exams. Frankly, this seems like an odd (i.e., stupid) time to have final exams. Am not sure how I feel about new system where weird second semester starts in mid-February. But am looking forward to taking Drama, Phys Ed, Ancient Civilizations

and Art. Am proud of self for successfully planning such an easy second term for final year of high school. Really, ought to write a handbook on planning for high school students such that the last year is the most fun of all school years. Will remember to include a chapter on Not Volunteering for Councils or Committees. (Best-ish friends Jules and Kiki did not volunteer for any "council" or "committee" and are having more fun than me while I am corralled into lame meetings at inopportune times, such as during lunch hour and after school.)

3. Have survived bruising, chickenpox, meningitis, morphine and variety of other perils, including, but not limited to: bad hair, running and best friends.

(NB: Sometimes putting up with your best friends is a survival skill in and of itself, especially when one of your best friends, namely Jules, she of perfect hair, body, teeth and skin, steals the boy you've had a crush on since the ninth grade.) (Kiki, having decided to have a boyfriend-free graduation year, is clearly a better friend than Jules. Although have known Jules for longer, now like Kiki better, in spite of her beauty, brains and athletic ability, which all combine to make her really dislikable. Although she's too nice to dislike.)

(NB2: People may mock me for being a hypochondriac, but think about it: MENINGITIS! CHICKENPOX! I was born under an unlucky star. I'm not a hypochondriac, I'm VIGILANT.)

4. Have found my mother (should this have been further up the list?), who deserted me as a small child and devoted her life, oddly enough, to God. Which is fine. It is. I'm okay with it.

Sort of.

Okay, I'm not.

I tell people that I am, and that it's just ... unusual. (I'm used to hearing people say that, when I tell them. "That's, uh, unusual!" To say the least, "NO KIDDING.") It's almost sort-of unbelievable.

My mother, the nun.

You know, at some point, she had a choice. And she chose "Not Haley." I could be bitter, but I don't want to be, so I'm choosing not to think about it. Period. My mom is nice and everything, and would be pretty, maybe, if she got made-over. Some highlights and some makeup and some better fitting clothes. Not that she'd care about things like that. She is who she is, as my dad would say. It's just that she clearly has no maternal instinct or any fashion flair (though in all fairness that's hard to tell as she is forced to wear unfashionable clothing by the superior nuns). I suppose it's preferable to having a mother like Jules' who is a) very young and b) very pretty and c) has no compunction about stealing her daughter's boyfriends, as a random example. (Which is less of a problem now that Jules is dating JT, who is therefore no longer crushable. See above for Obvious Rant.)

5. Have convinced Dad to a) become vegetarian (sort of) (at least he doesn't regularly cook large slabs of beef in the kitchen anymore) (not that he was ever much of a cook) and b) seek work in a profession that is strictly legal and does not involve "activism" or "marijuana." This proved to be a bit tricky for him as he has no ...

um … obvious skills. He's very smart. He is. I swear. It's just that he's never done much in the way of, say, college. In related news, I am optimistic that he may cut his waist-length grey hair soon. Because I convinced him that he can't keep a job when he looks like an aging hippie. Progress!

6. HAVE BOYFRIEND NAMED BRAD.
7. See 6.
8. See above.

I always thought that I'd be one of those girls who never got to have a boyfriend. Someone who had a weird force-field that repelled boys for no clear reason. Like a magnet, but the opposite: Someone who was doomed to be alone forever.

But I'm not.

Nope, now I'm the Girlfriend of Brad.

Brad, Brad, Brad.

Me.

I'm somebody's girlfriend.

What can I say about Brad? Brad is soooo nice. Really. I know that sounds insincere, but it's true. Everyone says so. He's considerate, kind and caring. He says all the right things. If an old lady was crossing the street and needed some help, he'd help her. That's just the kind of boy he is.

Note to Self: Ask Brad if he was Boy Scout. (Can picture him in his little uniform proudly displaying all the badges. Cute! Brad is someone who would get badges. All of them. Even sewing.)

Brad has these blue eyes. Really blue. Blue as … well, the sky. Or the sea. Well, actually, they're a bit greenish. Or grey. Come to think of it, I'm not exactly sure I could describe them without looking at him. *I don't know exactly what colour Brad's eyes are.* No, I won't panic. It's no cause for alarm. It's perfectly normal, I'm just overthinking it. I once read somewhere that if you can't say what colour someone's eyes are, it means you don't love them. Not that I should read anything into this.

Of course I love Brad. He's my boyfriend.

Well, "love." Hmm. Not "love," actually. I'm not up for "love." The word is a bit like nails-on-a-chalkboard to me. Not to hear it, but to say it.

I mean, give me a break. I'm 16.

Anyway, I'm confident that Brad's eyes are blue-ish in colour and very smiley. When he smiles, they crinkle up, much like Andrew McCarthy's eyes in the '80s classic film *Pretty in Pink.* I love that film. (I know it's dorky, but my dad collects '80s movies. What can I say? He's full of surprises.)

Top Three Films from the 1980s:
1. *Pretty in Pink*
2. *Sixteen Candles*
3. *The Breakfast Club*

I wish I looked like Molly Ringwald.

And could make a beautiful dress out of a pink curtain.

Back to what I was saying about Brad. Brad is … perfect. He's what any girl would want. People are seriously jealous! Of *me.* (Even I can't figure that one out, so don't feel bad if you're surprised.) Once we were at Sophie's Cosmic Café having coffee and big pieces of pie. (It's really good there. I highly recommend it.) I went to the washroom to brush my teeth. (Always brush after eating. Otherwise you give all those bacteria plenty of opportunity to rot your teeth. Next thing you know, you're toothless.) I was flossing madly and a girl I didn't even know (blonde hair, looked like a model and/or a junkie, but pretty) came up to me and said, "What does *he* see in *you*?" Her lip curled up in a really horrible and rude way when she said it, too.

I was, well, stunned. I think I said, "Uh."

I wish I'd thought of something better, something witty. But I didn't.

Instead, I almost cried. (Luckily, I was in the washroom already, so I could fix my makeup before anyone saw me.)

Frankly, I don't know what Brad sees in me either. I'm not beautiful like Jules. Or smart and athletic like Kiki. I'm not even interesting. I can't remember the last interesting thing that I've done. And there is a possibility that I may be a slight (only slight) worrier/overthinker. Although I'm not interesting, things sort of happen to me. Like: I have a tendency to run into trees.

And I have a father who was in trouble with the law.

And a mom who is a nun.

And kind of a crazy life.

Is it my fault that I'm a bit paranoid?

It's always a good idea to look out for disease. And plague. (I'm sure that someone somewhere has a little vial of the Black Plague lying around ready to release into the air, like in that monkey movie with Bruce Willis). Think about it.

You wouldn't want something like "cancer" or "mad cow disease" to sneak up on you unawares.

But back to what I was saying about Brad. Brad is … I mean, he's … Well, he's just … For one thing, he plays hockey, which I didn't know when I first started kissing him. (We kissed before we were dating. It's a long story, but at least it got us past that awkward "first kiss" bit.) (Not to mention the first hickey.) (And I'm telling you, "Haley Hickey" is *not* a nickname that you want following you around for your entire graduating year.) I think he might be a really good hockey player, although I've only seen one game so far (there's another one later this month) and I don't know much about hockey. He's so modest, it's impossible to know from what he says if he's good or not.

Hey, maybe one day he'll play for the Vancouver Canucks or the New York Rangers and I'll be able to sit in the rink and watch him while wearing beautiful designer clothes and smiling prettily at him with my capped, perfect teeth. (Assuming, of course, that he'll be rich and he'll naturally want to improve my appearance by buying me nice things.) But why would he want to marry me?

Not that I'd think about marrying my high school boyfriend.

Honestly, I don't know why I'm even talking about marriage. What's got into me? Like Jules says, I just don't know how to be normal.

The thing with Brad is …

He buys me flowers. Okay, he bought me flowers once. But he does thoughtful things. Like, he doesn't even go to my school, but on the first day back after Christmas, he snuck in and stuck a card on my locker that said something cute and funny. Which I actually can't remember because when I first saw it, I thought it was threatening hate mail like in that movie *Swimfan* (but the opposite, because in that movie the girl was crazy and the boy was being stalked) except I hadn't cheated on Brad with someone in a swimming pool. (I'd never do that.) (And I hate swimming because water gets into my ears and gives me vertigo.) Brad also used red pen to write my name on the outside of the envelope, and for a second it looked like blood. Okay, not like *blood*, but it was ominous. I might have panicked. Just at first. Then I saw it was from Brad, and it was cute and funny.

He's very thoughtful. Thoughtful, cute *and* funny. It's just that he ... I mean, I feel like ...

I can't even say it, or type it. I can't because then you (if by "you," I mean "future me," as I'm the only person who should be reading this diary, and if you are NOT "future me" you should stop reading as this is very personal and if I wanted to tell you, I would, so give me a break, okay?) will think that I'm ... I don't know.

I don't know what I am.

It's just that sometimes Brad seems to like me so *much* that I kind of want him to go away. I mean, I like him. I do. I love having a boyfriend. But sometimes I can't breathe. I have to hold a paper bag over my face and take deep breaths.

And then when he goes home after a date, or drops me off, I can suddenly breathe again and I'm okay. Look, it's not like I can tell anyone about this. It's crazy. Everyone likes Brad. He's nice. He's funny. He's cute-ish. He's going to be a professional athlete, for heaven's sakes. AND EVERYONE LIKES HIM.

(It's possible that I don't like him much.)

I'm sorry. I'm an idiot. I'm going to pretend that I didn't say that and move on.

Maybe I'll delete it. I *should* delete it. I don't really mean it. Do I?

Argh.

List of Qualities about Brad that Make Him the Perfect Boyfriend:

1. Good looking, funny, nice, kind, athletic.
2. Probably smart, though have never looked at his report card.
3. Popular.
4. Understanding of weirdnesses, like when I suddenly can't talk on the phone anymore because it's making my ear feel funny.
5. Is JT's cousin.

List of Qualities about Brad that Freak Me Out:

1. Is very serious.
2. Possibly thinks he is in love with me.
3. Wants to be around me all the time.
4. Is very serious.
5. Wants to do, uh, more than I do.
6. Is JT's cousin.
7. IS WAY TOO SERIOUS.

So Junior, that's that. Do you remember why I called you Junior? It's because of JT. JT, the most perfect boy in school, the boy I had a crush on until he started dating Jules. But that's another story and you know it already.

I hate that I called you Junior. Am considering renaming you.

But that's not why I'm writing. I'm writing because I have Big News. Capital-B Big.

Dad got a job.

Am too excited to write more.

Love,

Haley, daughter of guy-with-real-job.

Sort of a real job.

Okay, I should explain. My dad, lovely hippie throwback to the sixties that he is, was caught last year growing and selling marijuana. (I'm so embarrassed. And please don't think that I support this in any way because I don't. I think marijuana makes you a) lazy and b) stupid. And c) hungry.) In a way, I was glad. I mean, I wasn't glad, because it was a terrible time for all of us, mostly for me. And I was in the hospital when it happened. It was v. dramatic, come to think of it. There was a giant roll of money and shady characters, jail and drugs, and a weird woman who kept visiting me and making me think I was *this* close to being put into foster care.

It seems surreal now. Almost like it didn't happen. But back to my dad, I'm *so* glad he doesn't grow marijuana anymore. It kind of freaked me out. I spent a lot of time waiting for him to get caught, and then it happened.

And it was horrible.

But that's over and now someone has to pay for a roof over our heads. And I'm only 16 (long story, I skipped the first grade.) (I'm not a genius or anything.) (Far from it.) (In fact, I have a recurring nightmare that I have to go back and complete kindergarten and Grade One as a result of not having done them at all because in a burst of unprecedented — and unrepeated — energy, my dad homeschooled me for exactly one year, during which time he taught me to read and how to do long division. And I couldn't very well go into Grade One already knowing third grade math. So the school randomly selected second grade because I was too young for third, and that's the whole story.) So what I'm saying is that I'm only 16 and can't be expected to be the wage-earner. I know I should get a job. But I should get a job to buy clothes, not to buy tofu and kitty litter.

I think Dad secretly wants to work like a normal person. I think he was sick of watching day-time TV (okay, he LOVES *Oprah* and *Dr. Phil*, but we have Tivo for heaven's sake, he can Tivo them) and operating a shady business out of the basement.

So he got a job.

It's all good, right?

▶ ▶ ▶

Monday, January 13

MOOD	Late, annoyed, edgy
HAIR	So short as to not matter — ok, it's sticking up
HEALTH	So far not bad

| HOROSCOPE | Today things will surprise you — remember, some surprises are good! Watch for the number 4. |
| ~~JT SIGHTINGS~~ | n/a |

9:07 a.m.

I was late for school this morning, but it wasn't my fault. It was Dad's first day of work and he refused to get up.

BUZZZZZZZZZZZZZZZZZZZZZZ.

That was, of course, the alarm. I hate alarms. I read on the internet that the stress of waking up every day to an alarm clock was the same as the stress you'd experience being held up at gunpoint. Every day. That can't be good for your heart, can it?

I turned the alarm off (by throwing it at the wall and missing entirely, managing to get it into the massively overflowing laundry basket) (no wonder I never have anything to wear) and cursed whoever decided that school ought to start at 8:45 in the morning. Why do they think we learn better by being sleep-deprived?

Then I remembered that it was Dad's first day of work, and I'd have to hurry to get to the shower first. (*NB*: The hot-water tank in this house is very old and sometimes only one person can have a hot shower and the water will remain cold for the rest of the day.) I had my shower and then perhaps spent a bit of extra time on my hair (due to an unfortunate incident with a candle last year, my hair was cut short ... and then shorter ... and then shorter ... and now it's so short, it's barely even there and yet takes more time to style than ever before). I should mention that it's now very dark brown, which gives it the illusion of being shiny and healthy even though it falls out in alarming handfuls when I blow it dry.

Note to Self: Look up "alopecia" on the internet at first opportunity.

Next thing I knew, it was 8:30. Perhaps I was wrong, but I thought Dad was supposed to be at work at 8:30 (the job he got is at a bakery), so I ran upstairs to his room (he sleeps in the attic on a mattress on the floor). He was sound asleep.

"Dad!" I said.

Okay, maybe I yelled.

Dad: Mmmmflfmmm.

Me: Dad! Get up! You're late for work!

Dad: [sitting straight up in bed, his long grey hair sticking out wildly] Oh.

Me: *Hurry up!*

Dad: It's not a very good job anyway.

Me: DAD.

Dad: Uhhhhhh.

Me: Dad, if you go back to sleep, I swear to God, I'll kill you.

Dad: Okay, sweetie. I'm up, don't sweat it.

Then I had to run for the bus, which I missed anyway. I only hope Dad made it to work. Honestly, I don't know who is the parent in this relationship. There should be a Dad Handbook. If there was, I'd give it to him for his birthday.

His birthday is coming up. Coincidentally, so is Brad's. THEY HAVE THE SAME BIRTHDAY. Both are Aquarians. Kiki says this is a sign. Kiki believes in astrology and karma and tarot cards. I believe in my horoscope. Sort of. I leave a lot of room for error, though. And coincidence. Like with Dad and Brad sharing a birthday. I think it's a weird coincidence, that's all. Life is full of flukes and only some of them mean something.

For example, I think it might be meaningful that JT and I arrived at school at the exact same moment. Albeit, I was on the bus and he arrived in what looked like a brand new Jeep.

"Hey," he said, pushing past me into the school (Sacred Heart High, aka SHH).

"Uh," I said. JT has green eyes. Dark green. Like the sea when you look down on it from the dock. Which is something I noticed, not meaningful. I don't even like him any more. So it simply shouldn't matter that I can't speak when he talks to me. That he makes the pit of my stomach drop to somewhere near my shoes.

That he smells so good.

I blame those things. You know, pheromones.

Brad, Brad, Brad.

Note to Self: Be better girlfriend to Brad.

12:14 p.m.
List of (Late) New Year's Resolutions Typed While Waiting for So-Called Best Friends to Meet Me for Lunch:
1. Lose five pounds.
2. Get job so can buy better clothes and maybe a car.

3. Learn to drive so that a car isn't such a weird thing to purchase.
4. Figure out reason for needing car, such as "going to college."
5. Figure out if want to go to college.
6. Explore career options so next time someone says, "What's next for you, Haley, after graduation?" I can say something other than, "Unnhhhhh."
7. Be better girlfriend to Brad and stop thinking things like "Please go away, Brad."
8. Abandon all feelings of crush for JT, which is OVER anyway.
9. Be better friend to Kiki and Jules.
10. Stop being jealous of Kiki and Jules.
11. Stop lying to self about ability to run 5k without throwing up.
12. Run more so as not to embarrass self during mini-marathon April 5.
13. Find reason to not run mini-marathon on Apr ...

Oh, there are Jules and Kiki. Never mind. Must go.

2:36 p.m.

Dear Junior:

Am glad to have "spare" period during which I can study and learn new things and NOT obsess about JT and unusual ridges on nails that suggest early heart disease. Oooh, which reminds me, must look up alopecia on internet.

Love,

Haleychondriac

(from mdadvice.com)

alopecia areata

DEFINITION: Sudden hair loss in circular patches on the scalp. Hair loss is not accompanied by other visible evidence of scalp disease. This is not contagious.

BODY PARTS INVOLVED: Hair; scalp; eyebrows; eyelashes; beard; genital area; underarm (sometimes).

SEX OR AGE MOST AFFECTED: Affects all ages and males more frequently than females.

SIGNS AND SYMPTOMS: Sudden hair loss in sharply defined circular patches. In rare cases, body hair loss may be total. No pain.

No itch.

CAUSES: Usually unknown, but heredity and emotional factors, such as anxiety, may contribute to hair loss. The autoimmune system may also be involved.

May be caused by thyroiditis or pernicious anemia.

RISK INCREASES WITH: stress; family history of alopecia areata.

HOW TO PREVENT: Cannot be prevented at present.

Cannot be prevented?

Hmmm. V. alarming.

And I definitely have the symptoms. I mean I have *no pain*. And *no itch*. And I certainly have stress. I wouldn't know about family history. It's just me and my dad and he doesn't exactly keep good records.

I tugged experimentally on the hair over my left ear and a couple of strands came out in my hand. When I pulled quite hard. I pulled on an eyelash to test and immediately got dizzy. I hate it when anything touches my eyelashes.

Note to Self: Check with doctor about alopecia if hair starts coming out in larger clumps.

What if I go bald?

That would most certainly turn TGYML (So Far) into TWYML (or Twimmel, as I like to think of it in my head). Which stands for The Worst Year of My Life. Obviously. Although this isn't TWYML. It can't be. How could it be? So far, it hasn't necessarily been perfect, but it's been good. I have a boyfriend! I have a mother!

I have every reason to be completely happy!

I have *no pain* and *no itch*!

Okay, maybe I'm not *totally* happy. But I should be. Unless I go bald. Bald! I couldn't carry it off. Some people can. Jules would probably look just as lovely bald as she does with a sheet of straight blonde perfect hair. But people like Jules don't go bald. People like *me* go bald. Just thinking about it made my eyes well up, which was embarrassing as I was easily in view of at least a dozen other people. Okay, of one other person, and I don't think he was looking at me as he was busy picking his nose. But he could have been. Probably he couldn't meet my eye as he didn't want me to know that he knew I was going bald.

Just then Jules wafted into the library. Jules doesn't walk. She wafts.

"What's wrong with you?" she said loudly.

"Shhh," I said. "It's a LIBRARY."

"Don't be so nasty," she said. "No one cares. You look like you've been crying." She peered at the screen and I hastily clicked a link on the bottom of the page so she wouldn't see what I was looking at.

"What are you looking at?" she said suspiciously.

"Nothing," I said, looking at the screen. "Locks of Love, actually," I said. Which was what now appeared on the screen. "Uh, for Student Council. For a charity thing. For, uh, to raise money for, uh, prom. Or, not for prom, for the Student Council. Not really for Student Council, just to raise money. For charity. You know, people with long hair cut it off and they make it into wigs for people who have cancer. When they go bald."

"Hmmm," Jules said. "I don't believe you. Unless you think you *have* cancer. Is that it? Never mind, don't tell me. Anyway, listen, we should go. If you want a ride home, that is. Unless you want to take the bus."

Jules has a way of making the word "bus" sound like "gross contagious skin disorder."

I hate the bus. It makes me dizzy. Once, I got on the bus when it was very full and the driver closed the door such that my arm was hanging out and then drove off and I couldn't get him to stop. I thought for sure I was going to fall out. Believe me, it was scarier than it sounds.

"Okay, okay," I said. I turned the monitor off and tried not to notice if any more of my hair had fallen out on the keyboard.

I'm sure it hadn't.

I mean, what are the odds of me getting alopecia anyway? I'm sure they're very remote.

3:09 p.m.

I followed Jules down the hallway, dragging my book bag on the floor. It was heavy. Jules didn't have a book bag. Jules never studies. I don't know how she does it. I guess, with her looks, it's hardly like she's going to college anyway. She'll probably be a movie star, natch. Or a model. Or someone who is famous for being pretty.

"Hurry *up*, Haley," she said. "Honestly. You are the slowest thing alive. I don't know how you muster up the speed to run anywhere. You do still run, right?"

"Of course," I lied. "I'm training for the marathon with Kiki."

"I don't know," she said. "I just can't imagine you running." She laughed.

Really, she is v. mean to me. Don't know why I like her at all. I picked up my bag and threw it over my shoulder and tried to walk like it didn't weigh a thousand pounds and wasn't causing my legs to shake with fatigue. We pushed the doors open and were practically knocked on our butts by a blast of cold air. (Which would have hurt me a lot less than it hurt her, what with all my natural padding and her complete boniness.) It's been an extraordinarily cold winter. It's not snowing (yet), but it's so cold that the ground is frozen. You don't want to stand around outside for more than 10 seconds or all your mucous membranes will freeze. (Can eyeballs freeze? Because that would be horrible.)

Naturally, that was the moment we bumped into Bruce Bartelson, Student Council Ring Leader. BB is unable to have any conversation that lasts less than 10 minutes. I pushed Jules, hoping that she would ignore BB and leap into the car and drive off with me as though we were making a getaway from a heist. But of course, she chose that moment to light a cigarette and stare dreamily off into space.

"Earth to Jules!" I hissed in a panic, but it was too late.

"Blah blah blah, Jules," Bruce yelled, running to catch up. He practically pounced on me. "Oh, and Haley? Blah blah blah Prom, blah blah blah."

"Huh," I said, politely. "Cold out here, isn't it?"

"Blah blah blah," he said. "And you missed blah blah blah. You have to blah blah blah." He looked at me expectantly. "Haley? Blah BLAH BLAH!"

"That's not nice," said Jules blowing a smoke ring at him. ("What isn't nice?" I wondered, shivering in my jean jacket and cords. I could use a winter coat, particularly if it is going to be abnormally cold like this.) "I mean, really. Grow up." (Can Jules understand Bruce? Perhaps I have perfected a way of blocking out his annoying voice.)

"Besides," Jules said. "Haley has a great idea for that charity Locks of Love."

"Yeah," I said.

I do?

Gah.

"I can't wait to hear about it," Bruce said. His face was practically touching mine. Honestly, has he never heard of "personal space"?

"I'll tell you at the next meeting," I said. "Uh, I have to make some calls first."

Note to Self: Make some calls.

I swear, sometimes it seems like my life is something that just happens TO me. I'm not in control.

Further Note to Self: Take control of life.

Which is easier to do when not being whipped around corners in Jules' car. Although at least a) we were *in* the car and making an escape, and b) the heat was on and my hands were turning purple and red, which indicated some circulation was coming back into them. I swear, I don't know where Jules learned to drive. I wish I had my licence.

7:45 p.m.
Phone Call with Kiki:

Me: Where were you after school? Jules nearly killed me on the way home. You have to help me practise driving so I can take my test.

Kiki: Sure.

Me: Really?

Kiki: Why not?

Me: Actually, I don't think you can, I think I have to be taught by someone older.

Kiki: Why? I'm almost 18.

Me: I know.

Kiki: I keep forgetting you're only 16.

Me: I know.

Kiki: It's going to suck when we can go to bars and you can't.

Me: I *know.*

Kiki: I have to go do some stuff to get ready.

Me: What stuff?

Kiki: Stuff.

Me: Get ready for what?

Kiki: Bye, Haley, I'll call you later.

I hung up the phone and lay on my bed for a while trying to figure it out. Kiki has "stuff"? What "stuff"? "Ready" for what?

Note to Self: Find out what Kiki is up to. Suspect she is reneging on her "no-boyfriend" deal and is embarrassed by it. Or perhaps she has joined an embarrassing cult or other group and doesn't want to admit it. Or perhaps she is just busy.

Busy doing *what*?

8:14 p.m.
Phone Call with Brad:

Me: Hello?

Brad: Haley! [He always sounds so happy to hear my voice that it's a bit disturbing.] How *are* you?

Me: Um, good. How are you?

Brad: I'm doing great. I miss you.

Me: Yeah. Um. Great. So, uh, what did you do today?

Brad: Oh, you know. School. Thought about you. Want to go out this weekend? I can't talk long, I'm getting ready for practice.

Me: Oh, right.

Brad: Want me to call you when I get home?

Me: Uh, sure.

Brad: Okay, honey.

Me: Bye.

Honey?

   HONEY?

   I whammed my face into my pillow and screamed. I just don't feel like I'm anybody's honey. Although it's certainly sweet that Brad likes me enough to make up a cutesy name for me.

   Not that "honey" is particularly cute.

   Perhaps he has forgotten my name.

   Argh.

   I screamed into my pillow again, then got up and changed into my running clothes. Okay, they aren't "running clothes" per se, they are just old sweats that serve as "running clothes." It's not as if I run often enough to have specific "clothes" for it. Maybe if I had proper "running clothes" that wick away sweat and streamline the body I would a) look thinner, and b) run better, and c) be more motivated.

   Hmmm.

   They have actual scientists making that fabric, you know.

9:02 p.m.

Dear Junior:

Ran too far (at least three miles) (or one). Threw up in shrub on front walk. Don't tell.

   Hate running.

Love,

HAH

9:37 p.m.

Dad is home from work (?). Must have very long shifts at this bakery. Will go downstairs like proper, nice, kind, thoughtful daughter and ask after his day.

9:40 p.m.

Dad does not want to talk about his day and does not have to get up for work tomorrow as he has been fired for refusing to cut his hair.

"I mean," he said, "is this a job at a bakery or the army?"

Then he went to watch *Oprah* and *Dr. Phil*. I think I will write to both Oprah and Dr. Phil to see if we can't get Dad a makeover and personality … jolt.

"We can't afford Tivo if you don't have a job," I said.

"I'll get another job, sweetie," he said.

"When?" I said.

"Shhh," he said.

Honestly, he's so pathetic. His socks didn't even match. I think one of them was mine, which believe me, is not unusual. In addition to mismatched socks, he was wearing jeans with a hole in the crotch and a shirt from Madonna's "Like a Virgin" tour, which I believe was also mine. In the eighth grade.

Some people are colour blind.

Other people are entirely fashion blind.

"Dad," I said.

"It wasn't meant to be," he said. "Besides, it was a horrible job. And it only paid eight dollars an hour. I'll find a better job than that, honey."

(Honey!!!!!??!!)

"Dad," I said. "You …"

Then I gave up. I mean, he'll get another job. I'm sure he will. If he doesn't, we'll end up living on the street, but I guess we'll cross that bridge when we come to it. I stomped back up the stairs. I have perfected the stomp such that the pictures on the wall shake but don't come down. It's v. dramatic. Perhaps I should investigate the possibility of an acting career.

Truthfully, I thought the bakery job sounded awful anyway. I can't see my dad selling cookies to children and elderly people. (You never see people of a normal age eating cookies. Why is that? Cookies are perfectly legitimate food. I wish I had a cookie right now, come to think of it.) On the other hand, I can't see my dad doing much of anything.

I slammed the door so The Bird couldn't flap his way in and get stuck in my hair, his/her (we're not sure which) favourite thing to do. (Dad does not believe that animals should be caged — or named, for that matter — so as a result, I am all but stalked by The Bird, who lies in wait to crap on me at every opportunity.) (I swear, he/she aims.) (It's a good thing I have such ridiculously short hair.)

I lay on the bed for a while and stared at the ceiling. There used to be a patch there that looked like Australia (where I will never get to go now that I am doomed to be destitute forever, or at least until I get my own job) but it has spread and now looks more like Africa, with a blob of Europe above it and a giant blob of Russia to the left. Am slightly alarmed about the ruin that the house is falling into, but couldn't spend too much time worrying about it because at that moment The Cat came leaping out from under the bed (carrying several dustballs), yowled horrifically, ran in a circle over me (nearly scratching out my eye in the process), landed in a heap on the floor and threw up on my running shoes.

"Great," I said. "Thanks a lot."

I seriously wish my mother was here sometimes, not because I think it would be nice to have a nun around the house (although maybe it would be, I don't know, I'm sure nuns are very nice people), but because I could freak out and have someone listen. Instead of hearing my dad say, "Well, I guess you just clean it up and move on, don't you?" And barely looking up from his stupid TV show.

Sometimes I get so tired of my life, I could just scream.

► ► ►

Thursday, January 16

MOOD	Improving
HAIR	Partly still attached to skull
HEALTH	Deranged with angst re: alopecia
HOROSCOPE	Friends are important to you today. Be considerate of other peoples' feelings! Today is going to be one of your best days for romance and fun in this whole lunar cycle.
~~JT SIGHTINGS~~	n/a (4)

9:03 a.m.
Reasons to Be in a Good Mood:
1. Am having good hair day.

2. Am only days away from being finished with stupid classes such as Math and Automechanics, and can look forward to spring semester of lame, easy classes, such as PE and Drama.

3. Horoscope says day will be good and have no reason not to believe in horoscopes even though they are rarely correct.

3:45 p.m.

Good mood lasted only until Student Council meeting, when I suddenly found self in charge of "Locks of Love" Charity Ball. Well, that's not entirely accurate. It's possible that when Bruce Bartelson, Student Council Head Devil, said, "Haley has organized a charity fundraiser for Locks of Love!" the idea of a ball popped into my head.

A Valentine's Day Ball.

For charity.

I *must* pay closer attention during boring Student Council meetings and stop stretching vigorously when bored. Apparently, have inadvertently volunteered to a) sell tickets and b) do introductory speech.

This was made worse by the fact that Bruce Bartelson, Master of the Parade of Hopeless Dorks, practically leaped on me as I tried to sneak out the back door and announced that he and I would be working closely on the Locks of Love Ball. At least, that's what I think he said. (It's so weird how he's a close talker and yet I can never really make out what he's saying.) (And he'd obviously eaten tuna for lunch.)

Side note: Luckily, own hair is too short to be shorn for charity, although am fully supportive and in awe of people who do it, because it's an amazing thing to do.

But Bruce Bartelson?

UGH.

Note to Self: Kill self at earliest convenience.

► ► ►

Saturday, January 25

MOOD	Restless
HAIR	Frizzy and dry
HEALTH	Headache / dizzy
HOROSCOPE	Take advantage of today's solar eclipse to get things re-organized! You'll be glad you did.
~~JT SIGHTINGS~~	n/a NONE

2:00 pm

Why is Jules my friend? Seriously, she makes me crazy.

2:15 p.m.

List of Jules' Qualities, Good or Otherwise:

1. She is shallow.
2. She is vain.
3. She is beautiful.
4. She is selfish.
5. She is incredibly self-involved.
6. She is dating JT.
7. She is going to be famous.
8. She is going to be on TV.

Wonder if I may like her *because* she is beautiful and might be famous, in spite of the fact she is often mean and unfriendly.

It was sort of, but not quite, snowing outside when I went to see Jules and Kiki at Jules' house. It seemed like there was nothing to do because the weather was so horrible (and cold). I wanted to play a game or something, but that didn't go over well.

"I'd rather stick spikes behind my nails," drawled Jules. "I mean, we aren't 12 years old any more, Haley."

"Duh," I said. "It's not like there's anything else to do."

"Don't get nasty," she said, blowing smoke in my face. We're allowed to smoke in Jules' house because her mother apparently wasn't alerted to the fact that you don't technically *have* to be smoking at all times in order to live. Jules' mother lives in fear of "getting fat." As far as I can tell, smoking and eating are mutually exclusive activities, but what do I know? I'm just the fat, non-smoking friend.

Well, I'm not fat, per se. But I'm fatter than Jules (who weighs in at a whopping 120 on a bad day, although she says "110.") And I'm fatter than Kiki, who sometimes has to get size two pants altered to fit. And I'm the only non-smoker.

Maybe I should start smoking.

No, I couldn't. I mean, *cancer*? Hello? Tooth yellowing? Even at that moment, I had a Crest Whitestrip on my teeth.

"I'm not being nasty," I said. (I may have lisped slightly. It's hard to talk with Whitestrips in your mouth.)

"God," Jules said. "Don't spit at me. You're gross."

"Don't fight," said Kiki. One day, Kiki is going to be a great mom. She's raised both Jules and me, even though we are all (almost) the same age. Jules is dad-less (well, she has one, but she might as well not have one. He sends money and comes around a few times a year to say hello and then ignore her for hours at a time. Jules hates being ignored, so she pretends he doesn't exist) and I'm mom-less. In any event, Kiki is like a parent to both of us. Sort of.

"I think I'm going to get into Harvard," Kiki said suddenly. "I think that's what I've decided."

"You don't just decide," I said. "You have to be accepted."

"She'll be accepted," said Jules. "She's smart. She gets A's! She's going to be Valedictorian, everyone knows it. Of course, she'll get accepted. She can pick and choose."

"I guess," I said, twiddling with the carpet pile. It was incredibly soft. I lay my face down on it. I wouldn't be going to Harvard. I preferred to not think too much about "what to be when I grow up." I mean, people are always asking me. I just shrug and attempt to look mysterious. I haven't got the faintest idea. I breathed deeply through my nose and closed my eyes.

"I'm going to do some travelling, I think. Hopefully my *modelling* career will take off soon," said Jules, flicking her hair at me. Sometimes I dream about shaving that girl's head to see if she'd be able to function without hair flicking.

"It's very competitive," I said. "Modelling, that is. I don't think you can just *do* it."

"Thanks," Jules said. "What's wrong with you today? I can be a model if I want. My mom's friends say that I should do it, at least for the money for college."

"Hmm," I said.

"You'd be a great model," said Kiki. (Kiki is v. supportive

and nice. Must try to be more like Kiki.)

"Yeah," I said grudgingly.

"Actually," Jules said, with a funny expression on her face. "I have an announcement."

"Mmm?" I said. I felt a bit panicky. Sometimes Jules' announcements are of the "I'm-dating-the-boy-you've-had-a-crush-on-since-ninth-grade" variety. Although, maybe she'd BROKEN UP WITH HIM.

My heart was pounding in my chest, to tell you the truth. Not that it would make any difference in my life if Jules broke up with JT. I mean, I'm not interested in him anymore. I have Brad.

"I have Brad," I said out loud.

"What?" said Jules. "I was going to say something."

"Oops," I said. "Did I say that out loud?"

"Obviously," she said. "Can't I make an announcement without you rambling on about Brad? Seriously, Brad, Brad, Brad. That's all you ever talk about."

"It is *not*," I said hotly.

"Is so," she said.

"Is not," I said.

"Is so," she said.

"SHUT UP!" Kiki yelled. She must have PMS. Kiki never shouts at us.

"*Anyway*," said Jules. "If Haley can stop talking about herself for a minute, I'd like to tell you guys a secret. But you can't tell *anyone*."

Which is how we found out that Jules, our Jules, had been chosen as a semi-quarter-whatever-finalist for the reality TV show *Who's the Prettiest of Them All*?

"For real?" said Kiki. "Oh my gosh, I'm so excited for you!"

"Argkjhg," I said.

"What?" she said.

"I'm very happy for you," I said. As sincerely as possible. I mean, I was happy for her. But if she got on TV? She's vain enough as it is.

Why does nothing good *ever* happen to people who aren't outlandishly beautiful? I looked at her staring at me with her giant brown eyes. (Was she wearing coloured contacts?) Totally clear skin. Baggy size two clothes.

"I mean, that's so great," I said. "You'll win for sure. I'm so so so happy. I mean, gosh. TV. That's really fantastic. That's great. I'm so so excited."

"Haley, you're babbling," Jules said.

"I'm not!" I said. "Actually, I've just remembered! I have to go! To … the mall! I've got to get, well, I've got to get Dad and Brad something for their birthdays. Tomorrow." Which I realized was true as soon as I said it.

"Bye," Jules and Kiki said. They barely even looked up from the portfolio that Jules had whipped out from under the bed so we could peruse her photographs and gush over her loveliness. But I can't say that I blame them for ignoring me.

"So I'm going to the mall," I said again. I kind of hoped that one of them would offer me a ride. It was practically snowing! And I was having a panic attack, which would be made worse by the bus.

But they didn't.

Huh.

List of Ideas for Dad's Birthday Gift, written on the bus to the
mall on the back of a takeout pizza receipt:

1. Book: *What Colour is Your Parachute?* (i.e., book about
    how to get a job)
2. Book: *Resume Writing for Dummies* (i.e., book about how
    to get a job)
3. Book: *I Could Do Anything If Only I Knew What It Was*
    (i.e., book about how to get a job)
4. Book: *Vegetarian Cookbook* (i.e., book about not eating
    meat)
5. Gift certificate for haircut (i.e., improve appearance to
    get job)
6. Tie (i.e., something to wear to job)
7. Book: anything by Dr. Phil
8. Card?
9. ...

Gift Ideas for Brad:

1. ...
2. ...
3. Card?

5:32 p.m.
Why do malls close at 5:30? I wasn't finished shopping.
Have purchased book by Dr. Phil. Clearly, this is a gift
for Dad.

I have nothing for Brad.

Am bad girlfriend with no hope of keeping boyfriend.

6:02 p.m.

Phone Call with Kiki:

Kiki: Look, why didn't you just get him a sweater? He'd be thrilled with anything you came up with, you know. He likes you so much it's …

Me: It's *what*?

Kiki: Nothing! I don't know! Can you buy him something on the Internet and say that it was late getting delivered?

Me: No! I don't have a credit card! And I don't know what to get.

Kiki: Why didn't you just get him a nice card and a gift certificate or something?

Me: I don't know! I don't know!

Kiki: Don't freak out. Why were you being so weird today?

Me: I wasn't being weird!

Kiki: Yes, you were. Did you run today?

Me: No! I mean, yes!

Kiki: You didn't, did you?

Me: Yes! I mean, no! I don't know!

Kiki: Are you hysterical?

Me: No! It's just that I didn't get Brad a gift and I feel horrible about it. And I'm … I don't know!

Kiki: Calm down. Why don't you make him something?

Me: Too late! Argh! [The Bird chose that moment to fly into my room and land in my hair.]

Kiki: Relax!

Me: The Bird! The Bird!

Kiki: I'll be there in 10 minutes.

Me: Why?

Kiki: We're going to Brad's game, remember?

Me: Oh, yeah. [Hung up in mad panic.]

6:15 p.m.

I forgot.

Brad's game.

The game is a proper girlfriend activity that I should be happy about. Instead, I chose to lie down on my bed and mentally freak out for nine minutes and then had only one minute to prepare. Which meant that I didn't have time to fix either my hair or my makeup or cover up the zit the size of a small hairless sasquatch squatting on my forehead. One of the many, many, many, many drawbacks of having short hair is that you can't arrange your bangs to cover unsightly blemishes. Brad will take one look at me and want to break up with me anyway. Who could blame him?

He must be v. jealous of JT, who is perfect looking and rich *and* dating Jules, who is bound to be the next *Who Is the Prettiest of Them All?* winner.

ARGH.

"Who is the grossest of them all?" I asked the mirror.

It answered, "Stupid, stupid, stupid." Honestly, I don't know who taught The Bird to say that but it is v. annoying. And I hate the way The Bird stalks me.

"Shoo!" I said, batting him out of the room. He squawked and flew into my hair.

"Argh!" I screamed. "GET OFF ME OR I'LL KILL YOU!" Honestly, it's like a horror movie in here only I'm not being chased by a guy with a chainsaw, but rather a bird with razor-sharp claws and a personality disorder. I swear The Bird laughed as he flew down to the floor.

I made a face at myself in the mirror just as Dad was walking by.

"You look nice," he said. "You're so pretty."

ARGH.

Note to Self: Encourage Dad to stop smoking drugs in the style of an aging rock star (albeit surreptitiously outside or when I'm out, followed by the wafting of incense through the house like *I don't know what it means*). Is making him delusional.

10:57 p.m.

The fact that Brad's team lost the hockey game didn't have anything to do with me.

Sure, if Brad hadn't been scanning the stands for me, maybe he wouldn't have let in that first, second or third goal. (Brad is a goalie. Privately, I wish he was something sexier, such as a forward. Or a defenceman. I mean, being a goalie is obviously very cool, but he doesn't do much skating around and you can't actually see him as he's hidden behind a mattress-worth of padding and a helmet that covers his entire body.)

But it's not my fault. I mean, I was *there*. I just had to keep going to the concession for hot drinks. (Hockey is played on ice. Very cold in there.) (And I wasn't sensibly dressed, but I looked cute.) (Well, cute-ish.) The boy behind the hot-drink counter was interesting, not that I'm interested in other boys. I am dating Brad and have eyes only for Brad.

The hot-drink boy's name was Andrew and he had black curly hair and nice glasses.

I bought several hot drinks. I was thirsty.

Note to Self: Check symptoms of diabetes.

And then, of course, I had to pee. (Could also be sign of diabetes.)

Reminder: Start carrying hard candies in purse in case of diabetic coma.

And then I had to go check to see if the cold air was making the blemish appear larger than it actually was. And then I had to go to the car and get my cell phone, which had dropped out of my purse on the way over. In case someone was calling. So I may have ducked out a couple of times. But I was there for most of the game.

To be honest, I don't really follow hockey that much. Now that I'm a hockey player's girlfriend, I'll have to get books such as *Hockey for Dummies* so that I can have proper conversations about the games and understand why the ref blows the whistle every 10 seconds and why 15 minutes in hockey translates to roughly half an hour in real time.

"Where were you?" was the first thing Brad said when he'd changed and met us out front. "You kept disappearing."

"I was there," I said. "Good game!"

Kiki glared at me. "The other team was tough," she said. "Their offence was really sharp tonight. And the ref made some bad calls." (Is Kiki some sort of expert on hockey? If so, when did this happen?)

I glared back.

Brad scowled. "I stunk it up," he said. "I couldn't concentrate."

"Why not?" I said.

"Because ..." he said. Then he stopped and kicked at some ice on the curb. He was wearing very odd looking shoes. Sort of *bowling* shoes, almost. Perhaps they were very stylish and I just wasn't up on them yet. I looked at my own feet: new boots. Now, *they* were really nice. I held out my ankle to admire them and fell into Kiki.

"Oof," she said. "Look, kids, I have to go. See you later."

"Uh, bye," I said. To tell you the truth, I felt a bit funny being there alone with Brad. We weren't alone much. There was always someone around, such as Jules and JT. Or Kiki. Or just ... someone.

"So, um, it sucks that you lost," I said.

"Yeah," Brad said. "Doesn't matter."

Of course, it clearly *did* matter. If by that, I mean that it put him in a really bad mood. Which was weird. I'd never seen Brad in a bad mood before. Not that I've known him for that long. I mean, I guess I've known him for a few months but I only see him a couple of times a week, and although that seems like a lot, really it isn't a lot in the bigger picture. I've probably only seen him 20 or 30 times. How well can you know someone after 20 or 30 hours?

"Haley," he said. "I'm sorry. I'm just mad at myself."

"Don't be sorry," I said automatically. I mean, was he apologizing for losing the game? Should I have been upset about it? I didn't know how to respond, never having been the girlfriend of someone who plays hockey before. (Or the girlfriend of anyone.)

We got into Brad's car, or more accurately his mom's car, and I flicked the heat on high.

"So what do you want to do?" I said.

"Oh," he said. "Let's hang out and talk." It was dark and the roads were sort of icy and as he was saying this, he put his hand on my leg. I picked it up and put it back on the steering wheel and he gave me a look.

"What?" I said. "It's icy. I don't want to be in an accident."

"We won't be in an accident," he said. "Besides, I'm going about 20 miles an hour and the road is totally flat."

"I know," I said.

He gave me another look. Sometimes I feel like I'm a huge disappointment as a girlfriend. I fished around for something to say.

"Kiki's going to teach me how to drive," I said.

"You know how to drive," he said.

"I know," I said. "I need to pass my driver's test though."

Then there was this awkward silence. I mean, Really Awkward.

"I never took the test," I said at last. "Dad was all 'You don't need The Man to tell you that you can drive'! He's a hippie."

"Uh huh," said Brad. I don't think he was listening. He looked really cute, though. Much like John Cusack in *Say Anything*, except damper (from his post-game shower) and more annoyed (from being with me, natch).

"Um, so you played really well," I said. "Nice uniforms, too!"

"Haley," he said. "We lost six to nothing. That's not *playing well*. You see, my job is to *stop the other team from getting goals.*"

"Right," I said, nodding vigorously. "Well, they only got six."

"Haley!" he shouted. "Shut up! You know, there were scouts there, I'm sure of it. This was a really important game. And I screwed it up. And I don't want to talk about it. I don't want to talk."

"Hmmm," I said, trying to sound like a thoughtful considerate girlfriend would sound. "Okay, honey." (Why is it that when I say "honey" I sound like an idiot?) "I mean, Brad," I added quickly. "Not honey."

"Forget it," he said, giving me a weird look. "You know what? I'll just take you home."

He seemed mad. I don't get it. I just don't understand other people sometimes. I was trying, but I swear, when we got to my house he barely slowed the car down enough to give me a peck on the lips.

"I …"

"See you around," he said.

"Hey," I said. "Wait!"

He looked at me. I was standing in the driveway, leaning into the car. The wind was whipping at my hair. (Luckily, my hair is only an inch long, so it didn't do anything inconvenient like blow into my mouth.) I don't know what came over me, but I knew I had to say something.

"It's your birthday tomorrow," I said.

"I know," he said. "I'm surprised you remember."

"Of course, I remember," I said (honestly, he can be very grouchy when he wants to be). "I totally have it all planned out. Everything. So meet me here at 11 a.m., okay? It's a surprise."

"Oh," he said. He looked happy, which made me feel bad because I hadn't technically planned anything. "See you tomorrow then," he said. "And Haley?"

"Yeah?" I said, but I was backing away. It was too cold to stand and chat.

"Thanks," he said. Then I slammed the door, and he drove off. He skidded a bit at the bottom of the hill and for a second I was scared he was going to go into the ditch. Then he was gone.

It gave me a weird feeling. Like I'd done something wrong, but I didn't know what it was exactly.

"Is that you?" Dad called as I stomped into the kitchen. It was twelve-thousand degrees in there, like always. Dad is always cold. This probably has something to do with the fact that he spends all his time sitting very still and not moving around. I needed warming up, but it was so hot that I immediately broke into a sweat.

Note to Self: Investigate possibility of thyroid disorder.

"Who else would it be?" I snapped.

"Listen," he said. "Don't plan anything for dinner tomorrow night, okay?"

"Why not?" I said. "It's your birthday, maybe I was going to surprise you with something."

"Were you?" he said, skidding into the room in his socks and underwear. Honestly, it's the end of January.

"You wouldn't have to put the heat so high if you wore some clothes," I pointed out. "Heat is expensive."

"Don't be bossy," he said. "Besides, tomorrow is my birthday and I want to surprise you."

"Fine," I said. "Okay. Whatever." I picked up The Cat off the counter and dropped him on the floor, where he hissed at me like mini-Satan. Sometimes, he frightens me. If we ever get too desperate, perhaps we could loan him to Stephen King or someone. I glared at him, and brushed a pile of crumbs after him. Seriously, this place is a disgusting zoo. There was a big orange cat hair sitting right on the dish of butter. "Dad," I said. "Can't you at least put the butter in the cupboard when you're done?"

"Did you have fun tonight?" he said, sock-skating around and putting the butter away. I couldn't help but notice that his sock-skates cleaned a streak in the floor. Gross.

"No," I said. "Good night." And I stomped up to bed.

I've been feeling stompy lately. I don't exactly know why. I looked up "irritation" on WebMD, but only found references to skin irritation. General irritability just doesn't count, I guess.

I'm falling asleep trying to think of some way to make it up to Brad. To make up for the fact that I'm a terrible girlfriend. To make up for the fact that I don't even think I like him very much.

Note to Self: Go to more of Brad's hockey games and *do not* develop inappropriate crush on hot-drink boy.

► ► ►

Sunday, January 26

MOOD	Weirdly nervous
HAIR	Not as horrible as it could be
HEALTH	Dizzy, lightheaded, probably v. sick
HOROSCOPE	Things that are falling may cause trepidation. Be careful of having too much of a good thing. Offer a family member a helping hand.
~~JT SIGHTINGS~~	n/a (countless)

11:45 a.m.
Oh, help.

11:47 a.m.
This was a terrible idea.

11:49 a.m.
See 11:47 a.m.

12:51 p.m.
Okay, let me backtrack for a minute. To summarize, I needed a surprise.

Fast.

I don't know why, but the only "surprise" I could think of was … well, it's so stupid, I almost can't write it down. It's crazy.

I don't know. I woke up this morning and the only thing that came into my head was …

…

…

bungee jumping.

I know, I know.

It's stupid. Possibly the World's Worst Idea.

But it was the only thing I could think of, and last night when I was half-asleep, it seemed like it might be an adventure. Wacky. Zany. Fun. Something that Clare Danes might do in a movie. Although now I can't think of a single movie where anyone has bungee jumped. Possibly because everyone — without exception — looks stupid jumping off a perfectly good bridge with an elastic band tied to their feet.

I don't know what I was thinking.

I was thinking that I'd look like the wild, fun girlfriend and not like the neurotic, strange girlfriend.

I forgot to consider a) the terror, and b) the cold, and c) the dizzying heights, and d) the actual jump itself.

But bungee jumping is free. (*NB*: Always read the fine print when something is going to be "free".)

Oh, PS — it's only free if you do it in your bathing suit.

Okay, here's the full story. First, Brad was late to pick me up. For a few minutes, I thought he wasn't coming, so naturally freaked out and called both Kiki and Jules, but neither of them were home. I thought about waking up my dad, but when I went up to his room, he wasn't there. Which, now that I think of it, was very odd. Dad has always slept until noon on Sundays. At least, I think he has.

I usually sleep until noon on Sundays and so assumed he also was asleep.

Note to Self: Check and see where Dad was and investigate possibility that Dad leads a double life I haven't noticed because I've been asleep.

Seventeen minutes later, when Brad pulled up in his old truck (his dad's old truck, actually, but Brad's dad gave it to Brad on his 16th birthday so he could drive himself to his early morning hockey practices). (I'm not shallow, but it's a v. ugly truck with large patches of rust and it makes an unusual sound when you speed up or slow down.) (Secretly, I'm afraid of the truck and am relieved when Brad borrows his mom's car, which was not the case today.) I was relieved.

And he was all huggy and kissy, which is nice, but I tend to get short of breath and panicky after the first five minutes or so. So I kind of pried him off me (he also gave me a rose, which was sweet considering it was his birthday and I didn't have anything for him, but also a little cloying. Only a little. I mean, it was a nice thing to do) and said, "Get in the truck! We have to hurry."

"Why?" he said.

"I can't tell you!" I shouted. So we got in the truck. Unfortunately, the heater in the truck was not working (big surprise) so it was freezing. It made it hard to talk, what with the chattering teeth. And violent shivering.

"What's the matter?" he said.

"Too cold to talk," I mumbled.

"Well, you have to tell me where we're going," he pointed out. He looked a little exasperated.

"Eighteen, huh," I said inanely. "You're like an older man."

"Not *that* old," he said defensively. (He's very sensitive about being held back in sixth grade. Which naturally I'd forgotten about.)

"Okay," I said. And then I said, "Go left!" And I pointed up the street as though I had a Very Specific Plan. At this point, I still hadn't made up my mind. I had my bathing suit in my purse, as well as some old swim trunks of my dad's that I thought Brad could wear. They're almost the same size, except that dad is about 20 pounds thinner than Brad and several inches taller.

The scenery whizzed by. There were strange icicle-like things hanging off the trees. You don't get a lot of that here, so it was unusual. Also, it was windy — a bitter, cold wind that blew us around.

I was beginning to rethink the whole bungee surprise.

I pointed randomly left and right. This went on for a bit, until Brad said, "Haley, where are we going?" Granted, it was cold, but still, I would have thought he'd be having fun driving around with his girlfriend on a Sunday morning. Perhaps he isn't as smitten with me as I thought. And who could blame him? I have a giant boil on my forehead and sometimes, when I'm cold, my nose drips in a very un-pretty way.

"I, uh," I said.

I was hungry. I mean, I hadn't eaten yet because I'd been getting ready. I thought if I looked like a proper girlfriend then I'd feel like a proper girlfriend. I know that sounds crazy, but it's true, so there you have it. I was wearing a very pretty blue sweater. Light blue. I love that sweater. Only it isn't very warm.

"Here," I said, pointing.

"International House of Pancakes?" Brad said. He sounded disappointed.

"Just for breakfast before your surprise," I said. I knew at that point I was going to have to do it after all. There was no way I could get away with saying that endless pancakes at IHOP was his surprise. And I could think of *nothing* else. It's like someone else had taken over my brain and all I could think was "bungee jumping." Bungee, bungee, bungee. I felt a little crazy.

"Okay," he said.

As soon as we got a booth, I excused myself to the washroom. I felt that it wasn't fair to panic (i.e., hyperventilate) in front of Brad on his birthday.

List Made on Gum Wrapper in Washroom of IHOP of Reasons Why Bungee Jumping Is a Terrible Idea:

1. Am afraid of heights.
2. Am afraid of falling.
3. Am afraid of falling from heights.
4. Am afraid of bridges.
5. Am afraid of being maimed.
6. Am afraid of dying.
7. Am generally afraid.
8. Am afraid might pee my pants due to uncontrollable fear.
9. Am afraid might throw up.

10. Am afraid might cry.
11. Am afraid that legs will completely detach from body.
12. Am afraid of fainting.
13. Am afraid of embarrassment.
14. Am really, really afraid.

I sat down on the toilet (covered with toilet paper. You can get really gross things from toilet seats, I'm sure) and perused my list. Then made another one:

Reasons Why I Have to Go Bungee Jumping:
1. Did not get present for boyfriend's birthday.
2. Did not plan anything else for boyfriend's birthday.

I left the stall, which was pretty disgusting, and stared at myself in the mirror. I looked pale and afraid (apart from the giant, red, pulsing blemish, natch). I slapped my cheeks to add some colour. This drew a strange look from everyone else in the washroom (i.e., the one other person in the washroom, who may or may not have had a permanently disapproving look on her face anyway).

"Are you okay?" she said.

"Fine," I lied. I'm not going to tell total strangers my problems, am I?

"It's just that I'm going bungee jumping," I said. "And I'm scared of heights."

"Hmmm," she said.

"I have to do it," I said. "Because I didn't get my boyfriend anything else for his birthday. I've never had a boyfriend before so I wasn't sure what to get. And I don't really have any money. I mean, I couldn't buy him anything. Besides, I didn't know what he would like. I guess I could have bought him a sweater. A sweater would have been a good idea, right?"

"Hmm," she said, drying her hands under the blower. She was still looking at me with disapproval. "I couldn't really say."

"It's just that I don't have a job and my dad's, uh, out of work," I said.

She gave me a funny look. "Well, good luck with everything," she said. Then she left. Some kind of "supportive stranger" she turned out to be.

So I did the only thing I could do. I called Jules and made her agree to come with us. I mean, if I'm going to jump off a bridge, I want her to do it, too. She's my oldest friend. It's only right that we should die together.

"Why me?" she said.

"Because you're my oldest friend and I want to share this experience with you," I said.

"Ask Kiki," she said.

"I can't!" I said. "Also, she's not home."

"Oh," she said. I could hear a muffled conversation in the background.

"What?" I said. "Hurry up, I have to get back to the table. My pancakes are getting cold."

"You eat pancakes?" she said. "Huh."

"What does that mean?" I said. "I have to *eat*."

"Whatever," she said. "We'll meet you there at the bridge at one o'clock."

Which is how I came to be bungee jumping with Brad, Jules and JT. JT! Let's just think about this for a minute.

Maybe we could make a list of *all* the things that are more humiliating than jumping off a bridge in January in a bikini in front of the boy you've had a crush on since the ninth grade (who happens to be dating your best friend), and in front of your boyfriend (who you suspect no longer even likes you), and in front of your best friend (who looks like a fashion model about to walk the catwalk and not like a freezing lump of Jell-O about to jump off a bridge to her death with a large elastic band tied to her ankles).

Oh God.

Oh God.

Oh God.

"Haley," Brad said. "This is the best birthday gift I've ever had. I love …"

And for a second I thought he was going to say "you," which would have scared me enough that maybe I would have jumped without the cord. But he said "it."

Brad and JT were having a great time. They were all cool and tough and manly. Jules just mumbled "I'm going to kill you! You owe me for this!" as she shivered prettily under JT's jacket and flipped her hair. I tried not to throw up. My legs were shaking. Sometimes I think that I must have fewer muscles in my legs than other people. They just don't want to hold me up.

Oh well, I thought, if I die then I guess I'm dead. At least I won't have to run that marathon in April.

On the other hand, I didn't much want to die.

The bridge was about a million miles off the ground.

You could see tree tops. It went over this gully with a river at the bottom. It's amazing the river wasn't frozen, but it wasn't. It looked deep and very cold. I peered over the edge and immediately got vertigo.

"Argh," I said and grabbed my head, which felt like it was pulling me over the edge. It was a very weird feeling.

"Don't look down," advised Jules.

"Shhh," I said. Somehow just hearing her talk was making it worse. Brad and JT were pretending to throw each other off the edge. Hilarious. If by "hilarious" I mean "seriously not funny." My knees were slamming together, I was shaking so much.

And I had to pee.

I dug my nails into my hand and, well, prayed. To whomever. Anyone who was listening. Because I'm telling you, it was a long way down.

Mostly, I wished I hadn't eaten those pancakes. I swear, I could see my stomach growing. It wasn't bad enough that I was about to die (I suddenly remembered a story I read about someone bungee jumping off a bridge somewhere with the cord around their ankles but they forgot to attach *the other end* to the bridge), but now I was going to die while looking gross (and also pasty and white) in a bathing suit. In January.

I tried to smile so as to distract people with my extremely white teeth. Maybe if they were blinded by my teeth, they wouldn't notice my stomach. "Stop grimacing, Haley," said Jules, smoking furiously. "You look like you're going to the chair or something. This is supposed to be fun, remember? Also, it was *your* idea."

"You're not afraid of heights," I pointed out, taking a puff of her cigarette and nearly choking to death. "Besides," I croaked, as coolly as possible, "this is your opportunity to look adorable in a bathing suit." It suddenly occurred to me that this is why she agreed to do it. (Naturally, standing next to me in a bikini, she looked like a gorgeous supermodel, whereas I looked like a soft sausage stuffed into a tiny floral casing.)

Brad, for the record, did not do any of the following: a) hold my hand until it was my turn, or b) tell me that I did not have to do it, or c) stand anywhere near me. (Perhaps I look so repulsive in a bathing suit that he did not want to associate with me.) He and JT were having a ball. He clearly had no idea what a huge deal this was to me.

Next thing I knew, I was out there alone on this wobbly platform with three boys (men) wrapping belts around my legs and shouting instructions about "not tensing up."

"That's hilarious," I started to say, and just as I was going to explain why it was such a ridiculous thing to say, they shoved me off the edge. Seriously. They give you this countdown and if you don't jump (which is difficult to do when you are paralyzed with fear), they give you a big old *push*.

I guess I screamed a bit. I mean, it was completely terrifying and I thought I was going to die. Believe me when I say it takes forever for that elastic to snap you back up and wallop you up and down like a rag doll of unusual weight. I had lots of time to think "I didn't get a chance to say goodbye to Dad" and "I hope a lot of people come to my funeral and cry a lot" and "I hope JT cries" and …

Then my head hit the water. I'm pretty sure the cord is

supposed to be measured so you don't hit the water but apparently I'm extraordinarily heavy, so my head got dunked. It was very cold.

Very very cold.

Extremely cold.

Possible Outcomes of Having Head Dunked in Ice Water in January During Ice Storm:

1. Pneumonia.
2. Head cold.
3. Broken neck (if water had been covered with layer of ice).
4. Frozen hair that dries in icicles and snaps off.
5. Abject humiliation.
6. Pneumonia.
7. Pneumonia.

Clearly, am doomed to get pneumonia, which serves me right for trying to be "wacky" and "fun."

Afterwards, Jules (who, by the way, fell like a ballerina and came nowhere near the water due to the fact that she's so light and graceful) said, "You know, even for you that was quite ... er, dramatic."

"Huh," I said.

But Brad was thrilled. At least, I think he was. I ended up getting a ride home with Jules because she lives closer and the roads were getting icy and I urgently had to sit in a hot bath and defrost so that I didn't die from pneumonia.

As Jules dropped me off, she said, "You know, Brad is really really nice. You should be nicer to him."

And then I felt mean. Aren't my friends supposed to be more supportive?

"Huh," I said. "Well, thanks for coming."

"Yeah," she said. "Anytime."

Honestly, sometimes I feel like everyone is mad at me for no apparent reason. I'm like the human equivalent of E.coli. I repel people. Even the people who are supposed to like me the best.

Dinnertime, approx.

Dear Junior:

As though my day has not been bad enough, what with nearly falling to my death in an icy-cold river, things have gone from bad to worse.

My dad has a girlfriend.

That was what his big birthday surprise was. *That* was why I had to keep my evening free. To meet *her*. I'd tell you more about it but I keep throwing up so I'm otherwise occupied.

Must go stomp angrily around the house until Dad offers up an explanation of this travesty.

Love,

Left-Out Girl

I mean, how could he not tell me? How am I supposed to act?

11:30 p.m.

Dad: Haley, I have to go to bed, I have a job interview

> tomorrow. Are you going to tell me what's bugging
> you or do I have to guess?

Me: Forget it. Nothing is bugging me.

Dad: Okay, then. Good night.

He has a job interview?

Nobody tells me anything anymore.

"What secrets are you keeping?" I asked The Bird.

"Pretty girl," he said. "Pretty, pretty, pretty."

"I think you have me confused with someone else," I said. "Like Jules. *Who's the Prettiest of Them All?*"

"Stupid, stupid, stupid," he said.

"That's more like it," I said.

Outside, it was starting to snow really hard. I could see flakes swirling through the traffic lights. It was pretty. I love snow. I mean, I like how it looks, not how it is a) cold and b) wet.

Come to think of it, I'm not crazy about snow.

I'm more of a beach girl. The kind of girl JT would like.

Not that I think about JT anymore. Very often. Not as often as I used to. Obviously I'm going to think about him sometimes as he is dating my best friend. And I'm dating his cousin. It's not my fault that our paths are going to cross. It's destiny. Well, not *destiny*, but coincidence.

That's all.

List of Reasons to Be Happy (cont'd):

1. Have boyfriend.
2. Dad has job interview.
3. Dad has girlfriend, which makes me very annoyed,

although should ostensibly make me happy so will include it on list.

4. Albeit, girlfriend who is 30 YEARS YOUNGER THAN HIM, which is to be expected. After all, what normal-aged woman would date my dad? (More on The Girlfriend later when I'm ready to actually write about The Horror that was Dad's Birthday Dinner.)

5. Must think positively, is good that Dad has girlfriend who can share clothes with and giggle with on the phone.

6. Have beautiful, supportive friends.

7. Albeit, beautiful, supportive friends who don't call.

Note to Self: Find out where Kiki was all weekend.

8. Have bright and brilliant future as ... doctor? Lawyer? Interior designer? Artist? Welfare recipient?

Note to Self: Make appointment with counsellor to talk about career options.

  Whenever you're ready. Really, there is no rush.

▶ ▶ ▶

Monday, January 27

MOOD	Twitchy
HAIR	Spiky and pointless
HEALTH	Plagued by insomnia
HOROSCOPE	Don't know as the paper is not out yet.
~~JT SIGHTINGS~~	n/a

1:07 a.m.
If I go to sleep right now, I can get six hours of sleep.
Almost.

3:09 a.m.
Or four. Four hours of sleep is a lot, really.

6:14 a.m.
One is okay. One hour of sleep.

7:02 a.m.
BUZZZZZZZZZZZZZZZZZZZZZZZ.
  Argh.

10:05 a.m.
Things I Dread About Today:
1. Suspect Brad is annoyed with me but he is now away
   for a week on some kind of hockey tour thing so can't
   talk to him unless he calls later from wherever he is.
2. Have had no sleep and therefore look awful. Dread
   seeing Kiki and Jules looking perfect.
3. Have Student Council meeting after school.
4. Must start studying for final exams which are in 10 days.
5. General feeling of impending doom.

Search results for "impending doom" (from WebMD):
  Anxiety
  Feeling worried or nervous is a normal part of everyday life.
  Everyone frets or feels anxious from time to time. However,
  anxiety that becomes overwhelming and interferes with

daily life is not normal. This type of anxiety may be a symptom of another problem, such as depression.

Physical symptoms of anxiety include:
- Trembling, twitching, or shaking.
- Feeling of fullness in the throat or chest.
- Breathlessness or rapid heartbeat.
- Lightheadedness or dizziness.
- Sweating or cold, clammy hands.
- Excessive startle reflex.
- Muscle tension, aches, or soreness (myalgias).
- Fatigue.
- Sleep problems, such as the inability to fall asleep or stay asleep, early waking, or restless, unsatisfying sleep.

Emotional symptoms of anxiety include:
- Restlessness, irritability, feeling on edge.
- Excessive worrying.
- Fearing that something bad is going to happen; sense of impending doom.
- Inability to concentrate, "blanking out."
- Constant feelings of sadness.

1:01 p.m.

I'm not crazy. I'm not.

At least, I don't think that I am. But do crazy people *know* they are crazy? I mean, do they walk down the street thinking, "I'm crazy, I'm crazy, la la la"? Or do they look around and wonder why everyone else is crazy?

And would it be so bad to be crazy? Maybe crazy people are happier than everyone else. Just being crazy and oblivious to it.

So clearly, I'm not crazy, because I'm thinking about it. I'm just anxious. That's okay. "Anxious" sounds completely normal. This cheers me up immensely. I won't even get angry with Jules for not meeting me for lunch as we'd arranged. Or with Kiki for not even coming to school. What *is* with Kiki lately?

Note to Self: Investigate what is with Kiki. And find out why everyone seems to have a secret life, except for me.

Further Note to Self: Develop secret life.

8:52 p.m.
Dear Junior:

I'm sorry I didn't write more before now, but I was in shock. I will now go back and describe Dad's birthday dinner. Which was vegetarian, by the way. I thought that he was being vegetarian for my sake, or because maybe he finally figured out that eating meat was really gross. But it turns out that his new girlfriend, MELODY, is a vegetarian. So he's doing it to impress her.

Which is gross.

Because she's so *young*. I mean, I just about fell over when we walked into the restaurant. Well, I didn't at first because I thought she was the hostess. I thought she worked there. But of course she doesn't work there. She's a doctor.

But not a real doctor.

She's a NATUROPATH.

I should also state, for the record, that she's not particularly pretty. Well, she is PRETTY, but not overly pretty.

For example, her teeth aren't as white as they could be and she was wearing no makeup at all. And she was wearing one of those hippie skirts with the tiny mirrors sewn into them. I'm sorry, but I just don't understand those skirts. How do you wash them? What is the purpose of the tiny mirrors?

Also, she smelled a bit like garlic. And BO.

But she was nice. She was. She smiled a lot and touched my dad's hand, which frankly I found disturbing. She was CREEPY. But nice.

I'm sorry about all the capital letters, but I can't help it. I'm feeling EMPHATIC.

MY DAD IS DATING A TEENAGED (okay, she's 35) NATUROPATH NAMED MELODY.

Hmmm, if they get married (perish the thought), she'll be Melody Harmony.

Actually, that's kind of funny.

Love,

Haley

PS — Am suffering from extreme anxiety so cannot type any more tonight.

PPS — If they get married, will I have to call her MOM?

10:14 p.m.

I miss Brad. It's so weird, but when he's here I sort of wish he was away and now that he's away, I wish he was here.

10:15 p.m.

Phone Call with Kiki:

Me: Where have you been? It's terrible. Everything's gone wrong and the stupid Valentine's Ball is this

week and I have nothing to wear and I'm supposed
to be, like, in charge.

Her: Why do you volunteer for things like that?

Me: Never mind. Where were you?

Her: Nowhere.

Me: You must have been somewhere.

Her: I had a … meeting.

Me: A meeting? What kind of meeting?

Her: Oh, uh, an interview.

Me: What kind of interview?

Her: It's not a big deal.

Me: Of course it is. I mean, maybe it is. What is it?

Her: I was, uh, in Boston.

Me: What?

Her: In Boston. At Harvard. I had an interview.

Me: What?

Her: At Harvard. And I think it went really well. I mean,
       I think…

Me: HARVARD?

Her: Yes, I …

Me: You can't go to Harvard.

Her: Yes, I can. That's …

Me: No, you can't!

Her: Haley, I want to …

Me: Forget it. I have to go.

Then I hung up. I know I'm a lousy friend. But if Kiki goes
to Harvard then it will just be me and Jules left here alone.
And Jules will drive me crazy.

Or maybe Jules will go away, too.

Jules will go away and my dad will marry Melody and Brad will be on some hockey team and everyone will be gone except me.

Hmm. Except me *and* JT. I mean, I doubt JT is going anywhere. He isn't smart enough to get into college. Maybe if JT and I are the only people left in town, then he'll fall in love with me and ...

Oh, stop it. I don't even like him anymore. I'm just anxious. Maybe am also depressed.

(From WebMd):

What is depression?

Depression is a mood disorder that causes symptoms such as low energy, prolonged sadness or irritability, and lack of interest in daily activities. It can be triggered by a chemical imbalance or stressful, emotional situations. Depression is a medical condition, not a character flaw or weakness. Many people with depression do not seek treatment because they are embarrassed or think they will get over it on their own. If you feel you have depression or have been diagnosed with depression, there are many successful treatments available to help you. You do not have to live with depression.

What causes depression?

The cause of depression is not entirely clear. It is thought to be caused by an imbalance of certain brain chemicals (neurotransmitters). Depression seems to run in families and may be triggered by stressful life events and lack of social support, and it tends to recur.

LACK OF SOCIAL SUPPORT!

Hmmm. Perhaps am depressed *and* anxious.

Note to Self: Investigate therapists. Have lots of time to do so, what with being friendless and alone.

▶ ▶ ▶

Friday, January 31 (Day off from school, whoopee)

7:30 p.m.

What I Did Today:

1. Trimmed hair. Bangs now too short. Impossible now to be seen in public for six to eight weeks.
2. Bleached teeth. Teeth have taken on bizarre bluish tint and are clearly transparent around the edge. Must stop bleaching teeth. Perhaps will concentrate on growing out leg hair such that waxing is an option.
3. Plucked eyebrows. Eyebrows now surrounded by enraged, angry skin.
4. Cleaned room.
5. Cleaned bathroom.
6. Cleaned kitchen.
7. Tried to clean The Cat, but The Cat did not want to be cleaned.
8. Cleaned The Bird's cage.
9. Cleaned Dad's room (containing suspicious amount of women's clothing, presumably Melody's) (gross) (unless Dad is cross-dresser) (which seems unlikely, but you never know).
10. Cleaned the living room.

11. Cleaned out the fridge.
12. Ran out of things to clean.
13. Contemplated how sad it is that 16-year-old girl spends Saturday cleaning instead of going out with friends, especially considering this is TGYML. (Ha.)
14. Remembered that no one was going out because everyone is studying for exams that begin on Monday.
15. Piled textbooks on desk to begin studying.
16. Baked cookies.
17. Ate cookies.
18. Went for run in attempt to stop cookies from making fat roll grow.
19. Cleaned up cookie-making mess.
20. Made this list on computer.

I don't think I was cut out for studying. Perhaps will watch fascinating 1970s romantic comedy on television and study when Dad gets home.

If Dad gets home.

Legs feel peculiar and strange. Stringy and wobbly. Hmmm. Should do some sitting until this unpleasant feeling passes. Will check internet first:

(From MDAdvice.com):

diabetic hypoglycemia
GENERAL INFORMATION
DEFINITION — Hypoglycemia means low blood sugar. When the blood sugar decreases considerably below normal, a group of symptoms develop. Hypoglycemia develops when there is too much insulin or not enough

food for the condition you are in at any point in time. It is more frequent in insulin-dependent type diabetes.

BODY PARTS INVOLVED — Endocrine and metabolic.

SEX OR AGE MOST AFFECTED — Both sexes; all ages.

Signs & Symptoms

MILD:

- Hunger, weakness, nervousness.
- Emotional ups and downs, difficulty in concentrating.
- Sweating, headache.

MODERATELY SEVERE:

- Increased weakness, excessive perspiration.
- Skin cold and clammy to touch.
- Numbness about mouth and/or fingers.
- Pounding of heart.
- Loss of memory.
- Double vision.
- Staring expression.
- Difficulty in walking.
- Unawareness of surroundings.

SEVERE:

- Twitching of muscles, unconsciousness, convulsions.
- Passing urine unknowingly.

I am hungry. Sweaty? Check. But it is hot in here.

Will not panic.

1:37 a.m.

Am panicking.

Dad did not come home.

Gross.

And what if I'd fallen into a diabetic spasm? Passed urine unknowingly? Twitched?

Some father *he* is.

Good news: Feeling has returned to my legs.

Bad news: Legs are completely spasming in terrible cramping pain.

2:35 a.m.

Me: Hello?

Brad: Haley?

Me: Brad?

Brad: Where are you?

Me: I'm at home. You just phoned me here.

Brad: It's a cell phone. You could be anywhere.

Me: Where would I be?

Brad: Out with some guy?

Me: What?

Brad: I was just kidding!

Me: Why are you calling me in the middle of the night?

Brad: I miss you.

Me: I miss you, too.

Then we stopped talking. It was weird, but it wasn't awkward at all. And I think it's true. I think I do miss him. I even sort of fell asleep.

Hmm. Maybe am not depressed, maybe am just stressed from exams and will return to regular life/mood shortly.

FEBRUARY

MOOD	Blah
HAIR	See: Mood.
HEALTH	Blah
HOROSCOPE	Get out and exercise today! Meet friends and have fun. Today is a day for celebrating life!
JT SIGHTINGS	*None*, not even thinking about JT

Noon

Dear Junior:

Hate studying.

Hate studying.

Hate studying.

Love,

Haley-who-is-doomed-to-flunk-Automechanics-which-was-Jules'-dumb-idea-anyway

► ► ►

Monday, February 3

MOOD	Stupid
HAIR	Limp
HEALTH	Lacking
HOROSCOPE	Typical rubbish about study, work, friends, and health. No romance. Sigh.
JT SIGHTINGS	None yet, expect several

9:35 a.m.

I am going to fail Automechanics final and will never live it down. Also, plans for Locks of Love Charity event have been taken over by the perky and intolerable Izzy Archibaud (aka one of JT's many exes) who makes me want to poke my eyes out with sharp sticks. Taken over because, according to Bruce Bartelson, I don't show enough "gumption" to do it myself.

Gumption!

Technically, she's supposed to be "helping" me, but really I've let her do it all. Mostly because she said, "Aren't you going out with Brad?" And her look said, "What does *he* see in *you*?" Which made me mad and so I gave her a list of "her" share of things to do, which was pretty much all of it.

I don't feel bad, because she loves that stuff and I don't.

On a related note, I have not heard the word "gumption" since my grandmother said it once in 1987.

But back to my Automechanics final, which I'm going to fail. Will I have to repeat 12th grade to retake Automechanics?

Very dumb, very smelly, very weird boys are going to get A's in this class and I am going to get *zero*. Do they offer

Automechanics in summer school? If so, won't it ruin the last, best summer holidays of my life? Although, can they really be considered "summer holidays" if I don't have anything to "go back" to in September?

More immediate problem: Have no idea what/where carburetor is.

Why didn't I study? Why? What is wrong with me?

Am doomed to life of slinging chicken wings and frying burgers as have no hope of getting into either a) college or b) automechanic school.

On the bright side, I didn't want to be an automechanic anyway.

1:47 p.m.
Oh no, oh no, oh no.

Should have studied more (some?) math.

Wonder what career options are open to someone who fails entire semester of 12th grade. Come to think of it, wonder about career options, period.

Have no career options.

Oh no, nooooooooooooo.

3:05 p.m.
"What's the matter with you?" Kiki asked as the bell went, plopping herself down next to me in the hallway. It was much, *much* too cold to be outside. Even the smokers had come in from the cold. And Sacred Heart High does not believe in making students comfortable while they are "loitering," or as I prefer to think of it "waiting for Jules to give us a ride home." In any event, there we were,

sitting down on the floor watching peoples' knees as they walked by. I can see now why the floors are red. This is so that dirt doesn't show as easily. The floors are, on close inspection, very dirty.

"Why are you staring at the floor like that then?" Kiki asked.

"No reason," I said loftily. "I was just thinking about interior design."

"Interior design?" she said. "Why?"

"I don't know," I said. The idea spontaneously popped into my head. "I'm thinking about becoming an interior designer after graduation."

"Hmm," she said.

"What?" I said. I mean, really, I was quite insulted that she clearly believed I would be a terrible interior designer. How hard could it be?

"Nothing," she said.

"We can't all be doctors or brain surgeons or whatever," I said.

"I know," she said. "I'm sure everyone doesn't want to be. It's a lot of work. I'm kind of not sure myself."

"What?" I said. "I thought you were all set to go to Harvard and leave forever."

"I am," she said. "And it's nothing to do with leaving, you know. It's to do with, I don't know, *doing* something with my life."

"Hmmf," I said. I mean, obviously she was implying that I wasn't doing anything with my life. Which wasn't very nice. I used to think Kiki was so nice. Now I'm not so sure.

"How's Brad?" she said.

Which is when I burst into tears. For no apparent reason. And this naturally coincided with the moment that Jules and JT sauntered up (Jules in designer denim, looking like a million dollars, and JT looking studiously casual in loose cords and a bulky leather jacket). (Hate them, and their fashionable good looks.)

"What's wrong?" said Kiki, swiping at my face, presumably to either a) slap me or b) wipe away my tears.

"Nothing," I said. "I have a cold. I have runny ... uh, eyes." I looked at JT. "From having a cold." I coughed and got up as quickly as possible, which was difficult as I had a pile of books (English and Science finals tomorrow and I AM going to study for them) that immediately fell on the floor. Which was when my nose began to drip unbecomingly, so I swiped it with my sleeve. I could feel JT looking at me, quite possibly laughing, which naturally made it all worse. Much, much worse.

"Haley, what is it with you?" said Jules, passing me my pile of books.

"Nothing," I said again and made a run for the bus stop. Which was stupid because obviously I hate taking the bus and also because I slipped on the way and skinned my knee, then proceeded to fall up the stairs of the bus and land head-first on the driver's lap.

It would have been less humiliating if it hadn't happened to me once before.

Oh help, I thought miserably, staring out the window at the grey, slushy streets.

Oh.

HELP.

List of Things that Are Wrong with Me:
1. Am a bad girlfriend.
2. Am a bad, unsupportive friend.
3. Am a totally rude, unsupportive daughter.
4. Am possibly suffering from brain tumour, masquerading as "anxiety."
5. Am possibly going to end up graduating from high school and doing nothing for the rest of my life.
6. Am possibly never going to graduate from high school.

When you look at it like that, it looks very bad.

It's no wonder that I spontaneously burst into tears at the slightest provocation. Who wouldn't?

I scrumpled the list up into a ball and stared forlornly at my lap. Which apparently looked like some sort of seizure as the kid next to me said, "Uh, what's wrong with you? Do you need help?"

I glared at him as frostily as possible. He was about 12 years old and had so much acne, it was hard to discern his facial features. Hmmm. That's horrible, I thought. At least I have good skin. I mean, compared to some people, you could argue that my life doesn't look so bad. I can see that abject failure as a human being could get some people down, but in that moment I decided to take Dr. Phil's advice (or is it from a song?) and start looking at life differently. In that vein, I made a second list.

Reasons to Be Happy Being Me Right Now:
1. Have very white teeth.

2. Have lost three pounds without trying ~~possibly due to brain tumour~~.

3. Never have to look at another car engine as Auto-mechanics elective is over.

4. Have upcoming semester of fun and interesting subjects.

5. Have boyfriend, who will be home this weekend.

6. Will have date for Valentine's dance ~~which still have to plan and will inevitably be a disaster.~~

Note to Self: Scratch all negative thoughts.

Accidentally missed bus stop and had to walk home. Which is fine as could use the exercise. Never mind that it began to hail.

Ouch.

Or that my legs don't work as well as they ought to due to some sort of wet-noodle muscle disease.

It's very hard to maintain a positive outlook when being pronged in the eye with frozen rain-balls and wobbling on ruined legs. That's all I'm trying to say.

I'm doing my best, okay?

5:48 p.m.

Have looked up "unexplained emotional outburst" and "muscle weakness" on the internet and now am almost certain that I am dying of a brain tumour. I saw a movie once where there was a lovely video sequence played at a funeral. It showed the dead person when they were young running through a field of daisies wearing a floaty dress.

I wonder if I should buy a floaty dress, just in case.

(From adam.com):
Symptoms of Brain Tumours:
- Headache: recent onset of new type; persistent; worse on awakening
- Vomiting: possibly accompanied by nausea; more severe in the morning
- Personality changes and behaviour changes
- Emotional instability, rapid emotional changes
- Intellectual decline: loss of memory; impaired calculating abilities; impaired judgement
- Seizures, new onset
- Reduced level of consciousness (decreased alertness)
- Neurologic changes
- Vision changes (double vision, decreased vision)
- Hearing loss
- Decreased sensation of a body area
- Weakness of a body area
- Speech difficulties
- Decreased coordination, clumsiness, falls
- Fever (sometimes)
- Weakness, lethargy
- General ill feeling (malaise)

Granted, I don't have *all* of those symptoms, but I certainly have *some* of them. Enough that I'm slightly freaked out. As I've pointed out, the point of being a hypochondriac is to ward off disease and not actually *get sick*.

"This is dire," I told The Cat, who was flopped out

obliviously over my feet. I got up and went to examine myself in the mirror to see if there was physical evidence of illness. I looked much the same as usual, except my cheeks were exceptionally red.

Note to Self: Check "rosacea" on the internet. Perhaps should get some sort of cream.

Okay, well, I don't actually have a headache. Or any of the other symptoms.

But I *cried*. In front of JT! (i.e., emotional outburst.)

And my legs are shaking! (i.e., weakness in one part of the body.) (Not that my arms are very strong either, come to think of it.)

I'll never live it down. No wonder my friends only pretend to like me, but actually probably can't stand me. In fact, they probably laughed when I ran out of the school.

No, they wouldn't do that.

Would they?

The thing is, you can't really count on your friends. I've been friends with Jules for long enough to know *that*. We've been friends since ballet school when we were four. We've been friends through everything: through all the weird family stuff and boy stuff and general stuff.

It's like we're practically married. Only different.

Like we're sisters.

Sisters who would stab each other in the back at the earliest opportunity. I mean, I wouldn't stab *her* in the back, but I'm sure she'd trample *me* down if she had to. She stole my boyfriend, for heaven's sake.

But family … family is allowed to do that, I guess.

Speaking of family, where is my dad? He's never home anymore. He spends way too much time with Melody, or la!la!la!, as I sometimes think of her.

"Nobody loves us," I told The Bird, who was conveniently pecking the crumbs off my keyboard. Sometimes The Bird comes in very handy.

So, to summarize, both my friends *and* my family have abandoned me.

I must do something to win them back, in case I am really sick and need attendees at my funeral. I'll start with my dad. I mean, how bad can this Melody person be? When exams are over, I will have all sorts of time, except for the time that I have to spend with Brad in order to maintain girlfriend-status and the time I have to spend planning the Valentine's Ball (i.e., telling Izzy what to do).

Maybe wouldn't be so bad to be friends with this Melody MYG (Much Younger Girlfriend) person. Maybe she could give me motherly advice. And hugs. Well, not the hugs. She's a little smelly.

Dear Junior:

Have made plans to cook vegan dinner for Dad and his MYG on Saturday night. Also for Brad, as he is going to be home from his hockey meet. Tournament. Thing. Whatever.

Must go and find recipes on the internet. Have pots of time now that have likely flunked exams that accidentally forgot to study for as much as possibly should have.

Love,

Chef-Haley-R-Dee

▶ ▶ ▶

Saturday, February 8

MOOD	Positive!
HAIR	Medium cute
HEALTH	Great! Ish. Okay, poor
HOROSCOPE	Be careful of sharp objects today. A trip to the store could prove to be lucky!
JT SIGHTINGS	None, and it doesn't matter

10:45 a.m.
Will just go to the grocery store and pick up the following ingredients:

- meatless chicken broth
- tempeh
- meatless sausage
- meatless crawfish
- Tabasco
- bunch of spices
- vegetables (peppers, celery, onions, tomato, garlic, artichokes)
- rice
- tofu
- etc.

12:57 p.m.
Have spent over $80 on ingredients for one dinner. Am I crazy? That $80 could have been spent on any of the following:

1. Highlights (hair is currently the colour of thick mud).
2. Laser treatment (to remove hair on top-lip — fear growing a moustache).
3. Cute T-shirt from anthropologie that have been coveting for three weeks.
3. Any number of more interesting things than vegetables.

1:46 p.m.

Not sure exactly how to follow recipe and prepare vegan jambalaya. Have put all ingredients into wok and stir-fried and then poured into a larger pot to "simmer" until dinnertime. Dad says the house smells like old socks. But I think he just hates/fears a) vegetables, and b) tofu, and c) tempeh.

He must really be in love.

So naturally, I pretend not to notice when he drives off in the direction of Burger King two hours before dinner. He's trying, and that's all that counts. Secretly, I hope that Melody (why is it that when I think of Melody, it's like her name is in quotes? "Melody"!) will smell the meat on his breath and run from the house screaming. Is that wrong? I mean, I want my dad to be happy. I *do*. I swear. I just, I don't know. I mean, she's almost the same age as *me*. Okay, not exactly almost the same age as me, but she's the same *size* as me. Which, now that I think of it, is a good thing because we can share clothes. So if I ever have an occasion to wear a batik skirt encrusted with tiny mirrors, maybe it's best to keep her in my corner.

Reminder to Self: As part of new plan to be more mature and generally likeable, get to know "Melody" before deciding you don't like her.

3:14 p.m.
I called Brad to see what time he was coming over, and the conversation was very disturbing. I'm making a special dinner just for him! And he doesn't seem happy about it. Can't he see that I'm trying to be a better girlfriend? Honestly, I don't understand boys at all.

Will now go get ready for dinner so that I look the best I can possibly look, and hope that Brad forgets that he's mad at me because he would rather have been going to JT's party.

JT's *party*?

Why wasn't I invited?

Contemplate phoning Jules to find out, but am distracted by bubbling-over burning smell from kitchen and have to hurry to prevent deadly house-fire.

▶ ▶ ▶

Sunday, February 9

MOOD	Numb
HAIR	Flat
HEALTH	Better than some peoples'
HOROSCOPE	Total rubbish about feeling beautiful and doing a charitable act.
JT SIGHTINGS	n/a

9:30 a.m.

Okay, it's necessary to recap last night's dinner so that I can figure out exactly what went wrong. First, let me just say that the jambalaya was really good. How was I supposed to know that Brad was allergic to tofu? I guess I should be happy that he didn't go into anaphylactic shock and die. (*Obviously*, I'm happy about that.) But I feel badly because of the hives and swelling. He took it really well, though. He apologized to me. Like it was his fault that I tried to kill him.

To backtrack a bit, it was snowing hard all afternoon. I was worried that no one would be able to come, if by "no one," I mean "Melody and Brad." Dad was upstairs "getting ready."

Note to Self: Dad must really like this Melody MYG person because the last time he spent more than 10 minutes getting ready for anything must have been before I was born.

He appeared in the kitchen (where I was making biscuits) at about five-ish. He looked suspiciously good. Naturally, I'm using the word "good" loosely in this context to describe a 60-ish hippie wearing a polo shirt (featuring a tiny horse) (where on earth did he get *that*?) and jeans with only a few holes in them. His socks even matched and he smelled good-ish. A bit like the Old Spice soap-on-a-rope I gave him when I was eight. Exactly like that, come to think of it.

I, on the other hand, did not look good, thanks to the giant blemish on my forehead (which was getting infected and as revolting as possible, and was made redder by all the steam in the kitchen) and the fact that I must have somehow gained some weight because my pants (Okay, they're Jules' pants) were slightly too tight. Which, now that I think of it, was probably because Jules weighs approximately the same as my right leg.

You should never wear clothes that are too small. They just make you look fatter than you are. And I'm not fat. I'm healthy.

Okay, I would be healthier if I exercised, but I'm trying.

Okay, I wish I were thinner and fitter. But I'm not, and I didn't have time to do anything about it before dinner anyway.

I was making some biscuits to go with the jambalaya. I reached into the oven to turn them over and maybe I kept my head in there for too long because suddenly my lungs were full of hot air and I thought I was going to faint. So I reached out to catch myself and accidentally pulled the pot of jambalaya off the stove and spilled half of it on my (Jules') pants (off-white), scalding my leg (and ruining said pants). Which wouldn't have been so bad, but I somehow then lurched forward and burned my neck. I don't know how it happened, exactly. It happened so fast! One minute, there I was, calmly stirring and look-ing thin-ish in my best friend's pants, waiting for my dad and his girlfriend and my boyfriend to come over for dinner, and the next thing I know, half of dinner is on my leg and I'm burned in several places.

"Stupid, stupid, stupid," The Bird screeched from the planter in the corner.

"Oh, shut up," I said.

"Happy Birthday," he said.

"It isn't anyone's birthday," I said.

I went upstairs and quickly changed into whatever was available. Which was a pair of mostly clean jeans, which maybe weren't as dressy as Jules' off-white wool pants, but they'd have to do. And I mopped up the floor as best I could.

Then, of course, I had to stretch the jambalaya, because there wasn't that much left. So I added some stuff to it. Some noodles. I thought if I served it on noodles, then it would at least fill people up. I didn't know that the noodles were flavoured.

Honestly.

Brad showed up first and he looked nervous. I guess I hadn't thought about it but it was sort of his first formal meeting with my dad. It hadn't occurred to me that Brad would care, to be perfectly frank. And I was a bit on edge myself. I don't know why. Maybe it was because I was wearing really unflattering jeans that were crawling up my butt and Brad was dressed up. (It can throw the balance off, when one person is dressed up and the other person isn't.)

"You look nice," he said. Which was very sweet (of course), considering I didn't. I looked the opposite of "nice." I looked "gross."

"I sort of spilled," I said, touching my neck, which to tell you the truth was really hurting.

"What happened to your neck?" he said, all alarmed. Like I had the plague or something.

"It's just a little burn," I said. I tried to change the subject. "My dad's girlfriend is a deranged hippie!" I blurted out.

Which is, of course, the exact moment that "Melody" and my dad came through the door. I swear the words "deranged hippie" were just hanging there in the air between us like a giant flapping bird. Like The Bird, in fact, who chose that moment to flap into the room and land on the edge of the jambalaya.

Luckily, he didn't fall in. And it was really no problem to fish that feather out before anyone noticed.

"Haley," Melody gushed (she doesn't speak, she gushes and oozes). "This looks fantastic! I can't believe a girl your age would do something so sweet for her dad! When I was your age, I was, like, partying every weekend!"

"Gosh," I said. "That's lovely. But it's not a big deal. This is Brad," I added.

"Hi," said Brad, shaking her hand. HE SHOOK HER HAND. What are we, 35? At a business meeting? Suddenly, I was even more uncomfortable. The whole thing was wrong.

Then I noticed that Melody was wearing bells around her ankles. I'm not making that up. She *rang* when she walked.

"What the hell is that noise?" I hissed.

"It's harmony bells," she said promptly. "Harmony!" she repeated. Like our last name was the funniest thing on earth. When she laughed, I could see food caught between her teeth. Poppy seeds, I think. Gross.

"Okay," I said. "This is fun and everything, but why

don't you all go sit down while I get the dinner finished?"

"Good idea, Haley," said Dad. He looked a bit worried and kept eyeing the pot on the stove nervously. You'd think I didn't cook for him practically every night of my life or something. "Uh, I think that might be burning."

"Get *out!*" I yelled. And they all sort of scampered into the living room, where luckily I couldn't hear what they were talking about. I could hear laughter, though, which struck me as odd and also made me paranoid. I mean, I'm the most obvious thing to be laughing about, aren't I?

I just sort of stood around by myself in the kitchen for a while watching it snow. The flakes were really pretty, swirling through the lights from the streetlamps. There wasn't anything more I needed to do to prepare for the dinner except put the biscuits into a basket and take the dish of goo into the dining room. I took my time, though. I could hear my dad saying something about hockey, and Brad answering really earnestly and … well, nicely. Of course. I don't actually know what I was thinking, but for some reason, I picked up the phone and dialed JT's number. I mean, if he was having a party he wouldn't answer.

But he did.

So naturally I hung up.

I hope he doesn't have call display.

What am I, 12 years old?

At least he didn't call back. That would have been embarrassing, not to mention "extremely difficult to explain."

Dinner itself was going fine, in that everyone was chewing and swallowing and talking and what have you. Then Brad stood up and said, "I feel a little funny. I'm just going to go outside for fresh air."

I looked at him and he was all red and puffy-faced, and Melody jumped up and said, "I'm a doctor!" (Which she *isn't*, as I've mentioned, she's a *naturopath*.) And my dad ran out of the room to call an ambulance because Brad was kind of gasping for air.

I didn't know what to do. To tell you the truth, I'm usually the one *having* the emergency. I don't really know how to *handle* an emergency. And then the ambulance guys came and when I opened the door, one of them said, "Hey, I remember you!" which was embarrassing. I felt really stupid. But I let them in and they gave Brad a shot and then took him in the ambulance for observation.

Seriously, how was I supposed to know he was allergic to soy? I felt horrible.

Melody said that she'd go to the hospital because it was on her way home, but I shouldn't go because of the snow and she'd call later. And then she hugged me (she smelled like patchouli, which makes me nauseated) and said, "It will all be all right."

"I know it will," I said irritably.

I stomped upstairs. I felt horrible. I did. I could hear Dad cleaning up the kitchen and a little later Brad called to say he was fine and that he was sorry. It all worked out. I just felt … terrible.

"Pretty, pretty, pretty," The Bird said from the doorway. So I slammed the door (on my finger) and checked my e-mail (none) and called Kiki (no answer) and Jules (busy) and cried for a while.

Reasons for Living:

1. This is the Greatest Year of My Life So Far! Or NOT.
2. I have a boyfriend WHO I NEARLY KILLED.
3. I have good friends WHO HATE ME.
4. I have a nice family OF HIPPIES.
5. I have a bright future. Maybe. If I can ever think of what I want to do.
6. ARGH.

▶ ▶ ▶

Tuesday, February 11
AKA
THE WEEK BUILDING UP TO VALENTINE'S DAY, A DAY THAT HAS
SUDDENLY BECOME BIGGER THAN CHRISTMAS

I swear, the neighbours have decorated their house with red and pink lights. I mean, since when was Valentine's Day such a big deal?

It's making me nauseated.

Although, nausea is part and parcel of having a brain tumour, so perhaps should get used to it.

MOOD	Stressed
HAIR	Perky. Quite good, actually
HEALTH	Ailing — am surprised to be alive
HOROSCOPE	An unexpected "blast from the past" will knock your socks off today!
JT SIGHTINGS	None yet, expect several

Note to Self: Find new source of horoscopes as horoscopes in daily paper are becoming UNSPEAKABLY LAME. (Also, stop using caps because it looks like shouting.)

7:15 a.m.

Valentine's Day was clearly a day that was invented simply to remind people that no one loves them. Or even likes them, for that matter. I miss Brad. I do. I know it's crazy. But my dad has Melody (la!) and Jules has JT (lucky cow) and Kiki has Stephano. Hot Prince Stephano. (More about *this* alarming development in a minute.) And I have no one. I mean, I *have* Brad, but he's away again (he was released from the hospital). (He was fine.)

And also, I think Brad and I might have broken up. I'm not sure. I was mad when I found out he'd be away for Valentine's Day playing hockey in who-knows-where.

You'd think the coach would understand. Valentine's Day is *important.*

But I tried to be nice about it. I did. I just said, "Do what you have to do! Don't worry about me!"

And he said, "That's so passive-aggressive. I *have* to go. I'm sorry about your little dance. I'm just glad I'm *alive.*"

And I said, "Little dance? I've killed myself organizing this dance." (*NB:* By that I meant, I've nearly killed Izzy organizing this dance.) "And you didn't nearly die. You had a reaction! It's over!"

And he said, "I thought Izzy did all the work for the dance. And I *could* have died. Not that you'd have cared."

And I said, "Forget it!" And hung up.

I haven't talked to him since.

WHO GOES TO A BALL BY THEMSELVES? That's what I want to know. I guess we know the answer to that: Me. Haley Andromeda Harmony. Girl Uninterrupted. I mean, it's not like there's anyone in my life who might interrupt me.

I curse Valentine's Day with the heat of a million suns.

So there.

▶ ▶ ▶

Friday, February 14
ARGH.

MOOD	Depressed beyond words
HAIR	Very, very good
HEALTH	...
HOROSCOPE	Love is in the air! Your romance is flourishing. Enjoy! Bask in the light of your love.
JT SIGHTINGS	7, but who counts these things?

Ha ha ha.

Barf.

8:45 a.m.

Hair looks surprisingly good. How can it be that on the one day no one will actually care what my hair looks like, it looks good? And also, will be ruining it later with bright red hair dye in honour of shave-your-head-for-charity day, because I can't shave my head.

Because hair is already nearly all gone.

Am re-thinking the hair dye.

8:47 a.m.

The Bird has just crapped in my hair. May as well go back to idea to dye hair bright red as have nothing to lose and am going to look like a fool anyway going to a ball BY MYSELF.

Also, dying microscopically short hair is the least I can do, considering all the people who are going to get their hair cut off for Locks of Love. I swear, if I had long hair, I would do it.

I would.

I mean, I *probably* would.

It's just *hair*. It grows back.

Am still shocked that seven people signed up to cut off all their hair for Locks of Love. Totally impressed, but still shocked.

9:16 a.m.

At least Drama class provides me with lots of time to write things down. It's not like anyone will notice that I'm not "being a tree." I wonder how much time Sarah Jessica Parker has devoted to "being a tree." My guess is "none." Because she is "beautiful" and doesn't have to "be a tree."

Must go now. My oak-like skills are being called upon.

BE the tree.

BE it.

Question: Why am I taking Drama class? I have no future as an actress as am neither a) pretty, or b) thin, or c) (less importantly) talented.

Hmmmm. Kiki actually is doing a very good job of resembling a palm tree. How is it that she can even make "being a tree" look intelligent?

Must get back to looking stoic and serious in the style of an ancient oak tree possibly festering with unknown rare oak-tree disease.

Update:

After falling over in Drama class and receiving sharp lecture about the "seriousness of the craft" and how "people with real talent shine through" and the "need to be outside of yourself," Kiki (probably feeling sorry for me for being such a pathetic loser) invited me to come to her house after school to get ready for the ball. Yay! Naturally, it will be awkward going to the ball with Kiki and Stephano, but it's better than showing up alone with weird bright-red hair and ill-fitting white dress, which would fit if I had time to do a million sit-ups between now and seven p.m., which clearly cannot happen as I have an assembly to get through, followed by a gripping hour of art history. If by "gripping," I mean "senselessly boring and without any tangible point."

Sidenote:

I said I was going to talk about Stephano and then I didn't. This is because I'm a) jealous, and b) annoyed with Kiki for going back on her word about staying single for the twelfth grade because she didn't want to be attached to anyone. I love Kiki, I do. She's great. She's so nice. And smart. And pretty.

And then she met a handsome prince. Naturally. And I use the word "prince" here to mean "an actual prince." He's some kind of Italian royalty. I didn't know there was still royalty in Italy, but apparently there is.

And he's drop-dead gorgeous.

She met him at her Harvard interview. They were on the same flight.

They're both going to be doctors. Harvard-educated doctors. She thinks she might "love" him. "Love!"

I'm happy for her. I am. And he's really nice. And funny. And wears nice clothes. (I think he irons his jeans.)

I just, well, I just miss Kiki. That's all. I miss going for runs with her. I miss all the time she used to spend making me laugh and just, well, doing stuff. Not that she's known him for very long. It's been, like, two weeks.

But still.

I'm just jealous. I should pull it together. After all, I have Brad. And he's great. Sure, he's never here and is missing the most important dance of the year (except prom, natch). And he's not European royalty. And he doesn't make me blush when he looks at me (like Stephano does).

But he's sweet.

So there.

2:01 p.m.

NEWSFLASH:

Oh. My. God. I seriously can't believe it. Well, first of all, it's important to point out that I almost made it completely through the lame speech that Bruce Bartelson, Student Council Demon, wrote for me, before I got the hiccups and turned the colour of a ripe tomato and had to take a drink of water from the bottle, which I realized as I raised to my lips was marked with someone else's lipstick, which of course caused me to spit it out and accidentally drop it on the floor. Don't worry about me, though. I'm used to this sort of humiliation. I don't think I would have been surprised if all my clothes had suddenly fallen off. That's the kind of year this is: not actually TGYML, but TMHYML (tim-himmel). The Most Humiliating Year of My Life. In any event, that's not the news.

Nope, it's hardly newsworthy when I trip over an extension cord and rip it from the wall and cause feedback to deafen the entire class.

What is newsworthy is Jules.

It was the Valentine's assembly. We had the people in from Locks of Love to talk about their charity, and some hair-people to cut hair. We had eight people signed up. It was a big deal. Even the local news cameras were there.

Come to think of it, that's probably why Jules did it.

I'm not kidding, I thought I was going to have a heart attack when she calmly got up and walked up to the microphone, took it from me, and announced that she was going to be first. And she did it.

That beautiful perfect sheet of blonde hair.

I was horrified.

I was totally proud.

It's possible that I cried. Then I thought about it. I mean, I'm sure she did it just so she would be on the news. And being Jules, naturally she looks fantastic with just-above-the-shoulders flippy hair in the style of Julia Stiles in that dance movie where she learned how to do hip-hop.

She looked really, really good.

Which is great. I mean, I wouldn't want her to look bad. Would I? Okay, maybe a tiny part of me wanted her to look … less good. And it was a bit of a knife in my heart to see JT clapping like crazy and telling everyone, "That's my girl!" and hugging her. And both of them being interviewed while I stood there with my already-short-hair and one wet pantleg from the water, hiccupping and generally looking stupid.

But I guess that's what I do, right?

I look dumb so other people can be heroes.

6:50 p.m.

Should never have let Kiki talk me into drinking vodka-and-orange-juice before getting ready for dance. Have peculiar red stain from Valentine-red hair dye on forehead that I can't quite seem to remove, and funny itchy feeling in scalp. This dress is different than I remember it being, quite short and sort of squidgy, and Kiki looks so pretty in her black dress, and I think you can see my underwear, although what does it matter? Who will care?

I miss Brad. I do.

"I miss Brad!" I wailed, staring at myself in the mirror and tugging at my dress hopelessly.

"Pull yourself together, sweetie," said Kiki worriedly. "Are you okay? It was just one drink."

"You know I can't drink," I sobbed. "I have no tolerance for alcohol, I think maybe my liver is … ish … I don't know."

Which is when she slapped some cold water on my face. You know, I never realized how effective that is until she did it. Really very refreshing. Although she didn't need to slap me. I was hardly hysterical.

"I never should have had such a stupid fight with Brad," I said to Stephano as we wobbled out to his car. His lips hovered near my face. V. nice lips. Like plums or some other sort of fruit. "Kiss me," I said, tipping towards him.

"What?" he said. (Although it sounded more like "Wot?" Which made me giggle.) He held me at arm's length and inspected me as though I had suddenly become afflicted with lice.

"Nothing!" I said. "I said that I was happy about Brad!"

"I thought he finished with you?" he said. Tosh, tosh, pip, pip, I thought. I think this every time he talks. Honestly, maybe I don't like Stephano that much. Apart from his devastating good looks, he's cold and somewhat suspect. I don't care if he's an Italian prince with a British accent and charming and good looking and smart and rich.

"Hmmf," I said snarkily, falling into the back seat. Really. I mean, Brad *might* have finished with me, but I drove *him* away. He didn't choose it. It was my fault.

Mine!

I choked back a sob and closed my eyes and half-listened to Kiki and Stephano laughing and chatting in the front seat. They seemed very far away and ... happy. Mmmf. I snuck a drink from the mickey I'd put in my purse. Wouldn't hurt and besides would need courage to get through the dance ALONE.

► ► ►

Saturday, February 15

MOOD	Humiliated
HAIR	Very … red. Like face
HEALTH	V. ill
HOROSCOPE	Middle of the night, so newspaper not available.
JT SIGHTINGS	000000

12:06 a.m.

Dear Junior,

Have never been so humiliated in my life. Have been suspended from school for being drunk on school grounds. I WAS NOT DRUNK. I can't walk a straight line when people are looking at me. This is a *psychological* problem. I had TWO DRINKS. I was very tired. And sad. Okay? I was sad about not being with Brad on Valentine's Day.

I guess I should elaborate so you know what I'm talking about, but please know that this isn't normal behaviour for me! Don't judge me. For real. Okay, after I possibly drifted off in the car, I finally woke up with a start. My head was crushed into my purse and I was freezing.

Kiki and Stephano were nowhere in sight and I appeared to be in the backseat of Stephano's car (which was v. nice and smelled of leather and other delicious boy-smells).

Bloody, bloody, bloody, I thought, catching a glimpse of myself in the rearview mirror. Well, as much of myself as

I could see in the dark parking lot. I could hear music pouring from the school gym. They let me go to *sleep*? In the *car*? What kind of friends do I have?

I got out of the car and walked firmly towards the school. Okay, perhaps I stumbled just slightly.

Okay, fine. I can't walk in high heels.

But that was really NO REASON for Mr. DorkButt, School Principal, to grab me by the arm and frog-march me to the office. It's hard to march like that in a dress that entraps your legs, I can tell you that. I mean, I hardly did anything wrong. I might have looked a bit dishevelled and maybe smelled a bit like vodka. But I'm sure lots of kids were drinking.

Now am in trouble with Dad (and even Melody said, "What are we going to do with you?" I would like to know when Dad and Melody became a *we*. Frankly, it makes me sick to think about. Am feeling sick already, but will address the problem more properly in the morning after having a good sleep).

Love,

Haley, Reject-of-the-Universe

PS — wonder if suspension will result in being kicked off the Student Council, which would be a good thing. Would not have to make any more humiliating speeches or be involved in other "dances" or "events."

3:00 p.m.

"It serves you right," said Dad, leaning over and staring into my bloodshot eyes. I slammed them shut again. Will not listen to him.

"Can I get you some ginkgo?" said his MYG. Or rather, she chirped.

"Grrr," I said.

Have given up façade of being nice to Melody. And my dad. And to anyone else. Perhaps — in the style of my maternal nun — will take a vow of silence for two weeks.

Mostly to see if anyone will notice.

"Want to go to a movie with us?" Dad said.

"Shut up," I said. Okay, vow of silence will start NOW.

► ► ►

Sunday, February 16

MOOD	V. relaxed, after all have no pressure for two weeks
HAIR	Perfect, naturally, as no one will see it
HEALTH	Fine. Healthy as can be
HOROSCOPE	Today is a wildly social day for you, Gemini. You'll be the most popular girl in town today! Enjoy!
JT SIGHTINGS	None expected until March

Dear Junior:

I wonder if taking a vow of silence means I can't even talk to you. Not that "typing" could be considered "talking." Not really.

There is something v. boring about Sundays when you aren't dreading Monday. Am actually looking forward to Monday because Dad and his MYG will leave the house. So far today they've made breakfast, FED

EACH OTHER and done yoga in the living room.

I counted three farts. I don't know which one of them it was, but frankly, it's disgusting. Am thinking of going for a walk outside as is lovely and springy and daffodils are coming up. On the other hand, being "suspended" makes me want to crawl back into bed and go to sleep.

Love,

Outcast Girl

4:09 p.m.

Was having a great dream about JT when the phone rang and woke me up. Naturally, it was Brad. So I had to talk to him. He is my boyfriend, after all. But I was trying to talk as little as possible, what with the vow-of-silence.

I swear, I'd make a terrible nun. I don't know how my mom does it. Of course, I don't think she belongs to an order of silent nuns. She seemed relatively chatty the one time that I met her.

Note to Self: Perhaps you should visit your mom.

I was just idly thinking about how visiting the nunnery was almost like visiting a hospital when I noticed that Brad had stopped talking.

"Mmm?" I said encouragingly. (The last thing I remembered hearing was "and then he just pushed me into the net, and …")

"Haley," he said. "Are you even interested in what I'm saying?"

"Mmm," I said. I wanted to explain about the vow-of-silence, but it required too many words. The weird thing about not talking for days (okay, hours) is that you lose interest in talking.

"Are you still mad about Valentine's Day?" he said.

"Mmf," I said. Which may have sounded angry, but I was thinking more of the disastrous dance than the fact he wasn't there. Of course, if he *had* been there, perhaps the dance wouldn't have been disastrous.

"Look," he said. "I'm just not interested in playing stupid games. Call me if you decide to be normal, okay?"

"Mmm," I said. But he'd already hung up.

Great.

I sat down on the bed. Then the chair. Then the bed again.

Really, I was quite bored.

I put on my running clothes. The least I can do while being outcast from society and sworn to silence (well, sort of) is to get in shape, lose the 10 extra pounds I'm carrying around, fit into my new Citizens of Humanity jeans that I bought at the Thrift Store (suspect they may have belonged to Jules' mom at some point, but so what? They were only $4) and look cool, hip and trendy when I get back to school.

Think it is very important after missing two weeks due to massive humiliation that I be thin, glamorous and nonchalant when I get back to school.

I made a face at myself in the mirror to practise nonchalance. Hmmm. Good. Not bad, anyway.

I have several more days to perfect the look. In the meantime, I will cleanse my body by eating nothing but … um, vegetables. And water! Definitely water. Lots of cleansing water.

5:03 p.m.

Have peed a record 12 times in the last three hours due to excessive water consumption. Must rethink the cleansing plan while eating popcorn and watching an '80s movie marathon with windows wide open to air room out after Dad/MYG's yoga fart-fest.

▶ ▶ ▶

Monday, February 17

MOOD	Moodless
HAIR	Hairless – okay, have hair but haven't looked
HEALTH	Healthless
HOROSCOPE	Divert your energy today by doing some spring cleaning. YAWN.
JT SIGHTINGS	JTless

9:00 a.m.

At least I didn't have to get up and go ROWING this morning. ROWING is Kiki's new love. She's going to sign me up for it as part of my PE elective. Sounds fun, if by "sounds fun" I mean, "sounds like torture." Can't imagine getting up at five a.m. for any reason. However, as am barred from school property and school activities, sadly can't participate.

   La la la.

List of Things to Accomplish While Suspended from School (to be checked off as accomplished):

1. Paint bedroom a fresh, pretty colour, such as pink or

yellow or light blue. Oooh, *Tiffany blue*! Yes, Tiffany blue, with white trim.

2. Make effort to get to know Melody better.
3. Lose 10 pounds.
4. Stop crushing on inappropriate people (accomplish this by not leaving the house).
5. Maintain vow of silence, unless someone important calls.
6. Alphabetize movies. And watch them. All.
7. Read *Moby Dick*. (Sounds intellectual and impressive.)
8. Do *not* do anything to embarrass self.
9. Be nicer to Brad. Find some silent way of apologizing to Brad.
10. Give The Cat a bath and scrape The Bird's crap off the wood floors as is v. disgusting and hurts when stepped on with bare feet.

There. That makes it easier. It's always much easier to accomplish goals when you lay them out in an easy-to-follow list. Will get to the list right away, but first am going to make chocolate chip cookies and watch a bit of TV, just to get into the right frame of mind for accomplishing things.

5:46 p.m.
TV Shows Watched Today:
1. Wedding Story
2. Makeover Story
3. Baby Story
4. Dating Story

5. Trading Spaces
6. While You Were Out
7. Dr. Phil
8. Oprah
9. Ellen

My brain has officially turned to mush.

Luckily, there is no noticeable difference between my brain while mushy and my brain the rest of the time (See: Brain Tumour).

Also, I feel horribly sick from the cookies. *Must* do better tomorrow and be less lazy and accomplish more things, such as resumé writing and / or manicuring nails.

▶ ▶ ▶

Tuesday, February 18

MOOD	Eager to accomplish goals
HAIR	Fine
HEALTH	Excellent, if slight stomachache
HOROSCOPE	You'll accomplish many goals today! Use your powers wisely as the stars indicate an excess of positive energy.
~~JT SIGHTINGS~~	n/a – in fact, am scratching this category altogether as is not healthy to obsess about best friend's boyfriend

7:00 a.m.
Ping!

It's funny how when I don't have to get up, my eyes spring open and refuse to shut again. But that's fine. I have no time for sleeping in. I have a lot to do today. First thing I'm going to do is go for a run. Running is an excellent way to start the day and get circulation pumping.

I crashed into MYG at the bottom of the stairs. I was in my running clothes, and she was in her "Trust me! I'm a doctor!" white lab-coat over something that she clearly stole from a 98-year-old Russian farmer. She even smelled vaguely like dirt.

"What's that smell?" I asked, forgetting temporarily about my vow of silence.

"It's Dirt!" she chirped happily. "Do you like it?"

"It's *dirt*?" I said, incredulously.

"Yes," she said. "It's part of our new holistic aromatherapy perfume line. It's designed to make you feel at one with the Earth."

"Oh!" I said. I smiled. I was trying, really I was. But sometimes I was worried about Melody's, er, mental capacity. "Okay!"

"I can get you some if you like," she offered.

"Great!" I said. Meaning, "I'd rather die than smell like Dirt!" But whatever. She's trying, too. Anyway, I'd taken a vow of silence, so I decided to lapse back into it again and could then ignore her prattle without feeling weird about it.

"So," said Dad, slumping down in front of a bowl of cereal (getting up at regular hours and going to an office is hard for him — a bit like putting a lion in a zoo and expecting it to thrive. I looked at him sympathetically and patted his arm). "What are you doing today?"

"Mmmf," I shrugged. I pointed at my running clothes.

"Going for a run?" he said. "Taken a vow of silence?"

"Mmm," I assented.

"But you were talking a minute ago," said Melody, looking confused.

Honestly, some people just don't understand. I rolled my eyes at Dad. He winked.

There's hope for him yet.

3:15 p.m.

Dear Junior:

Really is amazing how much good TV is on during the day. I hadn't realized. But luckily fit in an energetic run/jog/walk around the neighbourhood. Or around the block, anyway. Okay, just up the street until I fell over the Dodgerson's poodle. Why they let that thing walk around on its own is anyone's guess. Anyway, it wasn't hurt, but I thought I'd sprained my ankle, so I came home to look at paint swatches. Naturally, I had to watch some home decorating TV for ideas.

I now have the idea to a) pay someone else to redecorate my room, or b) get that carpenter (v. cute!) (reminds me of my BOYFRIEND BRAD)* from *Trading Spaces* to come over and build some shelves for me.

Mmm.

Love,

Accomplished Girl

---

* Must remember to call Brad tonight to "make up," although don't understand why/how we were fighting and/or *if* we are fighting.

7:13 p.m.

Phone Call with Kiki:

Me: I've taken a vow of silence, what did I miss today?

Kiki: If you've taken a vow of silence, why are you talking?

Me: I have to talk to you. You and Jules are exceptions to my vow of silence unless Jules is being Jules, in which case, the vow of silence still applies.

Kiki: Not like you've overthought this or anything.

Me: I haven't.

Kiki: What did you do today? You sound hyper.

Me: Nothing. What did I miss?

Kiki: Stephano is taking me to a movie.

Me: Gee, that's gripping.

Kiki: I mean, I have to go. Talk to you later!

Hmmm. I miss Kiki. I wish that she'd stuck to her "I-won't-have-a-boyfriend-in-twelfth-grade" rule. Honestly, she can hardly mock my occasional lapse from my vow-of-silence considering she *totally* blew her vow of boyfriendlessness.

I wonder what movie they are seeing.

I sometimes wish Brad was a more regular boyfriend (i.e., one not totally occupied at all times with playing hockey).

Phone Call with Brad:

Me: Brad?

Brad's Dad: He's not home, Haley, he call you back later.

Well, *that* was hardly worth breaking my vow of silence over.

Grrr.

I'm bored.

9:02 p.m.

He still hasn't called! Why hasn't he called?

9:45 p.m.

Phone Call with Jules:

Me: Jules?

Jules' Mom: She's not home, Haley, she call you back later.

That's weird.

Theory-in-Progress!: Both Jules' mom and Brad's dad have been taken over by alien life forces, and therefore have limited access to the English language. The fact that they both made the same grammatical error gives them away. Must go downstairs and watch *The Stuff* and *Invasion of The People Snatchers* for research purposes.

▶ ▶ ▶

Wednesday, February 19

MOOD	Crafty
HAIR	Covered with scarf
HEALTH	Enh
HOROSCOPE	Change is good. Someone you meet by chance will change everything. Be prepared.
~~JT SIGHTINGS~~	~~Irrelevant~~

12:45 p.m.

List of Obstacles to Achieving Goals:

1. Am distracted by lack of call-backs from so-called boyfriend and must eat toast to compensate.
2. Too much good daytime TV.
3. Too many movies to watch.
4. Tend to sleep too late when I stay up all night waiting for phone calls.
5. Dad and MYG are on a day off and are annoying me.

"Hey DAD," I yelled down the stairs. "I want to paint my room. Can you take me to the hardware store for paint?"

"I'll take you!" cried MYG, practically exploding off her chair in the kitchen. Either a) they had a fight and she wants to go anywhere to avoid him, or b) she has another one of her crazy get-to-know-Haley days planned.

"Mmm," I said noncommittally.

"I'll just get changed!" she shrieked. "Be right back!" Honestly, her voice could strip paint. Which might be useful if I actually have to do that.

Nah, I'll just paint over what's there.

MYG kept up an endless stream of chatter during the ride over to the hardware store. Which would have been fine if it weren't so annoying. It was a bit like sitting next to a flock of birds. I closed my eyes.

"... blah blah blah ... just like a *mother* to you!" she yelped.

I opened my eyes a crack and glared at her. "I have a mother," I said.

"Oh!" she said. "Um, I know! I just thought ..."

"You were wrong," I said, as coldly as possible.

The rest of the ride was quiet. If by "quiet," I mean "icily uncomfortable."

Luckily, the paint store was v. distracting. For one thing, the boy who was helping me choose paint was extremely attractive in the style of Judd Nelson in *The Breakfast Club*. He even had slightly-too-long hair and an earring. I'm sure I was blushing. MYG disappeared into the fascinating "house cleaners" aisle, which gave me plenty of time to talk to JUSTIN.

JUSTIN had a name tag, and very dark brown eyes. High crushability factor. I think he was flirting with me (probably thought I was older than I was, what with me not being in school) because he scribbled his phone number on a paint chip.

"What's that?" I said.

"It's my number," he said, and winked. Of course, in that light, I could see a bit of grey in his hair.

Really, that's v. disturbing. I'm sure it's also illegal.

"Uh," I said, flustered and gesturing at a chip. "I'll take this one."

Which is why my bedroom is going to be chartreuse.

2:57 p.m.
I thought "chartreuse" was some sort of pinkish colour. It's *green*?

My room now looks exactly like the stomach lining of a cow, if the stomach lining of a cow is BRIGHT SCARY GREEN.

Oh well, at least is clean and smells fresh and new.

3:49 p.m.

Argh. AM DYING.

Would call for help, but vow of silence prevails.

Times I've thrown up: 8

Times I've wished for death: 4

Times I've thought I was dead: 7

Clearly, brain tumour has grown to monstrous proportions and formed aneurysm. I can hear MYG and Dad laughing downstairs. I wonder if they will repaint this room when I'm dead.

I wonder if they'll notice.

I dragged myself over to Junior and weakly typed in my symptoms.

(From www.mayoclinic.com):

Migraine

SIGNS AND SYMPTOMS

A typical migraine attack produces some or all of these signs and symptoms:

- Moderate to severe pain — 60 percent of migraine sufferers feel pain on only one side of their head, while 40 percent experience pain on both sides
- Head pain with a pulsating or throbbing quality
- Pain that worsens with physical activity
- Pain that hinders your regular daily activities
- Nausea with or without vomiting
- Sensitivity to light and sound
- When left untreated, migraines typically last from four to 72 hours, but the frequency with which they occur can vary from person to person. You may have migraine

headaches several times a month or just once or twice
a year.

Okay, so it's a MIGRAINE. Fine. Perhaps am not dying.
Am too blind to do further research. Hole is forming in
vision.

Help!
Help!
Argh.

7:46 p.m.

Me: Mmmf?

Brad: Jules said that Kiki told her you'd taken some kind
        of stupid vow of silence. Is that true?

Me: Mmmm.

Brad: Look, we have to talk.

Me: Mmmk.

Brad: Can we please talk?

Me: Mm.

Oops. Accidentally hung up on Brad. But that's only
because I had to go throw up. Migraines are horrible.
Horrible.
Horrible.
Horrible.
Wonder if should go ask MYG or Dad to drive me to
Emergency for quick MRI. Although I had one of those
once and it was v. frightening. That tube! The claustro-
phobia! The weird turkey-baster escape call-button!

No, think will sleep. Will call Brad tomorrow and explain.

Am sure he will understand as Brad is v. nice and understanding boy.

► ► ►

Saturday, February 22

MOOD	Alarmed, agitated, anxious
HAIR	Antenna-like
HEALTH	Ailing
HOROSCOPE	A friend tries your patience today. Be positive, or go it alone.
~~JT SIGHTINGS~~	~~Irrelevant~~

Number of times have called Brad since Migraine Day: 29
Number of times have talked to Brad since Migraine Day: 0
Number of times Jules has hung up on me because she doesn't want to hear about Brad anymore: 29
Number of times Kiki has said, "You weren't very nice to him anyway": 8

Dear Junior:

I wish I had *real* friends. Friends-without-boyfriends. I am tired of the smug and high-and-mighty attitudes of my boyfriend-laden friends. Really, they are v. unsympathetic.

I MISS BRAD.

How will I get him back?

Who will help me?

I wonder what he's doing?

Love,

Sad, Lonely Girl

► ► ►

Wednesday, February 26

MOOD	BORED
HAIR	BORING
HEALTH	BORED
HOROSCOPE	Everything is boring and no one likes you. (Okay, I made that up. The real one was boring.)
~~JT SIGHTINGS~~	~~Irrelevant~~

9:45 a.m.

Not going to school is surprisingly less fun than I thought. I miss everything. I even miss Student Council. Well, sort of.

I miss HUMAN CONTACT.

"I almost miss BRUCE BARTELSON," I told The Cat. (The vow of silence is completely off when no one is home, and Dad and MYG are at work, saving hippies from bunions and assorted hippie ailments.)

"Okay," I amended. "I don't miss Bruce Bartelson. I miss almost everyone else, though. I miss JT!" The Cat looked at me. I swear, The Cat is the reincarnation of someone v. wise and knowing, such as Confucius or Leonardo da Vinci. "AND BRAD!" I yelled, scaring The Cat out the window. Which was just as well. I mean, he wasn't very good company anyway.

List of Fun Things I Can Do Today:
1. ~~Go for run~~.
2. ~~Clean The Bird's crap off floor~~.
3. Dye hair interesting and beautiful colour.

12:30 p.m.

Now that my hair is comically short, it seems like a good idea to colour it every few months. Or weeks.

I thought platinum blonde was a good idea.

Reasons Why Platinum Blonde Is Not a Good Idea:
1. Hair was still dark red from Valentine's Day and bleaching it within an inch of its life has rendered it pale pink.
2. Pale pink hair does not look good on anyone, unless they are named "Pink."
3. Pale pink hair makes every blemish show up a thousandfold. Don't know why. Suspect it is some kind of scientific phenomena that I'm not aware of.
4. As if my social life isn't horrible enough, having pale pink hair is sure to render me a Social Outcast.

Passing Thought: Hair is now exact colour that I *thought* "chartreuse" was.

6:30 p.m.

MYG and Dad spilled through the front door. Laughing, as per usual. Now I have nothing against "fun," but seriously, do they ever stop? It's almost offensive. Luckily, they'd brought me vegetarian paad thai, which I love.

And Melody even said, "Your hair is *gorgeous*."

Okay, granted it was MELODY and she'd say anything to make me like her, but it did make me feel a tiny, tiny bit better.

Only a tiny bit.

9:50 p.m.
Brad still hasn't called. Suspect this means that we have, in fact, split up.

▶ ▶ ▶

Friday, February 28

MOOD	First-day-of-school nerves
HAIR	Still pink
HEALTH	Racing heart, sweating
HOROSCOPE	Focus on getting ahead. Take some initiative. Don't be afraid to try new things.
~~JT SIGHTINGS~~	~~Irrelevant~~

5:00 a.m.
This is a terrible idea, albeit a "new thing," as recommended by horoscope. I wonder if "taking initiative" includes killing Kiki for signing me up for stupid rowing at stupid 5:00 in the stupid morning?

Will kill Kiki at earliest opportunity. It's *dark* outside! DARK! And COLD!

Two-week suspension has passed in a daze of daytime TV and checking my e-mail and phone messages to see if Brad has called/written. I've concluded that daytime TV is better than I imagined. Those makeover shows are terrific.

I watched some with Dad and have very nearly convinced him to cut his hair. Victory!

In related "Dad" news, since he's started working at Melody's clinic he has become annoyingly knowledgeable about vitamins. If I never hear another word about vitamin E, I'll be happy.

But I digress.

I am looking longingly at my bed before reluctantly stuffing myself into my layers of tights and sweatshirts, as loudly as possible so I can be sure to wake up Dad and la!la!la! (doesn't she have her *own house*?). I mean, it's the least I can do. This is all Kiki's idea, or rather something she signed me up for because I wasn't there to do it myself. In PE, apparently you can choose from all sorts of "fun" sports, instead of actually going to a PE class. It sounded like a great idea when Kiki first told me about it, but now *before sunrise* on a cold February morning, it seems like a terrible, horrible, bad idea.

I don't know what I was thinking. Well, maybe I wasn't. My brain was making a strange humming noise (see: Brain Tumour) from subsisting entirely on Cheetos and talk shows. So when Kiki called and said how it was such a good idea for "people like you, Haley" (question: who are "people like me?"), and how we'd get to take a spare instead of PE class, I said, "Sounds great!" Or maybe I said, "Unh." But what I meant was, "Go ahead and sign me up, Kiki! There's nothing I like better than getting up *in the middle of the night* to participate in a sport I know nothing about."

I'm sure rowing is considered to be *au courant* at Harvard, but here? It's just a crazy thing that insane people do in

the dark. Did I mention that I'm afraid of the water?
And the dark. Just for the record. In case I die.

9:05 a.m.
I can't believe it's only 9:05. So far this morning, I've managed to ride my bike down to the harbour in sub-zero
temperatures in the pitch blackness, only to arrive and
find a bunch of other people there already, *including* JT.
Not that it matters, as he is dating Jules, but it made me
wish I'd spent some time on my hair.

No, it didn't.

I swear, I think he's just a habit.

So when he said, "Hey, Haley," I said, "JT, hi! How's it
going? I mean, it's early, isn't it? Blah blah blah," I'm sure
no one noticed. Never mind that he'd already walked away.

Maybe I imagined it. I was pretty tired. But why wouldn't
he say "hi" to me? I'm his girlfriend's best friend.

I slumped around to the back of the boat shed so that I
could avoid making eye contact with him (or anyone else).
If my ass looked any larger in the five layers of sweatpants
I was wearing, it would have to get its own postal code.
Kiki was nowhere to be found. It was odd to be down at
the docks in the middle of the night in the freezing cold
for no apparent reason.

Except, obviously, to *row*. For a PE credit. Now that I
think of it, the other, more obvious choices for my PE
credit include, but aren't limited to: bowling, frisbee golf,
cricket or lawn bowling.

Why rowing? Why? Bowling is *fun*.

Because I missed the first week of rowing due to the

Suspension, I had no idea what to do. Everyone else was rushing around grabbing oars and running down to the dock, which was frosty and slippery. I nearly had a heart attack when a giant seal flopped off the deck and into the ink-black water beside me.

There was a full moon. I suppose it was pretty, if you go in for bitterly cold night-time (or early morning) activities.

But it was so cold. I sighed and tried to make myself unobtrusive.

"Hey, why are you just standing around?" A man was peering directly into my face with a flashlight.

"Hey," I answered. "Don't shine that in my eyes."

"Get to work," he said. "You don't earn your grade by hanging around looking tired."

"I'm new," I snapped. "I don't know what to do."

"Then *ask* someone," he said. "Don't just stand there."

On closer inspection, he was quite cute. If you go in for Angry Young Men. Which I don't. (Or do I?) (He was extraordinarily muscly. From what I could tell in the dark.)

"Sorry," I said. "Please tell me what to do, kind sir."

"Don't give me attitude," he said. "Just tell me your name and we'll see where we can put you."

Which is how I ended up sitting in a giant boat with seven other people, hauling desperately at an oar. The water was cold looking. And black. I couldn't even look at it for long because I was frantically trying to keep up, while the person behind me (the lovely and annoyingly perky Izzy) kept bashing me in the back with her oar.

"Ouch," I said every time, but no one could hear me over the coach shouting instructions. Such as: "You in the pink! Sit up straight! Don't turn your wrists like that! Don't look at me when I'm talking, look at the person in front of you! Watch where you're going!"

In summary, "rowing" is now low down on my list of "sports that I enjoy."

Sports that I Enjoy:
1. ~~Running~~
2. ~~Skating~~
3. ~~Skiing~~
4. ~~Aerobics~~
5. ~~Soccer~~
6. Bowling
7. Walking. Okay, I don't really like walking either.
8. Typing. Which normally wouldn't be a sport but is today because my arms are completely BROKEN from ROWING.

Not to mention my back.

And ass.

And legs.

12:07 p.m.
"Ouch," I wailed to Kiki as we sat eating our lunch in the cafeteria. I use the word "lunch" loosely to describe the bruised apple I'd grabbed from my locker. The apple appeared to be only a few months old. Frankly, I'd been a little too tired this morning to whip up any great sandwich feast, or even to consider "lunch." Although we'd been up for so long, it now felt like "dinner."

"Wasn't that great?" Kiki enthused. "I really love it. It's like ... flying."

"Hmmm," I said dubiously. "Like flying if 'flying' involved a boat and murky water in the *middle of the night.*"

"Haley," she said. "Just think about how good it is for you. I mean look at the people who have been doing it for ages. They are, like, all muscle. It will be great to get you in shape for the marathon. By the way, how's your training coming along?"

"Great," I said.

"How's your time?" she said.

"Uh," I said. "Well, I don't like to time myself."

"Haley," she said. "Are you really running or are you just *saying* that you're running?"

"I'm really sort-of running," I said. "Besides, I may never move again. Every muscle in my body is screaming in agony. Please, just give me a break."

"Hey, did I tell you what Stephano said yesterday? It was SO funny ..."

To tell you the truth, I may have drifted off during her story. Not that it wasn't gripping. That Stephano! A laugh a minute, I tell you!

Okay, I fell asleep. It was rude, and I'm horrible. (I mean, I love Stephano. Well, I don't *love* him, but he's crushable, certainly.) (But he belongs to Kiki.)

It's just that ... well, *five* in the morning? That's just crazy.

I was woken up by my cell phone ringing loudly in the empty cafeteria. Empty? Kiki had left me asleep and I was late for *class*. Argh! I glanced at the call display. Brad.

Hmm.

Don't have time to talk now.

Must run to Drama. There are trees that require imme-diate re-enactment.

3:45 p.m.

"So," Jules said, blinking her giant eyes at me. "Guess what?"

"What," I groaned. We were sitting in my living room, watching The Cat run in circles. Jules was sort of perched on the edge of the couch as though it might infect her with its dusty hairiness.

"It's *clean*," I said snarkily.

"Cat hair makes me sneeze," she said, sneezing deli-cately. Three times in a row.

"Jules," I said. "Do you have to be pretty all the time?"

"What do you mean?" she said.

"Jules, come on. You do everything so ..." I searched for the word. "Forget it."

"Anyway," she said. "Guess what?"

"What?"

"I made it to the next round!"

"The next round of what?" I said, stupidly. I mean, obvi-ously she was talking about *Who's the Prettiest of Them All*. I just chose to pretend I didn't remember anything about her possible future as the star of a television show.

She leaned over and pulled a packet of cigarettes from her bag and lit one, blowing a long stream of smoke at The Cat, who (God love him) immediately leaped on her cigarette, knocking it out of her hand. "Acckkkk!" she screamed.

I laughed. "The Cat doesn't like smokers," I said.

"Don't be cruel," she said, grabbing the cigarette from where it had burned a hole in the couch. "Or I won't ask you."

"Ask me what?" I said.

"Ask you to come with me," she said.

"Seriously?" I said.

"Yup," she said. "I'm not allowed to take JT, and I get to take another person. And my mom … well, she's too … um, annoying, for me to deal with on my own, you know?"

"Me?" I said. I couldn't have been more shocked. I nearly collapsed from the weight of all the guilt I felt for being so nasty to Jules for so long. Jules, my best friend in the world, was taking me with her to …

"Uh, where is it?" I said. "Where are we going?"

"California," she said.

"California?" I said.

"That's what I said," she said. "Are you going to repeat everything I say?"

"California?" I said. "I mean, when?"

"May," she said.

"May?" I said.

"Oh, for goodness sake," she said. "Please shut up. Or I'll un-ask you."

I shut up.

Oh, I love Jules. Love, love, love her.

She is my new favourite person.

I was so happy that I didn't even care when my dad and

Melody came into the room. Holding hands. And grinning like weird, maniacal garden gnomes. And I didn't even care *that* much when my dad said, "Melody's moving her furniture in — we're going to make it permanent!"

Okay, I cared. I grabbed one of Jules' cigarettes and lit it and started smoking furiously.

Okay, I nearly choked to death.

(At least Melody wasn't wearing a ring. I don't think I could have survived a wedding, or even a gross hippie love ceremony.)

But my point is that no one noticed my near-death cigarette-choking experience. Or that I was smoking, for that matter. Jules was grabbing her stuff and saying, "I'll call you later, Haley" and my dad was hugging me like it was a big celebration, and Melody was getting all teary-eyed like she was overcome with joy in the style of someone who just won Miss America.

And The Cat coughed up a big hairball.

Reasons Why Melody Can't LIVE Here, Even Though She's Almost Always Here Anyway:

1. He just MET her, for crying out loud.
2. She SMELLS.
3. She wears HORRIBLE CLOTHES.
4. She has TERRIBLE DENTAL HYGIENE.
5. He's MY dad.
6. I don't LIKE her. I mean, she's nice. I just don't WANT her.
7. She'll change everything.
8. She's too young for him.

9. He's too old for her.
10. She'll want to share my bathroom.
11. She'll change SOMETHING.
12. She'll BE here.
13. Oh, yuck.

MARCH

Monday, March 3

MOOD	Grouchy
HAIR	Still pink, but fading to white
HEALTH	Weak, sickly
HOROSCOPE	Your ambitions may be thwarted by a so-called friend. Watch your back today!
~~JT SIGHTINGS~~	~~Irrelevant~~

9:32 a.m.

The good thing about stupid, crazy early morning rowing practice is that a) I don't see Melody in the morning, and b) I'm never late for school, seeing as I've already been up for ages by 8:45. So I wasn't late this morning. Which was great, because it was … wait for it … Career Day.

Oh joy, oh heaven.

Oh crap.

If there is nothing that is going to make you feel worse about your Future Prospects™, it's CAREER DAY. Especially when, like me, you have NO Future Prospects™. Which is pointed out to you about a billion times during "inspirational" Career Day speeches. I can safely conclude that the following are jobs I have no interest in:

- Lawyer
- Doctor
- Nurse
- Teacher
- Architect
- Pharmacist
- HIGH SCHOOL PRINCIPAL*

"Blah blah blah," Principal Porky Butt blathers. "Blah blah blah EXCITING blah blah blah GREATEST TIME OF YOUR LIFE blah blah GREAT AND EXCITING FUTURE."

Oh, save me.

So far today the only thing I'm excited about is:

1. I'm going to see Brad tonight and hopefully get back to the part where I was all excited to be his girlfriend and he, well, liked me. Instead of sort of tolerating me, which is how he's treating me now.
2. I did not fall in the harbour this morning during rowing practice.
3. I rowed in a boat in the seat right behind JT, and got to stare at the back of his head for an entire hour, not that I care as I no longer have a crush on JT.

---

* Being Mr. Porky Butt would be a fate worse than death.

4. I did not collapse from exhaustion, although my legs are barely holding me up.

Hmmm. Must remember to do further research on "weak muscles" on the internet. I wonder if there is some sort of career that involves looking things up on the internet as I'm v. good at finding things to buy on the internet, selling things on the internet (eBay!), diagnosing myself on the internet, and, well, stalking people on the internet. For example, I've recently found Brad's name mentioned on the internet on a website called "Junior Hockey Stars to Watch." (Well, the website was called something more like "hockeykidswhoplay" or some such crap, but the gist is the same.)

I am dating (sort of) a nearly famous hockey star! Lucky for me that he likes me a lot (or will again) and perhaps will want to marry me one day so that I don't have to have a career™.

I wonder if it's a giant backwards step for womankind that I'd rather not work. I blame my dad. I mean, he hardly set a good example for me, what with his lifetime career of pretty much never working. He told me in secret the other day that the main reason he likes working in Melody's office is that *there is nothing to do*.

Seriously.

He's like the opposite of hard-working. So it really shouldn't be a surprise that I'm the opposite of ambitious. We all become our parents, right? I'm sure I saw that once on *Dr. Phil*. And look at Jules. I mean, she'll become a model, just like her mom. And Kiki? Kiki will be a big old success. Just like her dad.

And Brad will be a famous hockey player. Not like his parents, but *because* of his parents. I'm sure it wasn't *his* idea at the age of five or whatever to learn how to skate.

Yes, I'll just be a big zero like my dad. I guess. Well, I'm hardly going to become a nun, am I? That's just crazy.

Although what do nuns really do? Perhaps could be a nun, after all.

I closed my eyes and started thinking about a nice, peaceful nunnery with a pretty garden where I could wander around drinking tea and singing hymns. Which wouldn't be all bad. Of course, there would be no boys. And the clothes were …

Fire drill!

Ack.

2:00 p.m.

"Haley," said Kiki, as we wandered half-heartedly back into the school. "Are you going to go to this 'what-you-were-meant-to-be' seminar-thing? It looks cool. They punch in all your answers to a bunch of questions and then tell you what career most suits you."

"I don't know," I shivered. It wasn't particularly cold outside, but I was only wearing a T-shirt and jeans. A very cool T-shirt, yes, but still just a T-shirt.

"You should," she said. "I mean, you might want to think about it."

"I guess," I said. "Are you doing it?"

"I'll do it with you if you want," she shrugged. I could tell that she was just being nice. I mean, she knows what she wants to do, right? She's known since birth. And she's worried that I'm not going to do anything. That I'm not going to *be* anything.

Which is ridiculous. I mean, I'll be something. I'll be a … I don't know. A writer. Or a counsellor. Or a … jewellery designer. Or maybe …

"Okay," I sighed. "I'll do it."

Which is how I came to be sitting at a desk an hour later concentrating fiercely on the answer to questions like "Is a hot lunch at noon important to you?" and "If nylons are being rationed and you have one ration coupon left, would you spend it on nylons or butter?" Then I looked down at the very bottom of the 40 page "test" and found that it said, "Copyright date 1941." Seriously. I yawned and stretched and then had to hop around for a minute to reduce the cramping in my calf. Obviously, I need more potassium in my diet. There were 10 or so other people in the room, including Izzy, who was chewing her pencil as though her life depended on the outcome of this "test," and Bruce Bartelson, who kept giving me significant looks. Now I could be totally off base here, but I'm starting to think that maybe Bruce Bartelson is starting to work up the courage to move from having a crush on me (go figure) to actually DOING something about it.

Argh.

I glared at him with as much evil as I could muster and randomly filled in the rest of the circles as quickly as possible so that I could flee the room. Bruce Bartelson's slobbery eyes were following my every move. Okay, maybe they weren't, but it felt like they were. It didn't help that my calf cramp had travelled all the way up my leg (*NB*: check for possible blood clot?) and was now hurting my hip. I thrust the paper at the tester, a bald sweaty man with a name tag that said, "Hello, my name is HERB." I wondered what horrible wrong turn HERB must have taken to have landed the job of distributing personality tests to reluctant teenagers. Probably he was on some sort of work release program from prison. His neck was approximately the same size as his head, which usually indicates WAY too much time for working out.

"Let's take a look-see, miss," he said. (Miss? Where does he come from? The Old South?)

He hemmed and hawed while I tapped my foot nervously, keeping one eye on Bruce Bartelson to make sure he wasn't staring. The sight (and sound) of Izzy chewing her pencil was making me want to scream, to tell you the truth.

"Okay!" Herb said, printing something off an insanely ancient dot-matrix printer. "Here you go! Good luck!"

I grabbed the paper from him without looking and escaped to the library, where, sadly, the librarian was giving a talk about how fulfilling it was to be a school librarian. Considering the only people in the library are usually me and the nose-picking kid, I felt a bit sorry for her. There were three people listening to her. Normally, I'd feel guilty enough to listen, but I'd had enough of "career day."

Especially when I took a look at the crumpled print-out.
I'm most suited to a career as:

- A funeral director
- A ballerina (obviously this test does not measure fitness or flexibility)
- A waitress
- A police officer

I crumpled the paper into a ball and threw it out.

"There is no hope," I mumbled into my arms, which immediately cramped up.

My body was falling apart and my life was in shambles. I dragged myself up and staggered over to an empty computer terminal.

(From WebMD):

Deep Leg Vein Thrombosis

SYMPTOMS

Deep vein thrombosis may not cause symptoms. Only about half of people with blood clots in their legs have symptoms. Symptoms of a deep leg vein thrombosis may include:

- Swelling. This could be generalized swelling in the leg or localized swelling along a blood vessel that creates a swollen ridge that can be felt.
- Warmth.
- Pain or tenderness. The pain may be in the calf or thigh and may be present only when standing or walking.
- Redness.

There are many other conditions with similar symptoms, which can make diagnosing deep vein thrombosis difficult. Sometimes a person will be diagnosed with a blood clot in the leg only after a blood clot in the lung (pulmonary embolism) is found. Symptoms of a pulmonary embolism include:

- Sudden shortness of breath.
- Chest pain that gets worse with a deep breath.
- A cough that may bring up blood.

I rolled up my pant leg to inspect my leg for redness. Hmm. It wasn't red, but it was certainly hairy. I should think about waxing, I thought, staring idly at my (throbbing) calf. Lovely.

Which naturally is the exact moment that JT plopped himself down next to me and said, "I'm coming to California, like, with my dad and, like with you and Jules but you have to like, tell me when you're going exactly, because I want to like, surprise her."

"Uh," I said. "Yeah. Um. Sure."

"Say hi to Bradley, Bradford, Bradorama," he said. And he left, leaving me sitting there with my mouth moving and no sound coming out.

California.

With Jules. AND JT.

Oh my GOD.

Explore possibility that I died and went to heaven. Of course, if I'd died and gone to heaven, I wouldn't be taking Jules with me.

6:45 p.m.

Brad: Hi.

Me: Hi. Are you coming to get me?

Brad: Uh, I can't. Something came up.

Me: Like what?

Brad: Uh.

Me: Are you breaking up with me?

Brad: No!

Me: Oh, because it seems like you don't want to see me.

Brad: Um.

Me: I wanted to, you know, see you.

Brad: Haley, I miss you.

Me: Yeah. Me, too. You. Um, I mean, JT says hi.

Brad: Oh. Well. Hi back, I guess.

Me: How was your game?

Brad: Good. We won.

Me: Good. [Insert long silence]

Me: It was career day today. Apparently I have a future as a funeral director.

Brad: Yeah? Cool.

Me: It's not cool. What are you talking about? It's like, a joke.

Brad: Oh. Ha ha.

Me: It's not a joke, I just took one of those tests and it said that's what I should be.

Brad: Well, what do you want to be?

Me: I don't know. Something. Nothing.

Brad: That's really great, Haley. I'm sure that will work out for you.

Me: Why are you being so mean? What did I do to you?

Brad: Nothing.

Me: Whatever. [I twiddled the phone cord tightly around
        my finger and watched my finger turn purple.]

Brad: So, um, my parents are going to be away this week-
        end. I thought maybe you and Jules and JT would
        want to hang out at my house.

Me: Sure. Great.

Brad: Look, I have to go. I'll talk to you later.

Me: Okay, bye.

I stared at the phone for a minute. It was baby blue. Who
has a baby blue phone, anyway? We do, that's who. This
phone probably came out of some garbage dump somewhere.

I called Kiki.

Kiki: Hey, girl, what's up?

Me: Nothing.

Kiki: Something's up, what is it?

Me: How are you?

Kiki: Same as I was all day. I'm great. I was just going to
        go for a run, want to come with me?

Me: I, uh, already ran today.

Kiki: No, you didn't. It will make you feel better, I swear.

Me: FINE. I guess. I mean, sure. That would be great.

Kiki: See you in a minute.

Me: [falsely] Great!

I hung up the phone and carefully flexed my leg to see if

it still hurt. Rowing twice a week is making me more muscly and less rubbery, but let's face it, I'm still not in good shape. I inspected my leg in the mirror. No evidence of clots. Good.

Reasons Why I Should Do More Running:

1. Mini-marathon (the word "mini" here gives me a false sense of security when really it means "impossible distance," but never mind) is in less than a month.
2. Will make me stronger and less rubbery.
3. Will make me leaner and less flabby.
4. Is good, social activity.
5. Impresses people.
6. Is good "outlet" for "anxiety" (according to on-line advice doctor).
7. Is good excuse to get out of the weirdly patchouli-smelling house and out of earshot of Melody and Dad exclaiming over Dr. Phil's latest batch of screwed up "guests."
8. Is good excuse not to do drama "homework" of writing a three-minute monologue to perform in front of the class (gulp) the day after tomorrow.
9. Is good way to get blood flowing and stop feet from being so blue. Have just found out that blue feet indicate bad vein pressure, something about valves, and something scary about "clots." Have avoided remembering details as was very disconcerting and feet are nearly always blue.
10. Can ask Kiki honest opinion about Brad and if this weekend at his house while HIS PARENTS ARE AWAY

means what I think it means. Hey, I read Judy Blume books. I know what it MEANS. I just, I guess, I don't know. I guess I don't much want to think about it right now. Okay.

8:34 p.m.

Ouch, ouch, ouch, ouch, double-ouch, triple-ouch.

Ouch.

Hate running. Hate Kiki for loving running especially as she can maintain a conversation without getting a) short of breath or b) sick WHILE running. She's *so* going to leave me in the dust on marathon day. Why did I agree to do it?

"You'll feel so good about yourself just for finishing it," she said.

"No, I won't," I gasped. "I'll probably just throw up on the finish line."

"No, you won't," she said, running in little circles around me while I dragged my leaden legs along the street. "You need to accomplish something in your life, Haley. Then you won't be so ..."

"So WHAT?" I said. Or tried to say.

"Nothing!" she said, perkily. "Hey, what are you doing this weekend?"

I stopped running. (Big mistake, by the way. You should never stop cold like that. I immediately got dizzy and had to lean on a fence for support.)

"Don't stop!" she said. Great advice, but too late.

I started jogging again. "Why don't you and Stephano

come to Brad's?" I said. "Brad's parents … away … movies … Jules … JT." [insert gasping noise here]

I flopped down on my front lawn, which was wet and cold, and therefore totally gross.

"Brad's parents are away and he's having people over?" she said, frowning as she bounced up and down in place.

"Yup," I said.

"Sure," she said. "Sounds … fun."

She jogged off down the road, adjusting her headphones. You know, when she runs, not a thing "jiggles" or even "moves" on her body. I lay back on the lawn and lifted my leg in the air so I could bat at the back of my legs, just to watch them … swing. Sort of like the underside of old ladies' arms.

I shivered. It was dark, and the stars were just starting to pop out. By adjusting my head slightly on the grass (okay, it was mostly dirt), I could see Dad and Melody through the living room window, flopped on the couch watching TV. They watch more TV than, well, anyone. Except maybe The Cat. The Cat likes TV because it's warm, bright and vibrates. I sincerely hope that Dad and his MYG like it for, um, better reasons.

I pray that when I grow up, my life is a little more interesting than theirs. I mean, they watch TV. That's about it. They work. They stink up the house with hippie smells. It's like living on a commune, except without all the people.

And the drugs.

And the good music and one of those cool VW van things. I love those.

Huh.

I got up and naturally got dizzy again. I shivered again too.

"So," I said to no one in particular, "I guess that's that."

10:49 p.m.

Dear Junior:

Am nervous about this weekend. I know it's lame and that everyone has had sex by the twelfth grade and it's not a big deal, etc. etc. But I just … I don't know. I don't really WANT to. It's just … too soon.

I'm scared.

Don't tell anyone. I'm embarrassed.

Sometimes I wish I was 12 again. Twelve was easier. Sort of.

I wish I had someone to talk to about this who wouldn't make me feel stupid, like Jules. Or like I'm hopeless, like Kiki. I can hardly talk to my dad. That would just be WEIRD.

I guess it's just you and me, Junior. I'm feeling weird about stuff. Just thought you should know.

Love,

Embarrassed Girl

11:58 p.m.

Can't sleep.

List of Things I Really MUST Get Around to Doing SOON:

1. Resume. Need job so as to avoid being home as much as possible.
2. Career planning.
3. Plan for California trip on first weekend of May. May!

Weekend! California!

4. Get into proper training schedule so as not to embarrass self during "fun run," otherwise known as "torturous leg-drag."

5. Make friends with Melody and stop avoiding her in the hallway.

6. Spend quality time with Dad as have not exchanged more than twenty words with him since the arrival of Melody with her fourteen suitcases of hippie clothes and ten boxes of "alternative remedy" books.

7. Stop postponing inevitable prom-planning with Bruce Bartelson as am sure crush is just imaginary and not real. Must stop thinking so much of self that imagine everyone loves me.

8. ~~Have "talk" with Brad.~~

► ► ►

Friday, March 7

MOOD	Unnerved
HAIR	Not bad — trimmed bangs and added flippy ends
HEALTH	Nervous
HOROSCOPE	Your mind will be drifting today towards fun, and away from work. Have a party!
~~JT SIGHTINGS~~	~~irrelevant~~

4:30 p.m.

Jules, Kiki and I have decided to have a girls' night. I'm totally relieved not to be seeing Brad. Is that wrong?

Of course it's wrong. I'm a terrible girlfriend, if I can even call myself that, considering I NEVER SEE HIM.

I never see him and he thinks I'm going to sleep with him.

I never see him, he thinks I'm going to sleep with him, and I don't think I want to. But then he probably won't want to see me anymore. And here I thought he was different from other boys. I thought that he maybe loved me.

But of course he doesn't. Brad loves: 1. Hockey. 2. Partying. 3. Himself.

Never mind that. Tonight is going to be capital-F Fun.

"What are we going to do?" Jules asked, blowing smoke out the car window. It was nice outside. I love Spring. No more frigid, cold, icy days. No more slipping off sidewalks and skinning my knees. (Not that this had happened or anything.) (Very often.)

"I don't know," I said. "Let's just have fun."

"Let's just hang out and eat and talk," said Kiki.

"Eat?" said Jules. "I can't eat. I can't afford to get fat before the auditions for 'Who's the Prettiest of Them All.'"

"Okay, don't eat," said Kiki quickly.

"I'll eat," I said.

"Let's shop first," said Jules.

I yawned. Nothing is more depressing to me than shopping with Jules and Kiki as it usually involves trying on a bunch of stuff that looks horrible on me and great on them. "Ugh," I said.

"Don't be a spoilsport," said Jules. "You'll have fun."

"Whatever," I groaned. I traced a picture in the steam of my breath on the window. "Where are we going?"

"You'll see," said Kiki, hitting the gas.

Which is how we came to be at The Mall. Now I have nothing against the mall, but just a few short months ago, Jules declared The Mall to be completely uncool. I looked at her suspiciously. It's not like her to go somewhere that is Not Cool.

In fact, the whole thing seemed a bit suspicious.

Especially when we got inside and they marched me with great determination to the drugstore.

Kiki struck a pose. "Now, Haley," she said, glancing at Jules and laughing, "our little girl is growing up. It's time we told you about..."

"The birds and the bees," Jules interrupted. "The first thing we need to do is get you some SUPPLIES."

"Right," said Kiki, waggling her finger under my nose. "We don't want any accidents, hmmm?"

"Oh GOD," I moaned. "Please may you be kidding."

"Nope!" shrieked Jules, laughing in a way I haven't seen her laugh for, well, ages. It was kind of contagious. So in spite of the fact that I was so embarrassed that hives broke out all over my neck, I laughed, too.

Which is how I came to end up with a basket full of ... girl stuff. And condoms, natch. And how I happened to be running down the aisle to grab some gum when I smacked into Bruce Bartelson, and the basket went flying.

I'm sure there is a Universal Rule that says when you're buying something embarrassing you MUST run into the last person you'd want to see.

"Haley!" Bruce said. I swear his face lit up.

"Bruce," I said faintly.

"Let me help you with that!" he said, cheerfully putting my CONDOMS and KY into the basket as though nothing was wrong.

"Uh," I said blankly.

"Listen," he said, flipping a box of Trojans into the air while he talked. "I was wondering if you'd blah blah blah and blah blah blah the Prom blah blah blah."

"Sure," I said, grabbing the box out of the air and dropping it in the basket. "Got to go! Whatever! See you later!"

I could see Jules and Kiki out of the corner of my eye. They were bent double with hysterics.

"Thanks a LOT," I hissed. "Some friends you are."

"But Haley," Jules said. "That was hilarious."

"No it WASN'T," I said. "I think he LIKES me."

"Of course he likes you," said Kiki, wiping her eyes. "EVERYONE knows that."

"Who's EVERYONE?" I said wildly. "Who knows that?"

She gave me a funny look. "Haley, it's pretty well-known. What were you and Bruce talking about, anyway? You were all red."

I immediately went red again. It's impossible to tell a blusher that they were blushing without the blusher turning puce. "Shut up," I said. "Nothing. I don't know. I couldn't really understand him."

"Why not?" said Jules. "Was he speaking some other language?"

"No," I glared. "I can't explain it. It's like I've got a mind-block against his voice. I couldn't really hear him."

She hiccupped loudly and started laughing again. "God," she said. "I love you, Haley. You're so HILARIOUS."

"I'm NOT hilarious," I said furiously. "Anyway, now I have to pay for all this."

Which is when I realized that I didn't have my wallet. Actually, that's not quite true. I realized that I didn't have my wallet right after the cashier (young, male, of course) finished bagging my stuff.

Honestly, sometimes I wonder if I was put on the earth just to be a laughingstock. Needless to say, I didn't get any condoms. Jules and Kiki, great friends that they are, had run outside to smoke while they waited for me. I looked at them through the window and debated about whether to borrow money from them. For a second, I felt a little sad. I mean, shouldn't this be something that I do with my mom? Or my boyfriend?

"Forget it," I told the kid behind the counter. I tried to keep my chin up as I left the store. Really, I was repeating the phrase, "Keep your chin up!" to myself. Which might explain why I tripped over that pile of baskets on my way out of the store.

"What took you so long?" said Kiki, looking faintly amused.

"You're BLEEDING, Haley," said Jules. "Honestly, how can you hurt yourself in a checkout line?" She dabbed at my chin. "You've cut your chin."

"Leave me alone," I said grouchily. "I fell."

Jules' chin wobbled. I could tell she was trying not to laugh.

"Don't laugh at me!" I said. But it was too late. She was already laughing. I didn't have much choice but to join in, but I can tell you that it hurt to laugh. As if I don't have enough problems, a big gaping wound on my chin will repel Brad from wanting to even kiss me.

Not that I'm thinking too much about that.

▶ ▶ ▶

Saturday, March 8

MOOD	Terrified
HAIR	Flat, greasy
HEALTH	Nauseated/dizzy/anxious
HOROSCOPE	Do something you've never done before! Change is good. Take a risk.
~~JT SIGHTINGS~~	~~irrelevant~~

9:50 a.m.
Having breakfast with Melody and my dad is a weird experience. Normally, my dad and I would scarf down as many bowls of the Cereal-of-the-Moment (right now it's Froot Loops) as we felt like eating. We traditionally don't do a lot of talking at breakfast. Like, none.

But now? Now everything is different.

"Good morning, Haley!" Melody chirped cheerfully from the stove. Where she was cooking eggs. Have I mentioned that eggs make me sick?

"Uh," I said, reaching for the Froot Loops, which she batted out of my hand like a crazy person.

"Hey," I said.

"Haley," said Dad, looking up from the newspaper with a frown, "Melody has decided that we're all going to have breakfast together on Saturdays."

"Has she now?" I said nastily, eyeing Melody as coldly as possible. She was wearing one of Dad's T-shirts that said "Hotel California" on it, with plaid pajama bottoms (MY PLAID PAJAMA BOTTOMS) and big, pink bunny slippers.

"Are those MINE?" I said aghast.

"Are they?" she said. "I just got them out of the laundry!"

Now I, for one, hate people who end every sentence with an exclamation point. But I didn't have the energy to get into it. Last night Kiki and Jules and I had stayed up until two in the morning before Jules' mom kicked us out. "Whatever," I sighed, reaching for the lifestyle section of the paper so that I could read my horoscope. Which I do EVERY MORNING.

Bam! She whacked the paper out of my hands. "WHAT IS IT?" I yelled.

"HALEY," Dad said. "KEEP YOUR VOICE DOWN."

"It's okay," said Melody, looking uncertainly at Dad. "I just thought it might be nice if we all, you know, talked. Instead of just ignoring each other and reading the paper." She looked so ... pathetic, that I have to say I felt a little sorry for her. I mean, she was trying. I, on the other hand, wasn't.

"Fine," I sighed, pouring another cup of decaffeinated ("Caffeine is poison!") coffee. It tasted like muddy water.

"What happened to your chin, sweetheart?" my dad asked.

"Oh," I said, touching it. It felt bruised and swollen. Great. "I, uh, fell."

"Doing what?" he said.

"In the drugstore," I said irritably. Desperate to change the subject, I said, "What are you two up to tonight?"

"I don't know," said Melody. "We thought we'd ask you if you wanted to see a movie with us!"

"I can't," I said. "I have plans."

"What kind of plans?" Dad asked.

"Uh," I said. "Nothing really. Going out with Kiki and Jules and their boyfriends. And Brad."

"Oooh," said Melody. "How IS Brad? He's such a nice boy." Honestly, she talks like an 85-year-old teacher. Isn't she only thirty-five?

"Yes," I said. "He is. ANYWAY…"

"So," she said, undaunted. "Tell us about school!" While she talked, she heaped up big rubbery piles of scrambled egg onto three plates. I looked desperately at Dad. "Dad," I said, "You know I don't eat …"

"Mel," he said. "Haley is allergic to eggs. But I'm sure she'd love some toast!" He winked at me. (Since when had DAD started talking with exclamation points?)

"Yeah," I said. "Toast would be great."

"Okay," she chirped. The Bird chose that moment to flap into the room like a bat out of hell, landing square on her head. Which made her laugh with delight.

"Get off me or I'll kill you," The Bird said.

I nearly fell off my chair laughing.

"Ooops," I said. "Ha. I might have said that to him once or twice."

"Honestly, Haley," Dad said. "That's just weird."

I snorted. Some people don't know what funny IS.

I crunched down on my (burnt) toast. Raisins. I spat them on to my plate. Nothing is more disgusting than raisins.

"Well!" I said, as chirpily as possible. "I'm full!"

"Haley," sighed Dad. "Eat some Froot Loops."

"Okay," I said, smiling politely at Melody. Inside, I was thinking HA HA HA. But I'm much too polite to say so. What is it about her that I dislike so much?

"So tell us about school!" she said. Oh, yeah. That's it. I dislike her because she's ANNOYING.

"School's fine," I said, crunching vigorously. Froot Loops are really quite delicious. The best part, clearly, is the weird-coloured milk left in the bottom of the bowl. I tipped and drank.

"Come on, Haley," said Dad. "Tell us more."

I burped. "Um," I said. "Well, it was career day."

"Ooh," said Melody. "Fun! I love doing career days! I'm surprised your school didn't ask me!"

"Yes," I said politely. "That's an enormous shock."

"Haley," said Dad. "Please."

"Come on," I said. "I have nothing to say about school. Besides, um, I have to go for a run."

"A run!" said Melody. "I've been meaning to ask you if I can join you! I'm getting a bit fat in my old age." She laughed like a hyena. I glared.

"Uh," I said. "Fine. Whatever."

I mean, she's old. I could outrun her. Right?

Wrong.

12:14 p.m.
Wish that I'd pushed Melody into the reservoir that we ran around.

Twice.

No longer have any feeling below my waist. Wonder if repeated impact of running has caused unusual paralysis of spinal cord.

12:45 p.m.
Can't move.
   Argh.

1:37 p.m.
Dad popped his head into my room. "Haley, phone!" he yelled, scaring me off the bed and into a heap on the floor. Really, there should be rules about who can sneak up on who.

   "Who is it?" I snarled.

   "I don't know," he said, not covering the receiver. I hate when people do that. Because obviously the person on the other end can hear and you can't make up a reason not to talk to them.

   "Hello?" I mumbled.

   "Haley Harmony?" a voice said. A voice that I didn't recognize.

   "Yes?" I said.

   "You applied for a job at The Big UnBurger?"

   "I did?" I said, having a vague flashback to preparing my resume and dropping it off at different places. I love UnBurger. It's entirely possible that I dropped one off there.

   "Right!" I said.

   "We'd like to have you come down for an interview," the voice said.

   "Uh, sure!" I said.

"How about 4:30 on Monday?" the voice said.

"Uh, sure!" I repeated. Apparently "uh, sure!" is all the English that I know.

Note to Self: Try to be more articulate.

A job interview! Money! Of course, working at The UnBurger is probably the opposite of cool.

Good burgers, though.

I frantically flipped through my closet and then called Jules and Kiki on conference. Obviously, they'd have to lend me something to wear. I mean, that's what friends are for, right?

7:30 p.m.
Dear Junior:

Am on my way to Brad's. Am very nervous. It occurs to me that I have not even seen Brad for two weeks. TWO WEEKS.

Am going to be sick.

Maybe should make some excuse not to go.

No, can't do that. That's silly. Will go and watch movies with good friends and will have fun. Am sure Brad isn't thinking anything. About ... well, anything.

Love,

Haley-feeling-stupid-Andromeda

Sometime Around Midnight
Dear Junior:

Oh God.

Oh God.

Oh God.

Well.

Okay. Fine, I'll tell the story. But then I should probably delete it to save mankind (or even Future Me) from the embarrassment of reading it.

Here goes:

I arrived at Brad's early. I mean, I'd said I'd get there at 8:00 and it wasn't 8:00 yet. I'd become sick of trying to fix my makeup so my chin looked less bruised, so I'd taken off early. Also, Melody was having some sort of weird women's "Koffee Klatch" (her words, not mine) in the kitchen, and the high-pitched squealing of their laughter was making me crazy.

Brad's house was dark and it didn't look like he was home, so I sat down on the porch. It was a pretty house, with a perfect garden. It wasn't big or anything, not like JT's, but it looked like a home. Maybe that's why Brad is so ... NICE, I thought. Because he grew up in a nice house. I could imagine him playing on the front lawn with his friends.

I leaned over and pulled a leaf off a shrub and shredded it aimlessly. The moon was up and a bunch of geese took off from the pond across the road and started honking, disappearing into the evening sky in a V-formation. I jumped about a mile. I'm sure they are pretty and every-thing, but boy are they loud. That's when I noticed that my hands were kind of itchy. I scratched them, and then held them up to the light. Giant red welts were raising up on my rapidly swelling fingers. I was having some kind of terrible reaction to the leaf. Who keeps POISONOUS

PLANTS on their front walk? What kind of hostile family did Brad come from anyway? I rubbed my hands on my pants, which didn't help, and started looking around for some sort of water. There was the pond across the street, of course. My hands felt like they were on fire.

"Crap," I said. I left my stuff and sprinted across the street to the pond. I don't know why that car was honking like that. I mean, it's not like he didn't SEE me. Besides, my hands were going to explode.

Unfortunately, I didn't notice that it was a bit muddy around the pond.

Okay, it was like the mud equivalent of quicksand.

So, OF COURSE, I fell. I mean, what could make TGYML any better than if, on the eve of what should be the most romantic night of my life EVER, I should fall on my knees in gross mud and have giant, swollen, itchy hands?

Oh, I know. It would be even better if I then reached up and SCRATCHED MY FACE with my filthy, plant-stung finger and got an equally itchy, muddy rash on my cheek.

"Oh my GOD," I pleaded. "Please, just give me a break, will you?" A frog leaped out of the reeds and nearly gave me a heart attack. I clapped my (muddy, swollen, gross) hand to my chest.

"Argh!" I screamed. Not only was I filthy and disfigured, but my SHIRT was RUINED.

"Haley?" I heard.

I turned around. And there was Brad, looking confused.

"Hi!" I said. He really was cute-ish in this light. And he looked so worried.

"I, um," I said. "Well, I fell. I was, um. It's hard to explain, really."

"I think you'd better come inside and clean up," he said. "I'm sorry I was late."

"No big deal!" I said. (I could hear that I was starting to talk like Melody, which frightened me). "I found things to do!"

"So I see," he said. "Look, I don't know how …"

"I know," I said. "I'm sorry. I'm just accident-prone. It's like it's out of my control or something."

He made a weird face.

"What?" I said.

"Nothing," he said. Then he burst out laughing.

"Don't LAUGH at me," I said. I was horrified. I mean, there I am, possibly dying from some fatal reaction to his POISONOUS PLANTS and encrusted with mud and nearly crying. And he was LAUGHING? "Is there ANY-ONE in my life who doesn't think I'm a JOKE?" I blurted.

"I'm sorry," he said immediately. And he did look sorry.

But that's probably because he was figuring that if I was mad, he wouldn't get what he wanted.

"Just get me a towel so I can have a shower," I said, try-ing not to cry. It was all falling apart. Kiki, Jules and everyone would be there any minute. "And maybe I could borrow a clean shirt or some sweatpants or something."

"Sure, sure," he said.

I took my time in the shower. When I looked closely at my hands, the swelling and redness seemed to be getting worse. I wondered if Brad would let me check his computer to see what kind of plant had poisoned me. I got out and dried off and snooped around the bathroom. It was obviously his parents' bathroom because there was makeup and perfume in one of the cupboards. I put some foundation over my bruise, which of course was completely the wrong colour for my skin. I washed it off and went with eyeliner and mascara instead. Maybe if Brad was looking at my eyes, he wouldn't notice the rest of me. The T-shirt he'd found for me had the name of his hockey team on the front. It was white, and made me look like a marshmallow. The sweatpants were about three thousand sizes too big, adding to the effect. I ran my fingers through my wet hair, which was sticking up all over the place without my hair products to flatten it down. To make matters worse, it was threatening to get fluffy. It must have been the weird shampoo I found in the shower. I stuck my tongue out at my reflection.

"Well," I said to myself, "here goes nothing."

By the time I got downstairs (after laughing at pictures of Brad as a kid which were ALL OVER the walls of the house. And I mean, ALL over. There were about a hundred on the staircase alone), everyone was already there. JT was hanging out the window, smoking a cigarette.

"You can't smoke in here," Brad was saying.

"Oh, don't be so boring," Jules said flirtatiously. (Honestly, wasn't it enough that she stole JT from me? Did she have to focus her attention on Brad, too?)

"Oh, there you are," said Kiki, looking at me funny. "Where were you?"

"I had to have a shower," I said.

"Oooh," said JT, winking at Brad.

"Shut up," I said, surprising myself. I mean, usually when I talk to JT, all that comes out is "uh" or "um." "I fell in the pond."

"Sheesh," he said. "Sorry."

"Anyway," he turned to Brad. "I invited a couple of the guys. Hope you don't mind."

"Uh, sure," said Brad. But he looked kind of worried. I can't say that I blamed him. His parents' house was nice and totally, well, tidy. And carpeted. I just imagine what "a few" of JT's friends would be like.

Three hours later, the place was packed with people. Most of them went to my school but there was a bunch I didn't recognize. Everyone was smoking and drinking. It's possible that I had one or two drinks. I don't really remember. I mean, I was nervous. And upset. And I was wearing sweatpants. All the other girls there were in nice clothes, jeans and pretty tops. Wearing makeup. And there I was, without makeup, with a swollen chin and giant red hands, and fluffy hair.

Okay, I had five drinks.

Which is a lot. For me.

Which explains why I had to throw up. And may explain why I fell asleep on the bathroom floor. And then when I woke up and tried to find Brad, I found him lying in his bed with his arms around …

Izzy Archibaud.

I nearly fainted.

Brad? And IZZY?

What was she doing there?

I didn't wait long enough to find out, that's for sure. I grabbed my coat and my keys and my bundle of muddy clothes and I left.

I wasn't even that upset, really.

Okay, I was.

V. upset.

V. sick.

Love,

Broken-hearted Blotchy Girl

▶ ▶ ▶

Sunday, March 9

MOOD	—
HAIR	—
HEALTH	—
HOROSCOPE	Oh, who cares.
~~JT SIGHTINGS~~	~~irrelevant~~

10:06 a.m.

I'm dead.

Did I die?

No, feel too horrible to be dead.

Am also inexplicably sad. Oh, I remember now. I am *explicably* sad.

But my head hurts too much to contemplate it deeply. Also, I feel like vomiting. Really, to serve justice, I should have thrown up on Brad and Izzy last night.

Brad? AND IZZY?

My life is officially and genuinely a horrible nightmare. TGYML has now officially become TWYML. How could it get any worse?

Ways in Which My Life Could Get Worse:
1. Could develop terminal cancer.
2. Dad could marry Melody.
3. Limbs could begin falling off, as with leprosy or similar disease.
4. Could flunk grade 12 and have to repeat TWYML.
5. Could be murdered in the night by The Bird and The Cat in a well-plotted act of revenge for all the years that I've not let them go outside whenever they want.

"Okay, okay," I said to The Cat, who was clawing my leg. I stumbled over to the window and opened it so he could go outside. "Not *you*," I told The Bird, who also made a run for freedom. "You'd never come back."

I stared at the phone. I wanted to call Kiki and tell her what happened, but I knew she was busy with Stephano. He had some kind of rowing regatta (naturally, the reason why she tricked me into stupid rowing was because HE rowed) (not that I'm jealous or anything) (or bitter) about three hours out of town. They'd left early, or at least I think they had. I had a vague memory of them leaving while I was talking to Bruce Bartelson. I was? I closed my eyes and tried to recall what on earth I would have been talking to HIM about.

Note to Self: NEVER DRINK AGAIN. I'M NOT KIDDING.

My head pounded. Oh, no, wait, that wasn't my head. It was Melody pounding on my door. For a small woman, she carried a lot of weight.

"WHAT?" I said.

"Want to go for a run?" she chirped.

"I ran yesterday," I growled. "Go away." Honestly, it sometimes seems like all the people in my life are plotting to make me into Miss Fitness America. As far as I'm concerned, I get enough exercise going back and forth to the end of the driveway to get the paper.

"Sorry!" she called, as though I was a thousand miles away and not simply on the other side of a closed door. "I'll see you later!"

"Fine!" I yelled. The yelling hurt my head. I collapsed on the bed and dialed Jules' number.

Jules: Hello?
Me: It's me. [insert sobbing here]
Jules: Why are you crying?
Me: B-b-b-brad. And Izzy.
Jules: I'll be right there.

Jules is really good friend, after all.

7:47 p.m.
Dear Junior:

Have spent the day with best friend Jules. She even found an outfit that fits me to wear tomorrow for job interview at UnBurger. And she made me feel better. Sort of. She cheered me up. Or she tried to.

The thing is that I don't understand is, what's so horrible about me? Why does everyone hate me?

Why did Brad choose Izzy?

Love,

Sad Girl

Number of times that Brad called and I didn't answer: 14

Number of times that Melody answered: 10

Number of long conversations Melody had with Brad: 10

Reasons why I hate Melody: Increasing

Reasons why I hate Brad: 1

Possible Plausible Excuses for Brad Having Arm Around Izzy on His Bed:

1. She was choking and he was giving her the Heimlich and they fell asleep.
2. He fell asleep and she snuck in and snuggled up to him because she's crazy. And a stalker.
3. He was trying to make me jealous.
4. She's prettier than me, and nicer, and generally more fun to be around.
5. He hates me.
6. He was only with me to be nice.
7. It was a practical joke.
8. Everyone is more attractive to him than me, and he was drunk.
9. She was drunk.
10. Everyone was drunk.

► ► ►

Monday, March 10

MOOD	Tired
HAIR	Covered with rowing hat
HEALTH	VERY BAD
HOROSCOPE	Too early to have verified.
~~JT SIGHTINGS~~	~~irrelevant~~

8:33 a.m.

There is something very interesting about being awake before sun-up. If by "interesting," I mean "torturous."

I like rowing. I do. I mean, it's better than running, for example.

But rowing practice is inhumanly early. What's really funny is that there are people out on the harbour before us. Is there a rule that says that rowing can only take place before or after dark? It seems v. dangerous to me. You can't see anything in the water and there is nothing creepier than the sound of a boat hull scraping over something in the dark. It's like a horror movie.

Which is what I was thinking about on my way to practice at 5:00 when my bike hit something and I tumbled off. (The word "tumbled" here can be interpreted to mean "crashed heavily.")

Damn.

I'd hit a RACCOON.

What are the odds? Aren't small fuzzy animals supposed to know to get out of the way of moving bicycles? I sat on the pavement for a minute, stunned beyond belief. (The

raccoon wasn't moving.) (It must also have been stunned.)
All my parts hurt. My legs, my butt, my back.

My brain.

Which is when the raccoon (which luckily I didn't kill),
leapt on me and bit my wrist. (Am now sorry I didn't kill it.)

I'm serious.

There I was, sitting on the road in the MIDDLE OF
THE NIGHT (okay, it was almost 6:00, but it was still
dark) with a vicious (and probably rabid) raccoon attached
to my hand. Then he let go and ran away. I was so shocked,
I didn't even make a sound. My hand hurt like the bejesus,
I can tell you that. (Whoever said that bad pain takes a few
minutes to start hurting was wrong.)

I was almost at the dock so I got back on my bike and
tried to ignore the pain that was now coming from everywhere. I was a little dizzy, I guess. I coasted into the
boathouse and

    … of course

    … as if it isn't already embarrassing enough to be me

    … FAINTED.

Yup, indeed. Right in front of Damon, no less. Of course.
Who else would I faint in front of?

When I woke up, he was standing over me looking worried. Actually, there was a whole pack of faces around me,
some looking worried (most people) and some looking
amused (JT) and one looking panic-stricken (Kiki).

"Oh my GOD," she said, pushing everyone else out of
the way. "What happened to you?"

"I fell," I said. Or, I think I said.

And she said, "Your hand is bleeding like crazy."

And I said, "That's where the raccoon bit it."

"You were bitten by a raccoon?" Damon said. "Who gets bitten by a raccoon?"

JT laughed. "Haley does." He smirked.

"My hero," I said.

"What?" he said.

"Nothing," I said.

"Look," said Damon, looking at his watch and scratching his head. His hair is v. cute. All mussed up, like he just rolled out of bed. (Come to think of it, I'm sure he DID just roll of bed. Who does their HAIR before early morning rowing practice? Well, except me, of course.) "I'm going to have to drive you to the hospital to get a rabies shot or a tetanus shot or whatever. Wait here for a minute and I'll get the boats in the water and then we'll go."

He started yelling at all the other coaches and I sat there in a daze and watched the boats get ready. By the time they were done, the sun was coming up a bit. V. pretty, I thought woozily. My hand had bled through the towel-thing it was wrapped in. I tightened it to try to stop the bleeding. What if the raccoon had hit an artery/vein? What if I bled to death?

I put my head between my knees. Just in case.

Which is what I was doing when Damon tapped me on the shoulder. "Uh, are you okay?" he said.

"Not really," I said, holding up my bloody hand.

He blanched. I actually thought that HE might faint. But he didn't.

He drove me to the hospital in his Jeep, which was really cool. I tried not to drip blood on the upholstery, although "upholstery" isn't really the right word for "cracked ancient vinyl," I guess.

"Don't worry about the seats," he said wryly. "They aren't that clean to begin with."

I relaxed a bit. I couldn't make conversation because I was, well, woozy. And possibly bleeding to death. So we just sat there in silence. It wasn't awkward, though. I kept sneaking looks at him. He had very dark brown eyes. With big bags underneath them. He must get up at 4 every morning if he coaches every day, I thought. He was probably only about 25.

Once, he was in the Olympics. I only know this because, while I was waiting, I was looking at the stuff on the walls and there was a picture of him. If I had a boyfriend like Damon, I'd be …

Well, that's just stupid. I don't need to develop a crush on my rowing coach. I mean, I have Brad. Had Brad. Am not sure if I still have Brad.

Am not sure if I still want Brad.

I was dying to ask if Damon had a girlfriend. But the timing seemed wrong. Anyway, by the time I'd worked up the gumption, we were at the hospital. And lucky I didn't because I caught a glimpse of myself in the mirror while the doctor stitched up my hand (five stitches!) and gave me a rabies shot (ouch), and I have to say that I really wasn't looking … good.

Ugh.

Note to Self: If ever am "damsel-in-distress" again, make
sure to be wearing makeup.

12:37 p.m.
Have received 14 text messages, 7 voicemails and 3 e-mails
from Brad.
He wants to "explain."
Ha.
Bloody.
Ha.

1:45 p.m.
Am in drama class with Izzy "the traitor" Archibaud. I keep
shooting her evil glares and she just smiles at me blankly.
Honestly, believe Izzy has the IQ of a stump.
Which is handy, seeing as today we get to pretend to BE
stumps.
Fun!
If by "fun," I mean "pointless drivel."
Am going to see if Kiki wants to help me make voodoo
doll of Izzy to stick pins in. As such, am going to try to
position myself as close to her as possible during stump
exercise in order to steal a strand of hair.

2:15 p.m.
Have been sent to the principal's office for hair-pulling.
Honestly, it couldn't have hurt that much. Izzy is being
over-dramatic about it.

3:30 p.m.

Kiki is very nicely driving me to my job interview. It's hard for me to look job-like, what with the giant white bandage that goes down my hand and wraps around the middle finger, thus forcing the middle finger to point straight up.

"They'll think I'm giving them the FINGER," I wailed.

"They'll understand," soothed Kiki. "Just explain what happened."

"Explain that I got bitten on the wrist by a rabid raccoon that I accidentally ran over with my bicycle?" I said. "That's a great idea. Very professional."

"Well, sweets," she said. "It is The UnBurger. It's not like you're applying for a job at ... I don't know. The UN or something."

"Huh," I said. Obviously, Kiki (who doesn't ever have to get a job as a result of lucky genes and rich parents) would look down on working at The UnBurger. Who wouldn't? It's fast food. Vegetarian fast food, but still fast food.

"Don't be like that!" she said. "All I meant was that they probably won't ask too many questions!"

"I wasn't being like anything," I said grouchily. My hand was pulsating like the strawberry pie in Stephen King's creepy book *Thinner*, except that it wasn't making me lose weight and didn't involve fruit.

Kiki pulled up in front of The Mall. "Are you sure you don't want me to wait?" she said.

"No, MOM," I said. "I'll be fine. I can take the bus home. I might want to shop. Or something."

The truth is that I'm in no screaming hurry to get home

and listen to my dad telling me that the phone is for me or have Melody gushing over me and asking me what's wrong, what's wrong, what's wrong a million times an hour. I have it in my head that maybe I'll hang out in the mall for a while. And just, I don't know, be by myself.

4:17 p.m.
The Job Interview — Starring Me and the Tallest, Thinnest, Scariest Boy I've Ever Seen

Him: So, Holly, why do you want to work at The UnBurger?

Me: It's Haley, actually.

Him: Okay, so it's important for us to really get to know what motivates our employees. What would you say motivates you?

Me: Um.

Him: Thank you.

Me: You're welcome.

Him: Can you think of an example of a challenging situation that you've recently had to face down?

Me: Um, I ran over a raccoon this morning with my bicycle?

Him: We here at The UnBurger are opposed to animal cruelty. [Please note, he spat when he talked and my face was becoming, well, WAY too wet. I wiped it off as subtly as possible.]

Me: Look, I'm opposed to animal cruelty, too. And I love The UnBurger. And I REALLY need this job. Really. A lot. I do.

Him: Why?

Me: Um, to pay for college.

Him: Oh! We here at The UnBurger [is he paid to mention
        the restaurant name every two seconds? I felt like
        I was on a commercial. I looked around subtly
        for hidden cameras. I swear, when he said, "The
        UnBurger!" it sounded almost like The UnBurger
        song from the ad] fully support continuing educa-
        tion for our employees!

Me: That's great. I'd really like to work at The UnBurger!
        [Oh no, I was doing it, too.]

Him: What are you planning on studying at college?

Me: Well, um, I was thinking about becoming a …
        vegetarian chef!

Him: Wow! That's great! [He sat back and beamed. I felt
        a little badly for lying, but he looked so happy it
        was almost worthwhile.]

Him: Do you do much cooking?

Me: No. I mean, yes!

Him: Hmm.

Me: I love to cook.

Him: Are you vegetarian? Because we here at The
        UnBurger are open to …well, all kinds of people.
        Even Meat Eaters!

Me: I'm vegetarian.

Him: Why did you leave your last job? I have to ask that.

Me: I've never had a job.

Him: Oh!

Me: Sorry.

Him: It's okay! It's just that at The UnBurger we prefer
        to hire experienced people!

Me: I'm a fast learner. I am. Really. It's my dream [!] to
        work at The UnBurger. Seriously. Please.

Him: Well, all we have left to do is for you to take The
        UnBurger test! Are you ready?

Me: No! I mean, yes!

Him: What?

Me: Yes!

Him: Okay, Holly, you just fill this out and leave it at the
        counter! We'll be in touch! And thanks for think-
        ing of working at The UnBurger!

Me: Uh, sure. Okay. Thanks.

5:45 p.m.

Oh my God, I failed The UnBurger test. How was I supposed to know? I thought that The UnBurger would be
proud of me for saving money by c) rinsing the UnBurger
off and returning it to the bun, instead of being wasteful
and d) throwing it way. Honestly.

Oh my God.

I can't tell anyone that I failed The UnBurger test. I'll
never live this down.

Never.

9:57 p.m.

Number of times this evening that the phone rang: 39
Number of times that I answered the phone: 0
Number of calls from Brad: 20
Number of calls from Damon: 1

[Hmm. Interesting. Although should stop thinking about
Damon as he is a) way too old for me and b) probably is

just calling to tell me that I owe him money for car-cleaning after bleeding on his seat.]

Number of times my dad and/or Melody yelled at me to answer the phone: 39

Number of times my dad laughed at me because of my bandage/finger: 16

▶ ▶ ▶

Tuesday, March 11

MOOD	Extremely bad
HAIR	*see:* Health
HEALTH	*see:* Mood
HOROSCOPE	Didn't see it as Melody had vanished with the newspaper into the bathroom. (Too gross to contemplate.)
~~JT SIGHTINGS~~	~~irrelevant~~

12:30 p.m.

"Honestly, Haley," Jules laughed. "How could you be attacked by a raccoon? That's hilarious."

"It is NOT hilarious," I moaned. "It hurts."

"No," she said. "I've thought about it and it IS hilarious."

I glowered at her and she blew smoke in my face. I think it would be better for my health if I hung out with non-smokers. Second-hand smoke is not filtered! "I wish you'd quit smoking," I said. "You'll get wrinkles."

"I'll quit before I'm old," Jules said. She ran her hands through her hair. (Her new habit, now that she doesn't have three feet of long hair to fling around at all times.) Even though her hair is short, it's longer than mine. Mine seems to be shrinking into my head, much like a reverse hair-grow Barbie. I tugged on it experimentally and some broke off in my hand.

Again.

"Ack!" I said.

"Why do you always pull on your hair?" she said. "Maybe you have that weird thing I saw on Montel. Where you pull all your hair out because you're a loon."

"Huh," I said. "That's really nice. I don't have that. I was just ..."

"You know," she said. "If you stopped colouring your hair, it would stop falling out."

"Hmm," I said. The thing is, I can't stop colouring my hair. I'm a Hair Person. Some people are Diet People. Some people are Exercise People. Some people are just plain VAIN (I'm looking at you, Jules). And some people are Hair-centric. I can't help it. And now that it's too short to cut without resorting to a brush cut, I have to colour it just so it knows that I'm still paying attention. I know that doesn't make sense, but it makes me feel better. All this stuff with Brad, and avoiding him, and IZZY, and avoiding her, and my dad and his MYG and, well, everything. It makes me anxious. So I bleached my hair again to get rid of the residual pink.

I just wasn't FEELING pink anymore.

Sure, it burned a bit.

And smelled a little funny.

But I think it's cute. It's almost transparent, it's so light. So maybe it's a little dry. I condition.

"I've got to go," I said, seeing Izzy running towards me, looking pale and frantic. (But still smiling. Really, I think it's creepy to be happy all the time, even when you look pale and frantic.) I turned and pushed my way into the school, only to run smack into Bruce Bartelson, My Worst Nightmare (MWN).

"Argh!" I said.

"Haley!" he said. "Your hair looks great! Blah blah blah! Saturday blah blah blah!"

I could feel Izzy closing in on me. Whatever she had to say, I didn't want to hear it. My heart was beating like crazy, and to tell you the truth, I was starting to hyperventilate. "Fine!" I said. "Whatever!" Then I broke into a run.

I think I lost her somewhere in the crowd in the cafeteria. I certainly didn't MEAN to step on that kid's hand. Why it was all splayed out there, I've no idea. And why aren't we allowed to run in the halls? You're always hearing on the news about how kids in schools are all fat and grotesque and out of shape and have more plaque in their arteries than 50-year-old smokers because they never exercise.

"Haley Harmony," said Mr. Dork Butt, staring at me sternly (or as sternly as he could muster) over his glasses (circa 1970 and taking up most of his face — why? Do his cheeks need corrective lenses?). "I don't know what's going on with you but I'm wondering if we shouldn't bring your dad in for a conference."

I almost threw up on his desk. "My dad?" I said. "I don't think so."

"Well," he sighed, flipping through my file. "We've got drunkenness on school grounds, a very strange hair-pulling incident, and now I hear that you broke an eighth grader's finger, pushed over a plant, and were caught running in the halls. Can you explain this?"

I lifted my throbbing wrist. Really, I was NOT giving him the finger. It's just that when my hand is down by my side like that, it hurts more. It's obviously to do with circulation.

"Oh for GOD'S SAKE," he yelled.

I was quite taken aback. He's not someone who yells.

"I wasn't giving you the finger!" I said, in a panic. "I was just elevating my hand! I was bitten by a raccoon! I have stitches!"

"I don't have the energy to deal with you today," he said. "Let's say detention for a week and some mandatory counseling. You DO know what mandatory means, don't you?"

"Argh," I said. "I mean, yes."

"Fine," he said. "Now try to stay out of trouble for the rest of the day, would you?"

"Okay," I said, nervously looking out into the hallway in case Izzy was still stalking me.

I skulked to the library. The pain in my chest was getting much worse. There's only so much stress a body can take, after all. Out of habit, I punched "chest pain" and "racing heart" into Google.

(From MDAdvice.com):

Symptoms:

- Chest pain; palpitations.
- Rapid heartbeat.
- Shortness of breath.
- Numbness or tingling around mouth, hands or feet.
- Emotional changes.

Possible Problems:

Severe anxiety

What to Do:

See Panic Disorder.

Hmmf. Panic disorder. Am fairly confident I don't have panic disorder.

Symptoms:

- Chest pain.
- Sudden breathing difficulty.
- Recent surgery.
  OR
- Recent injury or illness requiring bed confinement.

Possible Problems:

Blood clot from leg or pelvis that has lodged in lung.

What to Do:

Call doctor now.

See Pulmonary Embolism.

See Atelectasis.

Now THAT seems more likely. Blood clot from leg or pelvis!

Wonder if raccoon bites can cause embolisms that travel from wrist to lung. Probably I'm not long for this world and so it doesn't much matter that Izzy Archibaud is lurking by the door with an evil glint in her beady boyfriend-stealing eyes.

"Haley!" she yelled.

"Shh," I said, out of habit. "It's a library."

"Gawd! I've been looking for you, like, everywhere!" she said. "You were, like, avoiding me!"

"Like, it's possible," I growled. It was all I could do to not reach over and punch her directly in her cute button nose. I kept seeing her and Brad lying there, albeit fully dressed, but with his arm — his cute-ish arm — draped over her.

"You have to listen to me," she said. But luckily, just at that moment, the bell went.

"Got to go!" I said brightly, grabbing my stuff. "See you later!"

2:13 p.m.
Dear Junior:
Sort of wish I'd listened to whatever she had to say. I mean, what if there is an actual explanation?

There can't be an explanation.

Refuse to listen to anything either of the Two Traitors has to say.
Love,
Spurned Girl

3:30 p.m.

Detention is boring. Luckily, they don't make us do anything but sit here. And I can just type on my lapto...

3:32 p.m.

List of Reasons Why Detentions Suck, Written on Back Page of Someone Else's Math Text:

1. They confiscate your computer if you use it.
2. You aren't allowed to talk.
3. You aren't allowed to do anything.
4. These seats are very uncomfortable when you just have to sit in them without doing anything.
5. It's boring.
6. Gives you too much time to think about your life.
7. See 5.

3:45 p.m.

"Haley?" someone just now poked their head into the detention room. "The counsellor will see you."

Argh.

Even detentions are superior to counseling sessions. The things I would rather do than be "counseled" include having a root canal (have never had one, but how bad could it be?) and going to jail (have never been, but hear from Dad it's not so bad and they have satellite TV).

6:30 p.m.

Conclusions Drawn from Counseling Session:

1. Have no skills.
2. Have no ambitions.

3. Have no hope.
4. Have taken all the wrong classes.
5. Will be lucky to get a job at a fast food restaurant (did not mention how The UnBurger rejected me already) in lieu of having a Real Career.
6. Can see why Dad turned to life of TV and drugs as every other option is impossible.

Note to Self:
   You are a Loser.
   Go directly to Loser-ville.
   Do not pass GO.
   Do not collect $200.

"So, how was school?" chirped Melody, as she dished up big plates of unknown macrobiotic slime. (I mean, I'm vegetarian, yes, but that does NOT mean that I want to eat goo.)

"Fine," I said.

"Mel and I had a really funny experience today at work," Dad said.

"Good for you," I said.

"Want to hear about it?" he said.

"Nope," I said.

You have to hand it to Melody. I mean, she really is relentless.

"Brad called!" she said. "You know, I had a nice chat with him! I think you should let him explain! The thing that happened was …"

"SHUT UP!" I screamed. I knocked my chair over.

It was, perhaps, just a touch over the top. But I didn't want to hear it. Much less from HER. "SHUT UP! IT'S NONE OF YOUR BUSINESS! I DON'T EVEN LIKE YOU!"

Okay, so I don't know where that last part came from.

Okay, I do know. I DON'T even like her.

"HALEY," my dad yelled. My dad NEVER yells. Never. It was like he'd leapt across the table and whalloped me in the head. Naturally, I burst into tears (inexplicable emotional outburst! See: Brain Tumour) and ran out of the room.

Honestly. I mean, couldn't he have waited until I'd left home before importing his stupid, nosy, interfering MYG? I stomped upstairs, tripping on The Cat and whacking my stitches on the banister.

Great.

"ARGHGHGH!" I screamed into my pillow.

Sometimes I feel like I spend half my life screaming into my pillow.

Suddenly, my (chartreuse) room felt too small. I dragged myself up and put on my running clothes. I had this idea that I'd run over to Kiki's and she could make me feel better.

Kiki always makes me feel better.

8:20 p.m.

Kiki USED to make me feel better. What does NOT make me feel better includes (but is not limited to!) watching Kiki and Hot Stephano canoodling on the couch while sweating through my running clothes and worrying that the sweat will make my stitches infected.

I mean, eventually that gets uncomfortable.

I miss Kiki. Sometimes I think back on when we were all single, and I feel kind of sad.

11:05 p.m.
Can't sleep. Brad did not call at all tonight. Not once. Has Brad given up? Am I playing hard to get? Why do I miss him so much when he bugged me so much when I was with him?

I even miss his ugly stupid bowling shoes.

Maybe he's away. Am sure that's it. Am sure he is in some other town playing hockey and not thinking about me.

Will concentrate on plan to get back together with Brad once I discover "explanation" for his behaviour.

More Possible Explanations for Brad and Izzy Being "Together":
1. She drugged his drink.
2. She drugged his food.
3. She hit him over the head and he was unconscious and she draped his arm over herself to make me feel badly.
4. She's a witch and she cast a spell on him.
5. She seduced him with … ?
6. He has always had a crush on her and is now in paradisiacal relationship with Izzy Archibaud that does not involve Izzy ever falling into the pond across the road from his house.

ARGH.
Can't sleep.

Wonder if anyone has ever died from insomnia. Will check it out and then will get some rest.

Oh no.

Have discovered that insomnia is symptom of mad cow disease and that not sleeping can kill you. Have read fascinating story of entire family who died from not sleeping.

If I die from insomnia, Dad and Melody will probably be pleased to have my room. I know Melody has been eyeing it to set up as "home office" (am sure she will paint it right away as she believes that chartreuse is "jarring"). Think it's funny that Dad would hook up with someone ambitious enough to want to work even while at home. Think it's sad that he loves Melody more than he loves me. Think it's sad that he loves Melody at ALL, come to think of it.

Must concentrate on sleeping.

3:14 a.m.
Just had terrible flashback where I remembered agreeing to meet with Bruce Bartelson on Saturday to start planning for prom.

ARGH.

3:17 a.m.
Wonder if I'm too young/old to run away and join the circus. Have always admired those trapeze people.

The fact that I'm afraid of heights might be a problem.

4:50 a.m.
Wonder if Bruce Bartelson thinks it's some kind of date? Do I have a date with Satan?

Note to Self: Kill self. Am no longer kidding. Situation is dire.

► ► ►

Tuesday, March 18

MOOD	Morose
HAIR	Brittle, but cute
HEALTH	Medium
HOROSCOPE	Think carefully before making any big changes. Be careful of other people's feelings today!
~~JT SIGHTINGS~~	~~irrelevant 6~~

List of Things I Still Have to Accomplish During TGYML (as if, but I'm still hoping) Made During Boring Art Class in Lieu of Drawing a Portrait of My Foot:
1. Decide what to do after graduation.
2. Get Brad back.
3. Go to L.A. with Jules.
4. Stop having crushes on the following: JT, Damon, Stephano.
5. Run mini-marathon (have just found out that it is THIRTEEN MILES) (ha ha ha ha ha).
6. Get job.

Hmm. Have accomplished very little this year.

Things I Have Accomplished:
1. Had boyfriend (but lost him).

2. Have whitened teeth to max whiteness (according to dentist, teeth are beginning to look "scary").
3. Have tried to get job.
4. Have conquered fear of bungee jumping (albeit will never do it again).
5. Have pulled off charity fund-raising ball. Sort of. In a manner of speaking. Well, have successfully managed someone else pulling off fund-raising ball.
6. Have learned to row. Kind of. Wouldn't want to try it in a boat by myself or anything. Am certainly not going to turn it into a career.

Conclusion: I am a huge loser.

▶ ▶ ▶

Saturday, March 22

MOOD	Lumpy
HAIR	Limp
HEALTH	Gross
HOROSCOPE	Today is a good day to reorganize, restructure or even just repaint! It's a day to start over.
~~JT SIGHTINGS~~	~~irrelevant~~

10:37 a.m.

"So," Jules said, peering at her face in the mirror and wiping off an invisible speck of who-knows-what from her pearly complexion. "Shouldn't you be getting ready for your date with Bruce Bartelson?"

"It's not a DATE," I said. "I think it's something to do with prom planning. I don't really remember what he said."

"Weird," she said. "You're so weird. You know that, right?"

"I know," I said irritably. "Mostly because you're always telling me."

"Do I look fat to you?" she said, lifting up her shirt to reveal her totally flat belly.

"Huge," I said.

"Really?" she said.

"No," I sighed. "You look fine."

"It's just that I have to look perfect for …"

"I know," I said. "*Who's the Prettiest of Them All*? But it's not until May. You have almost two months to make yourself even more perfect. Don't worry about it."

"Maybe I should start working out at the gym," she said, flexing her non-existent muscle in her tiny noodle arm.

"Jules," I said. "Shut up. You're perfect. Listen, why don't you come with me to meet Bruce? You aren't doing anything anyway."

"I'm not coming with you on a DATE," she said, curling her lip. "Besides, me and JT are meeting Brad … whoops." She stopped. Well, mostly because I jumped off the bed and practically pushed her over.

"MY Brad?" I yelped.

"Well, he IS JT's cousin," she said. "Besides, WE aren't fighting with him. YOU are."

"Argh!" I screamed. "Traitor!"

"I thought you wanted to get him back," she said.

"Well, I don't," I said. "He cheated on me with IZZY ARCHIBAUD."

"No, he didn't," she said. "But you're too stubborn to listen to the explanation. You're such a dunce. He's the best thing that ever happened to you. Besides, I think he's cute."

"He IS cute," I moaned. "Tell me the explanation."

"Why do you think I know?" she said.

"Well, I'm sure he told JT," I said, cringing on the inside. "And I'm sure JT told you."

"Uh," she said. "Yeah, well, it's none of my business. Go! You're going to be late."

"Blech," I said. But I let her push me out the door.

1:01 p.m.
List of Reasons Why Bruce Bartelson Makes My Skin Crawl.
Written on five dollar bill while riding the bus (thanks, Jules!)
downtown to meet him:
1. Is too enthusiastic about everything.
2. Is weird looking.
3. Spits when he talks.
4. Smells like … socks.
5. Wears pink shirts.
6. Isn't embarrassed as often as he should be.
7. Mumbles.
8. Is close talker.

"Here," said Bruce, leaning over the table after lunch was over and TOUCHING MY HAND. "I'll pay!"

"No," I practically yelled. "I got it."

Which, of course, is how he happened to be holding the list of things I didn't like about him in his hand while we argued over the bill at the stupid coffee shop.

I don't think he read it.

I mean, I'm sure he didn't.

It's just a coincidence that he practically ran away and didn't give me a ride home. I'm not the most hateable person on the planet.

Or am I?

▶ ▶ ▶

Monday, March 24

Crack o' Dawn

(Can't comment on hair or mood as am undecided on both.) (No horoscope available yet.)

Now that stitches have been removed and bandage is off, I'm back to early morning rowing practice. Really, am amazed by how quickly the body heals. It takes WEEKS for a hickey to fade, but a wild-animal bite apparently can heal itself in no time flat.

Am worried about a) running over another raccoon, and b) that I've forgotten how to row. Am sure it will be fine.

Very pretty sunset this morning.

Am late.

Late Dawn

Well.

First of all, let me explain that rowing in a boat by yourself is considerably different than rowing in a boat with others.

With others:

By yourself:

Now, I don't know if I'm making my point v. well. (Is hard to draw with a mouse!) But let's just say that the single boat is much, much tinier. Second, the hull of the boat is much, much skinnier. It's like … skating. Only on the water. In the dark. On your ass. Very close to the surface.

Let me explain:

When I arrived at the dock, everyone was already bustling around doing their thing. So I went off to find Damon.

"Oh!" he said. "Haley!" Like he was surprised to see me. Which seemed a bit odd, but never mind.

"Hi," I said. I held up my hand and wiggled it around.

"I'm sort of better. I still have to keep it wrapped up, but it's pretty much fine. So, can I row today?"

"Sure," he said. "Right. We'll just get you a boat. It's just …"

Hmmf. As it turns out, he'd organized the boats for the year-end regatta, and he didn't put me in any of them. I know I'm bad, but that's just embarrassing.

"I sort of forgot about you," he said.

Bye-bye, crush, I thought sadly. (Possible cure for crushes: to be horribly insulted by crushee.)

He FORGOT about me? I thought about him at least once a day. Well then. I mean, maybe he hadn't been thinking about me, but it would have been nice to be REMEMBERED as part of the SHH TEAM.

"Want to try a single?" he said, his brow furrowing in an oh-so-cute way.

"Sure!" I said. Meaning, "Not on your life!"

Which naturally is how I found myself watching the sunrise from a dreaded racing single. Let me illustrate:

Obviously.

I mean, it should be no shock to anyone that I managed to wobble out to the middle of the harbour (barely) before

I flipped over. Let me say this: flipping over when your feet are ATTACHED to THINGS and you are in FREEZING COLD WATER is v. embarrassing and also v. frightening.

I could have drowned!

Of course, I didn't. That would have been too easy. THEN I wouldn't have been able to surface in time to see JT and his crew pull up beside me and start laughing themselves sick.

Honestly, in water that cold, hypothermia could have set in at any second. Finally, Damon pulled the coach boat up beside me and said, "Haley, are you all right?"

Naturally, I had to say "Fine!" As though bobbing around in the ice cold harbour at dawn had been my intent.

"Are you going to get out?" he said.

"Yes!" I said confidently.

Let me assure you that it is next to impossible to flip a boat the right way up while in the water, nearly drowning and suffering from hypothermia. And if you DO happen to be able to do this, it is TOTALLY impossible to climb back into said boat without flipping over again.

The plus-side is that this has a tendency to keep a person from noticing that they are freezing to death. The minus-side is that eventually the coach will get frustrated and tell you to get into the coach boat, which again is IMPOSSIBLE when your arms strongly resemble wet noodles and you have to pull yourself out of the water and INTO their boat without looking like a fat seal flopping onto the dock.

It's safe to say that I'll never be able to look Damon in the eyes again. I mean, we HAVE to wear spandex because otherwise our clothes get caught in the oars. How was I to know that my spandex had a hole in the bum? I can't see behind myself, can I?

If only I hadn't been wearing neon striped underwear, I'm sure he wouldn't have noticed.

Note to Self: Find some excuse — ANY EXCUSE — to never row again.

And/or Kill Self.

12:07 p.m.

"What's that SMELL?" said Jules, wrinkling her nose.

"What smell?" I said innocently.

"It smells like … salt water or … garbage … or something."

"It's HER," said JT, coming up behind Jules and flopping his perfect arm around her shoulders. "She fell IN!" He bent over bellowing with laughter. Honestly, it sounded like he was going to birth a calf.

"It's not that funny," I said. "I could have drowned."

"She did a good job of recovering," said Kiki. (Kiki is v. good friend. Love Kiki.) "It's hard to get back in those things when you flip."

"Have you ever done it?" I asked.

"Well," she said. "Not actually. But … they're very tippy! I could see how it could happen!"

"Ew," said Jules. "You SWAM in the gross, polluted harbour? I hope you don't get sick. Aren't there, like, chemicals in there?"

"NO," I said. "I mean, maybe. I had a shower, okay? Give me a break." I sneezed.

"You ARE getting sick," she said. "Knowing you, you'll probably get pneumonia and die or something."

"Ha ha," I said. "That's hilarious."

"How was your date with Bruce Bartelson?" Kiki asked.

"It wasn't a DATE," I said furiously. "It was just a student council thing. We talked about the prom." (Which was sort of true. I mean, I did mention the prom, but Bruce seemed to be operating under the strange misconception that we would be attending together. Which we are NOT. I chose to evade the whole topic by going to the washroom and staying there for 20 minutes and then coming out, claiming to have a stomach sickness. I AM NOT GOING TO THE PROM WITH BRUCE BARTELSON. AND IT WAS NOT A DATE.)

"Oh," said JT. "You're dating Bruce Bartelson? He's such a loser."

"Look," I said. "I'm not. Don't tell Brad. Not that there is anything to tell."

"Whatever," he said. "He's seeing…"

At which point Jules elbowed him hard in the gut and he fell on the ground. "HEY!" he said. "What did you do that for?"

"Who is he seeing?" I said.

"No one," said Jules, grabbing my arm and dragging me outside, pushing over some 8th grader in the process.

"Jules," I said. "I'm going to get blamed for that, you know. I'll probably get expelled. Are you okay?" I yelled at the kid over my shoulder. He flipped me the bird.

"Look," she said, once we got outside. Where, incidentally, it was pouring with rain. Pouring. Not drizzling, but

POURING. I immediately resembled a drowned rat and she immediately resembled a swimsuit model.

Anyway.

"You can't let JT know how you feel about Brad. He'll just turn it into a joke. You know what he's like." She stopped to roll her eyes. (I do?) "Just play it cool, Haley. For once in your life. You know, be the Ice Princess."

"Huh," I said. "Okay."

I mean, it must work for Jules, right? She landed JT.

Play it cool, I repeated in my head. So even when Izzy appeared in the doorway, I didn't budge, blink, or actually even breathe. (Which made me a tiny bit lightheaded, but that's to be expected.) I just walked right by her like she didn't exist. Ice princess, I said to myself. Play it cooool.

Note to Self: Concentrate all efforts on Plan to Win Boyfriend Back (and perhaps enlist him to get rid of Bruce Bartelson).

▶ ▶ ▶

Wednesday, March 26

MOOD	Filled with angst
HAIR	Must have it cut
HEALTH	Nothing hurts except broken heart
HOROSCOPE	Finances come together today, just in the nick of time! A family member will be there when you need them. Try not to worry too much.
~~JT SIGHTINGS~~	~~irrelevant 14~~

9:50 a.m.

Can't exactly remember why I thought Ancient Civilizations was going to be an interesting class. I immediately forget everything that took place the very second the bell goes.

Short-term memory loss IS, of course, a common symptom of brain tumours and also of mad cow disease. I never EAT meat anymore, but I probably did as a child.

If I have mad cow disease, I wonder if I can sue my parents for feeding me beef baby food.

Of course, that would be pointless, as they have no money either.

I can't help thinking that I'd be happier if I were richer, thinner and prettier. And I wouldn't have to work so hard to get Brad back.

Have come up with crack plan to get Brad back:

Plan to Get Brad Back:
1. Hang out at Brad's hockey games until he notices and falls in love with me.
2. Hang out in front of Brad's house until he notices and falls in love with me.
3. Hang out with JT so that Brad will eventually bump into me accidentally.
4. Tell JT that I'm seeing someone else so that Brad will hear about it and become overwhelmed with jealousy and remorse and try to win me back, in the style of what's-his-name in that movie with Drew Barrymore.
5. Get cute haircut.

4:30 p.m.

Problem:

Am at hair salon and hair is cut (It's quite cute and boy who cut hair is also cute for someone old. He's probably, like, 24. He looks almost EXACTLY like Justin Timberlake, only on him it looks cute. V. nice, also. Not that I'd notice. Hair is now like Ashley Judd's hair in that movie about the cows, but so blonde that it's white) and I have just realized that I don't have my wallet.

Solution:

Ask to use salon washroom and climb out back window, only to find self trapped in alley. Am forced to climb over wire fence to escape.

I swear, I'll mail him the money. I will.

No wonder my karma is so terrible.

Note to Self: Try to improve karma by doing more charitable things, such as helping the elderly or folding the laundry.

▶ ▶ ▶

Friday, March 28

or

The First Day of the Plan

MOOD	GREAT
HAIR	CUTE!
HEALTH	FINE

HOROSCOPE	Everything goes your way today. Just go with the flow and it will all work out.
~~JT SIGHTINGS~~	~~irrelevant~~

7:15 a.m.

Even the stars agree. My Newly Refined Plan is going to work.

I'm choosing my clothes v. carefully (jeans, cute camisole, leather jacket borrowed from Melody without her knowledge but is only nice thing she owns so am sure she won't mind) because I have to look great in order for it to work.

12:30 p.m.

"It's the worst idea I've ever heard," Kiki said slowly, chewing her sandwich thoughtfully after listening to my idea.

"No, it's not!" I said. "It's great!"

"What did Jules say?" she said.

"Nothing," I said. "I mean, I didn't ask her for her opinion. She'd just tell JT and then he'd tell Brad."

"Haley," Kiki sighed. "This kind of thing only works in movies. Besides, how do you know the guy you're thinking of will even do it?"

"Of course, he'll do it," I shrugged. "Why wouldn't he?"

"Haley," Kiki said. "I just don't want you to get hurt."

"I won't," I said. "It will work. It ALWAYS works."

"Okay," she said. "Fine, but I don't want to be a part of it."

"Please?" I begged. "I can't do it alone."

"Fine," she said. "But you owe me a favour."

"Great!" I said.

Everything was in place. It was going to come off without a hitch.

The Plan:

1. Go to Brad's game and make sure he sees me.
2. Spend duration of game flirting with hot-drink boy. (Justin?)
3. Get hot-drink boy to kiss me just as Brad is emerging from rink.
4. Brad gets angry and tries to save me from hot-drink boy and fight ensues like Colin Firth and Hugh Grant in *Bridget Jones's Diary*.
5. I nurse Brad's wounds and he comes back to my cool apartment (Okay, to my house) and stays with me forever. Or whatever.

7:02 p.m.

Here's what happens to "plans."

"So," I said to the hot-drink boy. "Justin. Do you, um, like working here?"

"It's okay," he said. "You like hot drinks, huh?"

Okay, so I was on my tenth cup of tea. I like tea. I was getting a tiny bit jittery, but I'm not used to drinking that much caffeine. I gritted my teeth.

"Are you okay?" he said. "My name is not Justin."

"Sure," I said, winking in a way that I assumed looked sultry, while trying desperately to come up with his actual name.

"Is there something in your eye?" he said.

"No," I said.

"Look," he said. "Can I get you anything? Because there are, like, people waiting."

In my plan, I hadn't taken into account the other hot-drink drinkers. Drat.

"Oh!" I said. "Sorry." I blushed. He gave me a weird look. It was possible that the plan was derailing slightly now that hot-drink boy (not JUSTIN) thought that I was completely crazy.

Jules came up behind me and tapped me on the shoulder. "What on earth are you doing?" she said. "You've missed the whole game, practically. It's freezing in there. I hate hockey. Come outside with me while I smoke."

"Uh," I said, following her dumbly. The hot-drink boy was leaning over the counter to serve some cute girl a hot chocolate with whipped cream. Flirt! He's like a boy-slut!

Crap.

"What's wrong with you?" Jules said.

I shrugged and batted her smoke out of my face. "Nothing," I sighed.

"Huh," she said. "You're all red. Do you have a crush on that weird kid who serves the drinks?"

"He's not weird," I said. "He's just different."

"God, Haley," she said. "You're capable of falling for ANYONE."

"I am NOT," I said. "That's just mean."

"Besides," she said. "I thought you wanted Brad back. You're hardly going to get him back by hanging over everything else in pants. Maybe if you, like, PAID ATTENTION

TO HIS GAME, he'd forgive you for being such a flake."

"Forgive ME?" I said. "Uh, let's not forget that he cheated on ME."

"Haley," she said. "Nah, forget it. You'll figure it out eventually."

Oh, so now that she's had two boyfriends, she's the expert? I stuck out my tongue. Which is the exact moment that Brad came through the doors. He gave me a weird look and then kept going.

He totally ignored me.

What was my plan again?

"Brad?" I said. But it was too late. He was already gone.

APRIL

Friday, April 4

MOOD	Foul
HAIR	Foul
HEALTH	Foul
HOROSCOPE	Today emphasizes written communication and may mean a raise or a new job! Enjoy a delicious meal with friends.
~~JT SIGHTINGS~~	~~irrelevant~~

Dear Junior:

How did it come to be April 4 already? HOW?

I'm serious. I want to know.

I don't even understand it. I mean, it was just SEPTEMBER a minute ago. I thought I had lots of time to prepare for this stupid marathon. I thought I had time to get fit. Instead, I've suffered: pulled muscles, black eyes, a broken nose, a severe wrist injury, and multiple side cramps. I've thrown up in shrubs, on lawns, and fallen over on park benches and random passersby.

I AM IN NO WAY READY TO RUN A MARATHON TOMORROW. Wonder if I can plead sickness and somehow get out of it with my pride. Well, with some pride. With a tiny crumb of pride.

Truthfully, have almost no pride left as most of my pride was spent "running" back and forth in front of Brad's house, even though I know he's away.

I swear those ducks were gunning for me.

Love,
Wimpy Girl

▶ ▶ ▶

Saturday, April 5

MOOD	ARGH!
HAIR	ARGH!
HEALTH	ARGH!
HOROSCOPE	ARGH!
~~JT SIGHTINGS~~	~~irrelevant~~

6:00 a.m.

When I got up this morning, The Bird crapped on my head first thing. In some cultures, that's considered lucky.

Not here.

Although to be honest, I was strangely buoyed by it. Also, it wasn't raining. It was even sunny. It was bloody cold (and early), but sunny.

I staggered down to breakfast, and — miracle of all miracles! — Melody was nowhere in sight. I think maybe she sneaks around so that she can be there whenever I go into the room to share "makeup secrets" and "boy talk." Where does she get these ideas? As near as I can figure, Melody herself was a teenager during the years when Molly Ringwald was in her prime. Ergo, she probably watched those films and emulated those people.

And yet …

And yet, she came out of the eighties being HER: A holistic tries-too-hard hippie with unfortunate teeth and bad dress sense. I can't understand it. I think that if I'd had the good fortune to be born in the seventies, I'd have been cool in the eighties. I missed my era, that's all.

Anyway, I'd borrowed some of Jules' spandex running stuff (not that she ever runs in it, she just thinks it looks cute) (which, of course, it DOES) (on her) (on me, it looks like really tight, unflattering clothing). But never mind that. I was feeling lucky because of The Bird omen and the good horoscope.

What was I thinking?

10:00 a.m.
Honestly, don't see how anyone can be expected to run anywhere in this kind of crowd.

10:35 a.m.
Have been elbowed in the face by very tall, bony, muscly elderly man and have been forced to trip him. Now probably will have bad karma.

10:37 a.m.
Okay, this is not so bad.

10:45 a.m.
How many miles is this?

11:03 a.m.
Threw up in potted plant on busy street. Pretended to simply be swooshing and spitting water like everyone else. SWALLOW YOUR WATER, PEOPLE. I'm not kidding. That whole swirl-spit thing is seriously disgusting.

11:10 a.m.
Am going to die.

11:35 a.m.
Can't feel legs.

11:40 a.m.
Am hallucinating. Where's Kiki? Am having heart attack. Will just duck over to this grassy area for short rest-stop to try to find breath, which lost around mile five. MILE FIVE. People should only run five miles if a) someone is chasing them, or b) doing so will cure cancer, or c) will save the world.

Just going to duck behind this …

ARRRHRHGGHGH.

3:30 p.m.
"I'm serious, Jules, just come and pick me up and promise

you won't laugh," I hissed into the phone.

"What?" she said. "I can't hear you."

"That's because you're LAUGHING," I said. "Come on, please stop laughing."

"I'm not laughing," she gasped. "Hang on."

She put the phone down and I could clearly hear her laughing heartily for what felt like 20 minutes.

"Okay," she said. "Just tell me again how you ran off the edge of the cliff?"

Then she laughed again.

But I swear, I didn't see it. It looked like a nice grassy area. How was I to know those shrubs were growing out of THIN AIR? I do feel badly about that picnic those nice people were having. Oh, AND ABOUT THE FACT THAT I BROKE MY LEG.

No matter. My life could not get much worse at this point, so having a cast encasing my leg from ankle to hip is really no big deal. And because my dad and Melody don't "believe" in cellular phones (it's not a RELIGION, it's a COMMUNICATIONS DEVICE), and Kiki is nowhere to be found (probably celebrating her win on the podium of Mini Marathon Hell), I have no one else to turn to except Jules.

"Okay," she said, finally managing to catch her breath. "I'll pick you up in a while. Wait for me outside."

"Thanks," I said.

"Don't mention it," she said.

Hmmm. Jules may not be a VERY good friend, but at least can count on her to pick me up from the Emergency Room when I've been casted.

4:05 p.m.

Jules is a terrible friend. How DARE she make me wait? Also, she is not answering her phone. HATE Jules.

Reasons Why I Hate Jules:

1. She knows that hospitals make me anxious, and she didn't bother to come get me.
2. She is too pretty for her own good, whatever that means.
3. She makes me feel giant, gross, lumpy, useless, ugly and comical.
4. SHE STOLE MY BOYFRIEND. Okay, my crush.
5. She forgot to pick me up from the hospital. Nasty cow.
6. See 5.

I tried to crutch my way to the bus-stop, but it was too far. Sadly, I only know, like, five people who drive.

Which explains why I called JT.

I swear, I wasn't trying to "get back" at Jules. I just ... I mean, I couldn't call BRAD. I had no one else to call.

4:45 p.m.

"Like, what happened to you?" JT said, as I hopped into his Jeep. Well, "hopped" is perhaps an exaggeration. As I DRAGGED myself into his Jeep (without his help, natch.)

"I accidentally ran off a cliff," I said, in as dignified a voice as possible. "I'm sorry to have bothered you, but I called Jules first and she clearly forgot about me."

"She clearly forgot about me," he mimicked, in an old lady voice, with an English accent.

"I haven't got an accent," I said.

"*I haven't got an accent,*" he said WITH AN ACCENT. Laughing like a hyena. (Possible alternate cure for crushes: WHEN THE CRUSHEE LAUGHS AT YOU.) (Not that I still have a crush on JT or anything.)

"Look," I said. "Settle down."

"Sorry," he said. "You just talk funny. It's … cute."

Cute?

Cute?

In that exact minute, my heart completely stopped beating. It's possible that I swooned. Or "fainted." Luckily, JT is too clued out to notice. I came to when he skidded into my driveway and all but pushed me out of his Jeep.

Cute!

"Uh, thanks," I said. But he was already gone. I stood there in the driveway for a long time. And not just because I couldn't actually go anywhere, since JT had driven off with my crutches. I hardly noticed. Sure, it was raining. And my leg was hurting in a million different ways. But I didn't care.

JT SAID I WAS CUTE.

Three years after the first day I set eyes on him and decided that he would be the very first love of my life.

Cute! Cute!

I was snapped out of my reverie by my phone ringing annoyingly in my pocket simultaneously with JT screeching to a halt in front of me and turfing my crutches onto the lawn. Not exactly gallant, but whatever.

"What?" I snapped into the phone.

"Haley?" Jules' voice crackled. "Where ARE you? I've been waiting here for an hour."

Which is when I realized that I'd sent her to the wrong hospital. She didn't take it well. It's not like I purposely set out to send her that way so that I could "get my claws" into her boyfriend.

I'm just not the type of girl to even HAVE claws.

Am I?

I mean, really. I'm just clumsy old Haley. Clumsy CUTE Haley.

Ha.

Oh my god, I'm CUTE.

7:38 p.m.
Dear Junior:

Broken leg is pain like no other.

PAIN.

LIKE.

NO.

OTHER.

But I'm cute, that's something.

Right?

At least someone thinks I'm cute. And isn't actively laughing *at* me. Quite unlike Dad and Melody who both burst into hysterics as soon as I hopped in the front door, falling over The Cat in the process. Why do the people who are supposed to love me best laugh at me so often?

Why?

Love,

Cute Girl

The Silver Lining List:

1. Will certainly be able to convince Melody to drive me to school every day until the end of year as anticipate being casted until end of June.
2. Will not have to row anymore and face humiliation of knowing that Damon does not even KNOW WHO I AM.
3. Will not have to run, ever again.
4. Will get priority seating on flight to LA, if Jules still wants me to go.
5. Have discovered that JT thinks I'm cute.
6. Can somehow translate broken leg/crutches into not having to go to Student Council meetings.

► ► ►

Wednesday, April 9

12:34 p.m.
"Haley! Haley Harmony!" a voice yelled down the hallway. Honestly, I'm the only Haley in the entire school. Using my last name is just … redundant.

"What?" I said, swinging around.

Only to see BRUCE BARTELSON barreling towards me.

"I heard about your leg!" he said. (Why is it that I can suddenly hear every word he's saying? Painkillers must somehow improve hearing ten-thousand fold.)

"Well," I said. "As you can see, it's clearly broken." I tapped on it with my pen. Which knocked me slightly off balance. Luckily, I caught myself on a locker before toppling over. "Anyway," I said, hoping to edge him towards some sort

of conclusion. The drawback to having a broken leg —
apart from the PAIN AND AGONY and risk of clotting —
was that I couldn't run away. Which I really wanted to do
at that moment. Badly.

"What?" he said, leaning in much too close.

I lurched backwards. "Okay, then," I said. "Got to go!"

"Wait!" he said. "Will you be at the student council
meeting after school?"

"No," I said (as sadly as plausible), "I've got a doctor's
appointment." I tapped again. Somewhere deep inside my
cast, my leg began to itch. I tried to wiggle my cast, which
caused me to nearly faint from pain.

"Are you okay?" Bruce asked, looking alarmed and
TOUCHING MY ARM.

If I could have clambered out of my own skin and
taken a very fast sprint away from him, I would have.

But I couldn't.

I was trapped.

So I was almost thrilled when I saw Izzy Archibaud.

"Izzy!" I yelled. She whirled around with wide eyes, as
though she'd just seen the ghost of Elvis selling Slurpees
at the corner store.

"Haley," she said. "You scared me. Oh, you POOR
THING! Can I carry your books? Let me walk with you."

For the first time in my life, I was actually grateful to
know Izzy. If that's not a miracle, I don't know what is.

Luckily, Bruce took the hint and disappeared. Honestly,
his crush is pathetic. Does he have any idea how pathetic
he looks? He BLUSHES when I talk to him. Frankly, it

makes me uncomfortable. I'm just not the kind of girl who makes people blush, no matter how "cute" some people (JT!) think I am.

I was so wrapped up in my own thoughts (as well as the act of hopping on crutches, which is more difficult than it looks) (it's very hard on the armpits) that I was only half-listening to Izzy as she rambled on. Then I realized she was talking about Brad.

My Brad.

For a second, I saw red. You know, I'd heard that saying before, but I never knew what it meant. Now I knew: it meant that you saw RED. Literally.

"How is Brad?" I said.

"Haley," she said impatiently. "That's what I'm trying to tell you. He's not the right boy for me. I'm *so* not interested. But we were driven by, like, PASSION. We couldn't stay apart! But his heart, like, belongs to you." (Since when does Izzy talk like a Valley Girl soap star? Seriously, her Future Prospects ™ involve being cast as the crazy-of-the-month on *All My Valley Kids*.)

"Huh," I said. The pieces were slowly falling into place. Brad was seeing Izzy. He was.

My Brad.

Brad "Guys Like Me Don't Get Girls Like You" Brad.

Unexpectedly, a tear rolled down my cheek.

"Are you crying?" she said.

"No," I said. "It's just my leg. It hurts."

"I'm sure it totally does," she said. "Hey, can I sign your cast?"

"Uh, sure," I said. I really didn't know how to answer. I mean, if they were seeing each other, the incident at Brad's party really meant something.

He hadn't been giving her the Heimlich manoeuver.

I know it's stupid. I do. But somehow, I thought that — when I was ready — someone would tell me what had happened and I'd realize, "Oh, of course, he wasn't cheating on me, he was just being kind or thoughtful or whatever."

But that wasn't the case.

And now I wasn't so sure that I wanted him back.

I wasn't that sure about *anything* anymore.

But then, when WAS I sure?

5:50 p.m.
"Haley, is that you?" Melody twinkled from the kitchen.

"Who else would it be?" I said, crashing through the door and nearly falling to my death over a pile of laundry that The Cat was sleeping on.

"I thought it might be your dad," she said. "But I'm glad it's you! There's a message here for you from a ... Steven? Do you know a Steven?"

"No," I said. "It must be a wrong number."

"No," she said. "He specifically asked for you, hon."

Hon? HON? *Argh*, I screamed inside my head.

"Well, thanks," I said, still standing in the front hall wearing my coat and carrying my book bag. Crutches are all very well and good, but they make it v. difficult to go about your day. For example, on an ordinary day, I would have run upstairs and avoided MYG and any further questions/answers, and hid in my room. As it was, the stairs just looked like too much.

I hopped over to the couch and lay down and groaned.

"Want me to rub your back?" Melody said. "I just went to this great massage course and I'm sure that with your broken leg, your muscles are all knotted up."

I shuddered. "Uh, no," I said. "Really, thanks."

Just the idea of her gnarly hands touching me skeeved me out completely. Although they weren't dirty or anything. They were just … calloused. Why would she have such calloused hands? Seems v. odd considering she's a naturopath.

I flicked on the TV and listlessly flicked through the channels. Nothing, nothing, nothing and more nothing. I turned it off and lay back and tried to pretend the pain in my leg was something else. Which obviously didn't work as the pain in my leg was very clearly the pain in my leg.

"Melody," I yelled. "Come here!" (One advantage to being broken is that you can get everyone else to come to you, instead of having to approach them the normal way.)

Melody came running into the room like the house was on fire. "Are you okay?" she shrieked, causing The Bird to excitedly flap out of the half-dead banana tree in the corner and very nearly take my eye out with his wing.

"I'm fine," I said. "I just, um, well, I thought that maybe we could just talk."

"Oh!" she said. I swear, she blushed. She touched her hair. "What do you want to talk about?" she asked finally.

"I don't know," I said. "Whatever."

"Well," she said. "It's funny because there IS something

I wanted to talk to you about, you know, away from your dad."

I could practically see the red flags waving.

"Mmm," I said noncommittally. Frankly, I wasn't just sure that there was anything that I wanted Melody to tell me in confidence away from my dad. Where WAS my dad, anyway? V. unlike him not to be home at this time of day watching *Oprah* and *Dr. Phil*. "Where is he, anyway?"

"He's out," she said. Her eyes shifted from left to right and back again. Now I wasn't raised the child of a hippie for nothing. I know, for example, a thing or two about body language. And the left-right-shift means "I'm lying!"

"What do you want to talk about then?" I said impatiently.

"Well," she said. "I just ... well, I want... I ..."

"Okay," I said. I closed my eyes. Just for a second. Okay, I may have dozed off. There was a patch of sunlight and lying on the couch in the sun was v. relaxing. I can see why my dad enjoyed it for, oh, my whole life. Much preferable to getting a job. Hey, maybe after I graduate, I could make a career of following in my father's footsteps. Albeit without the ring of crime. And grime.

It took me a few minutes to realize that Melody was talking again. "Blah blah blah a family," she said.

Wha — huh? Family?

"What?" I said.

"I just..." She looked at her hands (probably noticing how weird and gnarly they were). She looked up and plastered her weird, maniacal Melody grin on her face.

"I'm sorry!" she chirped. "I've been going on and on. What is it *you* wanted to talk about?"

"Actually," I said. "I wanted to ask what you and Brad talked about all those times on the phone."

"Oh, honey," she said. "You miss him, don't you?"

I shrugged. Okay, I cried. I'm a big baby and my leg hurt and I did miss Brad even though we'd been apart for almost as long as we'd been together, and he was probably away playing hockey and not even thinking about me.

"Aw, baby," she said. And she stroked my forehead.

Okay, I hate Melody. I do. She's just the classic MYG of an aging hippie freak-show. But I have to say that it felt really nice to have someone stroking my forehead while I cried. So I sort of let her. If only for a few minutes.

Just while she told me The Truth.

7:06 p.m.

Phone Call with Kiki:

Me: How much of this did you know?

Kiki: How much of what?

Me: About Brad. And Izzy. And how she, like, went crazy. And stalked him. Why didn't you tell me?

Kiki: [sighing] Honestly, Haley. I don't know. You didn't seem to want to know anything about Brad. Maybe you seemed so ... I don't know ... stressed out when you were with him and so much more relaxed when you weren't that I ... I don't know.

Me: What kind of friend are you? How many other people knew about this?

Kiki: Um, me. And Jules. I guess, JT. And Melody. And
         probably your dad, I guess. That's probably it.

Me: But that's just …

Kiki: I know, it was weird. Especially when he caught
         her looking in his window. Creepy. I always knew
         that girl was a little off.

Me: Poor Brad! That's just crazy! How could you not
         have told me?

Kiki: You didn't want to hear it. I tried. Oh, hang on, it's
         my call waiting.

Hate call waiting.

Hate it.

Hate being put on hold.

Well, I guess it's safe to say that I'm not nearly as important as whoever Kiki had on call waiting. Hung up and
called Jules.

Jules: Hello?

Me: Hi, it's me. Can you talk?

Jules: Hang on, I'm just talking to Kiki on the other line.

Great. My two best friends have now abandoned me and
are talking to each other while I wait pointlessly. I hung up.

"Forget it," I said to no one in particular. My leg was
aching like nobody's business.

Wonder if pain encourages weight loss. After all, only
three weeks until trip to glamorous LA with Jules, the
Prettiest of Them All. And I know I'm the grossest of them
all, but it would be nice if I were a bit thinner for the LA trip.

Short-Term Goals:

1. Finish weird art-project sculpture self-portrait (should be easy, can just make clay effigy and encase one leg in giant white cast).

2. Lose weight in order to look très thin and glamorous in LA.

3. Get short-term job that earns much money in order to be able to buy clothes in LA.

4. Find out if Jules still wants me to go to LA even though am broken.

5. ~~Call Brad~~

6. Figure out how to shower with leg in garbage bag as "sponge bathing" is not good enough and does nothing to get hair satisfactorily clean. Besides, miss smell of cinnamon-bun shower gel. Mmm.

9:30 p.m.

Dear Junior:

Am going to call Brad. Feel weird.

I can do it though.

I'm cute.

Think I might have crush on Brad.

Weird.

Okay. Am doing it.

Bye,

Haley

9:38 p.m.

Have dialed first six digits of Brad's number.

9:40 p.m.
Twice.

9:49 p.m.
Three times.

10:01 p.m.
Eighteen times.

10:30 p.m.
Am too scared to call Brad. Am giant coward destined to never leave this house again. Will probably become agoraphobic and also really large, like people who never leave their houses and fry whole chickens in fry pans that they keep by their beds.

Question: Do they have people bring in raw chickens for this purpose? And if so, would it not be just as easy to bring in an already-cooked chicken to reduce the fire-hazard qualities of cooking a chicken directly beside bed? And if these people have raw chickens, do they also have small fridges within arm's length of their beds? And if so, what else do they keep in there?

Hmm.

Maybe will call Brad tomorrow.

▶ ▶ ▶

Saturday, April 12

MOOD	Okay
HAIR	Not horrible, could use conditioning

HEALTH	Broken leg, possible clotting
HOROSCOPE	Obstacles from the past will be removed, but be careful of starting new things.
~~JT SIGHTINGS~~	~~irrelevant~~

3:00 p.m.

"So have you called him yet?" asked Jules, critically eyeing her new highlights in the bathroom mirror. (They looked perfect, blonde and shimmery. For the record.)

"No," I said, making a face at myself. My roots had fully grown out, giving my head a weird, bleach-tip effect that might have been cute on a twelve year old. If that twelve year old was also either a rap star or a snow-boarding champion. I cleared my throat. It was on the tip of my tongue to ask if she was still mad at me for trying to steal JT, not that I *was* trying to steal JT, but she might have thought that I was. To be honest, she hadn't said more than a dozen words to me since. So I couldn't be wrong to assume she was mad.

"Are you —?" I started to say.

"God, I'm lucky," she said, picking an imaginary eyelash off her cheek.

"Uh?" I said.

"My features are totally symmetrical," she said. "Did you know that's how beauty is measured?"

"No," I said. "I mean, yes." I did know this. Actually, I think I told her this to begin with.

Jules flicked her hair back and moved closer to the mirror to inspect something in her eyeball. (Mostly so she could look at herself REALLY closely without looking

like she was examining herself REALLY CLOSELY.)
(At least she has the sense to know that her painful vanity
is annoying for others to witness.)

"I think you should," she said. "Especially if you're going
to be all moody about it. I don't want it to ruin the trip."

"Oh," I said. "Right. Well, I wouldn't want my life crises
getting in the way."

"Don't be nasty," she said. "I didn't have to invite you,
you know."

"I know," I sighed. "I'm sorry, Jules. I'm just freaking
out. It's stupid. I'm an idiot."

"What did Kiki say?" she said.

"Um," I said. I tried to remember. Honestly, I don't
think Kiki called me back after she put me on hold to talk
to Jules. Secretly, I think that Kiki is not nearly as good
a friend as she used to be, since the arrival of Prince S.
"I don't think she said anything."

"Yeah," Jules said. "She's really wrapped up in that guy."

"Stephano," I said. And blushed.

"Did you just BLUSH?" Jules said incredulously.

"No," I said. "I mean, I don't know. You can't ask me if
I'm blushing, it makes me blush."

"Oh god," she said, rolling her eyes. "Is there anyone's
boyfriend that you DON'T have a little crush on?"

"I don't have a crush on anyone," I lied.

"Haley," she said turning to face me. "You will ALWAYS
have a crush on someone that you can't have." Then she
turned and left the room. I didn't bother to follow her.

Was she right?

Was I THAT girl? The one who was always crushing on unavailable boys?

I stuck my tongue out at myself in the mirror.

Note to Self: Get your hair coloured. You look dumb.

Also, CALL BRAD.

Maybe.

5:12 p.m.

Dear Junior:

Good news! The "Steven" who was calling was not actually a prank call. (Prank callers rarely leave messages, anyway.) "Steven" is kind, lanky man from The UnBurger.

Steven has offered me a job!

It's not actually AT The UnBurger because, according to him, I "would not be safe" around food.

Nope, it's in the back office. Some sort of an accounting thing. How hard can that be? It's possible that I told him during the interview that I wanted to be an accountant when I grew up. And now he will "mentor" me.

Hmm. Sounds quite creepy, really. Wonder if tall, lanky Steven has suspicious and gross crush on me. Will be very careful. Anyway, have told him I'll be away for one weekend in May, but other than that, the weekends are all his!

Obviously, except for the late-sleeping parts and the social-evening parts.

Love,

Rich Girl

► ► ►

Monday, April 14

MOOD	Tired
HAIR	Tied back as is unfixable
HEALTH	Tired AND broken
HOROSCOPE	Hang out and have fun today! The stars say that today is your day to shine in a crowd!
~~JT SIGHTINGS~~	~~irrelevant~~

4:01 p.m.

This is no way to get rich.

For one thing, Steven is paying me "training" wage. Which translates roughly to "nothing," or six dollars an hour.

Gah.

Hate accounting. "Accounting" is apparently code for "entering pointless numbers into a computer without knowing or caring what they are and/or what (if anything) they mean, in a darkened, creepy room behind The UnBurger that smells of rotting UnMeat and other questionable rudenesses.

This has been the longest hour of my life. Made worse by the fact that every time Steven comes to "check" on me (read: leer at me), I must be a) awake, and b) typing.

This is horrible.

Perhaps will reconsider college.

5:14 p.m.

Note written on back of pizza coupon found in book bag:

Steven very rudely took away my laptop. Said I was not

being a "team player." Hmm. Don't suppose I will last very long at The UnBurger. No matter. Tonight is the night. Tonight is the night that I'm going to call Brad.

6:30 p.m.
When my shift finally ended (longest three hours EVER), I raced home to drop off my stuff. If by "raced," I mean "crutched slowly and painfully to the bus stop and took the longest-bus-ride-ever home as we stopped at every stop." I was supposed to be going over to Jules' to try on her new clothes (for the trip) and work up my courage (i.e., drink from her mother's vodka supply).

I crutched around the house as quickly as I could, dropping off stuff and stuffing a soy dog in my mouth. Gross. As I was leaving, I was snagged by my dad, who was looking quite morose, I must say. Even for him. He wasn't even singing, like he always is. Instead he was sort of humming. Glumly.

Glumly humming.

I glanced at my watch. I was late, but that was okay. I mean, it was just Jules, right? She could wait. I pushed The Cat off the couch and sat down next to my dad.

"What's up?" I said.

"Nothing, my beautiful daughter," he said, tapping his leg. (His leg being encased in a violent green/orange plaid golf pant of some sort.)

"Oh," I said. The house was weirdly quiet. It took me a minute to realize that the MYG was missing.

"Where's Melody?" I said.

"She went to visit her coven," he said.

"Her COVEN?" I said. "Seriously?"

"No," he said. "Nope. Just kidding. Her friends. She isn't a witch, you know. Anyway, she thought that you and I might, you know, hang out for a while."

"Oh," I said. "It's just that …"

"Go," he said. "I know you have to go out. Don't worry about your old dad."

And in that moment, it was weird. Because he did look totally old. It kind of freaked me out. I hugged him.

"Thanks, Dad," I said. I was kind of choked up. Really, I must be premenstrual or something.

"Sure," he said. "I've got stuff to watch anyway. Me and The Cat are going to do some room-temperature yoga."

"Sure, Dad," I said. I felt bad leaving him. I did. But I had to go.

"Bottoms up!" said Jules, raising her glass to me. It looked suspiciously like vodka. Straight up. I know from experience (does NO ONE remember the Valentine's Ball except me?) that vodka + me = disaster. Maybe I'd be okay if I mixed it with something, but I'm not a vodka-straight-up kind of girl.

"Uh," I said. "I don't think so. Not for me."

"Don't be such a baby," she said. "I know you're younger than everyone else, but you're not, like, 12." She looked amused. There is nothing worse than being the source of Jules' amusement. Believe me, I've been on the receiving end of it often enough to know.

"Okay," I sighed, "but just one."

► ► ►

Tuesday, April 15

MOOD	Snappy
HAIR	Trying to escape pained head
HEALTH	Wretched
HOROSCOPE	Be careful of friends and family today — they may be trying to tell you something you don't want to hear! Stop and smell the flowers.
~~JT SIGHTINGS~~	~~irrelevant~~

7:46 a.m.

Dear Junior:

Suspect made big fool of self last night. Don't remember anything.

Suspect vodka has exacerbated brain tumour and now can't move. Brain is like runny egg slopping around in skull, only skull is sharp. And swollen.

Gah. ON A SCHOOL NIGHT! What was I thinking?

Think may have phoned Brad. Must call Jules and find out after terrible cursed headache has passed.

On the plus side, my head hurts so much that I can barely feel my leg.

Hmm. Wonder if have any painkillers left …

3:17 p.m.

Have slept through the following:

1. The whole day of school. Okay, I went, but I wasn't really THERE.

2. Dad and MYG having huge fight and MYG taking a suitcase and leaving.
3. The phone ringing twenty-thousand times (according to dad, but could be exaggeration).
4. A small fire in the kitchen.
5. My hangover.

4:09 p.m.

I am very worried about Dad. He says that it isn't a big deal. That if you love someone as much as he loves MYG (he LOVES her? Really?), you have to let her figure stuff out for herself.

He's actually inordinately cheerful.

This could be because I caught him making a burger in the microwave. Am fairly sure that microwaving beef is just inviting E. coli, but he wouldn't listen to reason. Perhaps his cheerfulness is just a mask for his truly suicidal inner thoughts. Will stay home and be with Dad in his hour of need instead of going, well, upstairs and doing my homework.

Am sure I can make some sort of sculpture tomorrow morning before school that will meet art requirements.

5:36 p.m.

Movies I Have Argued about Watching with My Dad:
1. *Beetlejuice*
2. *16 Candles*
3. *Friday the 13th*
4. *Animal House*

Movies Actually Watched: 0

Feel sick, as though I've eaten too much junk food. Yuck.

Had to leave as Dad spontaneously burst into tears during the first gross killing scene in *Friday the 13th*. Am worried that he is sublimating his true feelings of sadness about Melody.

I almost miss her myself. Well, a bit. I mean, The Cat threw up and I had to clean it up myself.

Also, maybe she's not so bad. Anyway, is nothing to do with me. Will just keep my mouth shut and go back to the living room because I can hear the theme song to *St. Elmo's Fire* (Dad must have switched them out), which is a very beautiful and sad movie that I've only seen 47 times before.

Oh, the phone!

Brad!

Oh my God. More later.

6:10 p.m.

Hmmm.

Have spoken to Brad. Am not sure how the conversation went or what it means, so will write it down and analyze each syllable:

Me: Hello?

Brad: Haley? Are you okay?

Me: Sure. Why?

Brad: I thought you might have a hangover.

Me: Oooooohhhh.

Brad: Are you there?

Me: Yes? For a minute there I thought I might have died from humiliation.

Brad: Ha ha ha.

Me: Um.

Brad: So I was thinking maybe you wanted to come to my game tonight and then after maybe we can talk.

Me: Ummm.

Brad: I totally understand if you don't want to.

Me: No! No! No! I mean, yes!

Brad: Okay. So.

Me: So.

Brad: Okay, bye.

Now did I miss the part where he said, "I miss you and I'm sorry and I want to get back together?"

Are we back together?

Wish I had taped conversation so that Kiki and Jules could analyze with me. But Kiki is out with Stephano ("studying," as IF) and Jules is having a "wardrobe consultation" to prepare her for WITPOTA (*Who Is the Prettiest of Them All*) (or "wit-pota," as I prefer to think of it as). (Or "With Potato," which accurately describes how Jules will look when she shows up with me.)

In any event, my more immediate problem is how I'm going to get to the game, what with the encased-in-plaster-immovable leg and lack of available-friends-with-cars. I mean, I can't take the bus, can I?

Does Brad even KNOW about my leg? I'm sure he knows,

but did he think of that when he told me to meet him at the game?

Perhaps Brad is v. selfish and doesn't care that I have to hobble on one leg (note to whoever invented "walking" casts: HA BLOODY HA) and can't actually drive anyway.

Huh.

Was just contemplating asking Dad for cab money when the phone rang again.

Me: Hellllooo.
JT (!):   Brad says I have to give you, like, a ride to the game. So, like, I'll be there in like 10 minutes.

Click.

Wonder how it's possible that I've maintained a crush on someone who cannot complete an entire sentence without using the word "like" 10 times.

Note to Self: You do NOT have a crush on JT. You have a crush on Brad and you may be able to get back together with him tonight. DO NOT BLOW THIS, YOU IMBECILE.

Possible Outfits to Wear Tonight to Win Back Brad's Heart (while also staying warm):
1. Really cute pants with adorable cashmere sweater (problem: do not own such an outfit)
2. Really cute jeans with adorable sweater of any fabric (see above)

3. Really ugly jeans with old sweater (problem: cannot get jeans over cast)

4. Really gross sweatpants encrusted with some sort of raspberry jam spill and a sweatshirt (problem: this outfit looks/smells like it has been in a box of kitty litter for a week)

5. Pajamas

6. Some sort of skirt (as skirt may fit over gross cast) and tights. With one cute boot and some sort of wool sock to protect toes on broken side from freezing. Wonder if Dad will paint toes for me on bad side as can't reach. No, don't have that kind of time.

7. Nothing. Don't go as do not have anything to wear and will look too revolting for words causing both Brad and JT (it's NOT a date, he's just GIVING ME A RIDE) to a) get sick, or b) laugh at me, or c) wonder who I am.

Argh.

Time spent getting ready: 12 minutes
Time needed to get ready and look decent: 4 hours
Makeup: Not bad
Hair: Not totally horrible though should not have dyed it TODAY as naturally head now smells like gross chemicals, but at least is shiny, and am sure Brad won't notice that left ear is also unusual copper-ish colour. Copper hair makes eyes look greener and therefore was worth it.
Clothes: Stretchy black miniskirt (I know, I know) over tights with one leg cut off so cast can fit through and cute high-ish heeled Mary Jane on good foot. On bad foot, am

wearing large black sock. Red cardigan with silk flower on it over stretchy white tank-top (Brad's team colours are red/black/white, so feel like I look okay-ish, although will likely freeze to death).

Jewellery: None, as don't want to be overdressed or look as though I'm "trying too hard."

Of course, entire outfit looks as though I'm trying to hard.

JT beeped in the driveway. Which luckily gave me just enough time to trade cute sweater in for a not-trying-too-hard T-shirt that said "FCUK" on it.

May be cold in T-shirt but feel like "not-trying-too-hard" is more important than "not-freezing-to-death."

10:00 ish p.m.

Dear Junior:

We're back together! Not only did Brad's team win 6-1, but he played really well. (From what I could tell. Had to spend much time at concession getting hot drinks as it's very cold in an ice arena when wearing only a T-shirt.) (Also, cute concession boy remembered me and wanted to hear about how I broke my leg.) (Was v. sympathetic.)

Not that I care about the concession boy, for goodness sake.

I care only about Brad. My heart belongs entirely to Brad and my eyes will never again stray to any other boys.

Ever.

Brad took me for a romantic walk after the game (and gave me a jersey to wear to stave off the shivering) (although romantic walks are more enjoyable when not on crutches) (in the sand) and explained about Izzy. (Frankly, do not care if never hear the name "Izzy" again.)

And then he kissed me and I remembered why I liked him so much to begin with.

Really, he has very dreamy blue-ish coloured eyes.

Then we looked at the stars and talked and talked. Okay, we just sort of sat there, but it was v. comfortable. Okay, it might have been more comfortable if we weren't sitting on a flea-infested log, but am sure that antihistamines will reduce swelling brought on by allergic reaction to flea bites.

Saw three shooting stars and wished that Brad and I would stay together forever, or at least long enough that we can go to prom together.

Love,

Haley Stars-in-her-eyes-Girl

MAY

Friday, May 2

MOOD	Tired
HAIR	Flat and limp, much like self
HEALTH	Difficult to say
HOROSCOPE	Travelling long distances will make you homesick. Expect turbulence!
~~JT SIGHTINGS~~	~~irrelevant~~

6:00ish a.m.

"Haley, will you HURRY UP!" yelled Jules. She was smoking like a chimney. If every cigarette removes two minutes from your life, by my estimation she'll be dead in 16 minutes. Which is good because then perhaps she will stop yelling at me and help me instead.

It's VERY DIFFICULT to drag one of those wheeled suitcase things (borrowed from Kiki) while on CRUTCHES. Does no one understand this? Never mind that I'm beginning to get blisters under my arms. Have strapped sponges on to arm-things to make it softer, but they just look ugly and unfashionable and Jules made me take them off in the cab. She is really stupidly nervous and not even slightly excited about going to Disneyland (the hotel where the auditions are is right across the street from the Magic Kingdom), which I can't understand. I mean, we'll have a great time. Sure, I won't be able to go on rides or anything, but that's okay as am terrified of heights and of going fast. I'm just not a "ride" person.

She's mad that it's not "really LA." Well, she's right. It's Anaheim. But still, it's better than staying home, no? And it's free. Free-ish anyway. Her dad is paying. He thinks that if I go, too, we'll be "safe" because I'm a "good influence." Naturally this is because he hasn't seen me since I was six.

I was a serious six-year-old. What can I say? I was mature for my age.

To be honest with you, I think neither Jules nor I are ready for LA. At least, I'm not ready to run around after Jules IN LA, what with all the movie stars and the like who are probably rushing in and out of the Starbucks there. I'm especially not ready because I'm on crutches. It's v. hard to be glamorous while hopping with sore armpits.

No thanks to Jules, who just went on ahead, it took me 45 minutes to get through security. Apparently they believed that it was possible for me to be smuggling some sort of bomb in my leg cast. Now I'm all for heightened security. God knows I'd hate to be on a crashing plane. But think it was v. unnecessary for them to make me take off my tights so that they could attempt to peer down my cast with flashlights. Finally, they let me go.

But reluctantly.

As though it was common for 16-year-old girls to carry war weaponry in their BROKEN LEGS.

When I finally caught up with Jules, she was in the departures area, flipping through *Vogue* and running her hand through her hair. Question: how is it possible that her hair grows this fast? My hair is still well above my shoulders, in that it barely reaches my chin. And HER hair, shorn off above her shoulders in February is now almost back at her bra strap. Wonder what vitamins Jules takes? Ask her when she is in better mood.) I personally find *Vogue* quite boring. The clothes are expensive and the articles are dull. I prefer *YM*. And *Jane*. I mean, I love that "prank" column. That's funny. *Vogue*? *Vogue* is not funny.

I would have gone to the newsstand and bought a magazine of my own, but seeing as I couldn't walk, it seemed like too much trouble. Instead, I satisfied myself by hanging over Jules' shoulder and making comments about the clothes in *Vogue*. That is, until she turned on me like some kind of enraged cat and shrieked, "Would you BACK OFF?"

"Hmmf," I said. "You're welcome for coming with you so you have someone to yell at when you start to freak out."

"Well," she said. "You weren't my first choice. But Kiki couldn't miss class and my dad wouldn't let me go with JT. Although SHE would have liked that." (She glowered at her mother, who was sitting somewhere else so we could "pretend to be on our own" but also probably so that she could pretend to not be the mother of a teenager.) "So I was pretty much stuck with you so as not to be stuck entirely with HER."

"Gee, thanks," I said.

"No worries," she said. "I wish we could smoke in here. It's stupid that you can't smoke in airports. I hate it. And you can't go outside, so ... argh. I'm having a nic fit."

I giggled. I admit it. There's something about the phrase "nic fit" that cracks me up.

"WHAT?" she said.

"Nothing," I said. "Uh, your hair looks good." (The best way to diffuse Jules is to heap compliments on her. She is much nicer when she feels pretty.) (Though how Jules could ever feel less than pretty is beyond me as she is indisputably pretty.)

"So what do you have to do when we get there?" I said. "Is there some sort of program?"

"Haley," she rolled her eyes. "It's not a circus. It's just an audition."

"Sorrreee," I said. Like I know what an audition's like.

"Oh," she said. "I forgot that you wouldn't know what that's like. Well, you pretty much just walk into a room and the judges look at you and ask you questions and then put you through to the next round."

"Huh," I said. "Cool."

She went back to *Vogue*.

"You think we'll have time to go to Disneyland?" I said.

She shot me a withering glance. "I doubt it," she said. "We won't have time to do much of anything."

"Drag," I said. I looked around. It had suddenly occurred to me that JT had told me ages ago that he was going to surprise Jules. I wondered where he was. I craned my neck to check out the crowd by the windows.

"Haley," Jules sighed. "Would you stop making such a spectacle of yourself?"

"I'm not," I snapped. Really, I get v. sick of Jules talking down to me all the time. Besides, I was just looking for HER boyfriend.

"How's JT?" I said.

"He's fine," she said suspiciously. "Why would you suddenly ask me that out of the blue?"

"No reason," I said.

"You've got to let it go," she said.

"Let what go?" I said.

"Your stupid crush on MY boyfriend," she said. "Honestly. He's with ME now. Even though you keep, like, calling him up. That doesn't mean that he's, like, interested in you."

"Of course he isn't," I said. "He's with YOU. What would he see in me?"

"Exactly," she said. "How's Brad?"

"He's great," I said loyally. "He's perfect. In fact, I've never been happier. He's so thoughtful. He's so nice. He's so …"

"Okay," she said. "Great. I'm glad you're happy. Now could you be quiet? I need some time to READ."

"Why?" I said. "Is there going to be some sort of fashion test?"

"Don't be stupid," she said. "God."

I stuck out my tongue and lay back on the chair. There was another hour before we were set to depart. Why we had to be at the airport four hours early is a complete mystery to me. They could satisfactorily strip-search every single passenger here in four hours and still have time left for coffee.

And for reading *Vogue*.

I sighed dramatically and took out my cell phone. It was only six-thirty in the morning, so it's not like I could call anyone. Instead, I started flipping through the ring signals to choose a better one. I love those ring signals that are songs.

"HALEY," screamed Jules (causing everyone to turn and look at us). "You're getting on my VERY LAST NERVE."

"SORRY," I yelled back. "IF YOU DON'T LIKE IT, GO SIT WITH YOUR MOTHER."

Honestly, don't know how Jules became my "best friend." Wait, I do know. It's because when we were four years old, she hadn't learned to be a TOTAL COW yet.

Hmmf. I hate Jules.

Terrible Ways to Die (List Made on In-Flight Magazine While Jules Ignored Me All the Way to Anaheim):

1. Plane crash (is this turbulence normal?).
2. Bungee jumping (still have nightmares of horrible falling-off-bridge feeling).
3. Snake/spider bite. Especially if out in the jungle with no way to call for help.
4. Killed by crazed masked psycho while camping in cabin in woods with friends on summer vacation.

Reasons Why I Hope Jules Gets Over Herself So We Can Have Fun in Anaheim:

1. Am slightly bored of myself.
2. Am quite bored of this plane.
3. Am bored.

Things I Miss about Home:
1. Dad
2. Brad
3. Kiki

I know, will fill out this fancy Alaska Air postcard and send it to self at home.

Dear Haley:
   Having a great time, wish you were …

We finally got to the hotel at 2:30 in the afternoon after nearly being killed by a psychotic cab driver. Okay, he may not have been psychotic, but suspect he learned to drive by reading *Driving for Dummies*. Although, who am I to judge?

Note to Self: MUST get driver's licence before graduating from high school.

The hotel was gorgeous. Really lovely. For one thing, it was HUGE. I've never seen a hotel that big before. Sure, I'm just a girl from a medium-size, unglamorous city, but we don't have hotels like that. It must have had a thousand rooms in it. And swimming pools everywhere.
   Also, millions on millions of a) small children wearing Mickey paraphernalia, and b) beautiful girls. I felt about as attractive as a piece of chewed gum on someone's shoe. Which is fine. I mean, I'm used to that. But the giant cast

that made my leg resemble a marshmallow was not helping my self-esteem.

Not that I have any self-esteem.

Anyway, after an exhausting check-in procedure (it must
have been exhausting because Jules' mom managed to
break a sweat doing it), we finally managed to get to our
room (on a separate floor from Jules' mom). I flopped down
on the bed.

"I'm exhausted," I said. "Who knew travel was so tiring?"

"I'm used to it," said Jules.

Right, like she travels ALL THE TIME. Not.

"Whatever," I said. Frankly, I'd had it up to my eyeballs
with Jules.

"You know," she said. "You used to be nice."

"So did *you*," I said.

To be perfectly honest, I didn't really know that I was
in a fight with Jules until I was actually IN it. It didn't feel
like a fight.

I know it WAS a fight, however, because Jules turned on
her heel, grabbed her purse and room key and said, "See
you later." And left. Slamming the door behind her (sort of).
Hotel room doors don't exactly slam.

Huh, I thought. I flicked on the TV. It was showing a
constant loop of Disney cartoons. I'll just watch for a
minute, I thought.

When I woke up, it was dark. The TV was off, and Jules
was a snoring lump on the next bed. And I had to pee like
crazy. Honestly, sometimes I think I was born with a
smaller than normal bladder.

Or perhaps I had a bladder infection. (Symptoms: urgency, frequency, burning on urination, etc.)

I tiptoed to the bathroom.

Fine, I stood up and immediately tripped over Jules' suitcase and fell to the ground screaming. I assure you that when YOUR leg is broken, you will know exactly how horrible the pain is when you fall on your already shattered limb.

"Shut up," said Jules.

"Grrr," I growled. Then I lay on the floor and cried for a bit. It was v. uncomfortable. Finally, I got up and peed and went to bed. If Jules thought I was going to be supportive of her tomorrow, she was TOTALLY WRONG.

I'd had enough of Jules.

And I MEAN it.

▶ ▶ ▶

Saturday, May 3

MOOD	California sunny!
HAIR	Oddly frizzy!
HEALTH	Sarcastic!
HOROSCOPE	Not available … at least, haven't found one yet
JT SIGHTINGS	???

10:00 ish a.m.
We were woken up by a knock on the door.

"Room service!" a voice yelled. Which was v. disorienting because I'd been dreaming that I was at home.

"Dad?" I said, hopefully.

"It's ROOM SERVICE," Jules said disdainfully. "Ohmygod what time is it, am I late?"

The last part all came out in a single blurt.

"Um," I said. "It's 10:30 a.m."

The knock on the door was repeated. "ROOOM SERVICE!" the voice yelled.

"Shit," said Jules. "Shit shit shit shit shit shit. Why didn't my stupid MOTHER wake me up? What is the point of her anyway?"

She buried her head in her pillow. Which was fine. I mean, there was nothing that I wanted to do more than walk on my broken leg to the door in my pajama top (the bottoms didn't fit over my stupid cast.)

But I did it. I mean, I'm the SUPPORTIVE FRIEND.

"Supportive friend," I mumbled under my breath.

"WHAT?" screamed Jules. Honestly, she was v. hysterical. We still had half an hour before she had to be at her stupid audition anyway.

"Nothing!" I chirped, doing my best impression of Melody. (Hmm. Has just occurred to me that perhaps Melody hates me and her chirping is not, in fact, her normal way of talking, but rather her way of talking to ME because she HATES me.)

I opened the door as well as I could without falling over.

"We didn't order…" I said.

And then I stopped. Because there was JT holding an armful of flowers (okay, it looked like he'd stolen them from the front lobby and they were dripping all over his clothes, but still) and grinning like crazy.

For a second, my heart quit beating altogether. And then

I remembered that he was Jules' boyfriend. I stepped out of the way without saying anything.

Really, it was all I could do not to throw up.

"JT!" Jules cooed. "What are you doing here?" She got up out of bed (wearing cute pink tank top and boy shorts, looking gorgeous. Naturally.) "THANK you! Oooh! How did you get here?"

Seriously, it was nauseating. I went into the bathroom, as there was nowhere else to go in the tiny room. Which only lasted about 10 seconds, before Jules came blowing in like a hurricane to "get ready."

Which left me, grossly unclean and half-naked, alone with JT.

"Uh," I said.

Luckily, he totally ignored me. I don't even think he noticed when I took an armful of clothes and hid in the closet to get changed. If he did, he didn't say anything or really change position on my bed (!) where he was completely glued to the TV.

"Uh," I tried again. It was easier to talk to him when I was dressed. I mean, it's hard to talk to anyone when your bum is hanging out.

"Shh," he said.

Which nicely put an end to that.

It took Jules an hour to get ready. I wanted to point out that being half an hour late for an audition was bad form, but I didn't bother as I didn't want her to say any of the following:
1. How would you know?
2. Shut up!

3. Don't be a cow.
4. Go away.

Actually, I wouldn't have minded "go away." Secretly, I still
wanted to go to Disneyland. Sure, I was on crutches. And
sure, it would suck going by myself. But it would be considerably better than trailing after Jules. Of course, I ended
up standing (all the chairs were taken) in a room full of
bizarrely pretty girls who were all waiting their turn and
flicking their hair. I've never seen so many people flicking
their hair simultaneously. It was really v. scary. I rolled my
eyes at JT, but his own eyes had glazed over. Probably, for
him, he'd died and gone to heaven. In any event, I'd become
immediately, completely and totally invisible.

I sighed.

Jules huffed back from the table. "That fat woman was
a total cow about me being late," she snarled.

"Well, you WERE late," I pointed out.

"Yeah," she said. "But she didn't have to be rude about it."
She leaned against the wall and sighed. "Now I have to
stand here for, like, four hours."

"FOUR HOURS?" I said. Okay, I screamed.

"Oh, sorry," she said. "Does that BORE you?"

"No," I said. "I mean, yes. I mean, no. I mean…"

"Haley," she said. "You're making me nervous. Go away."
So there it was.

"Fine," I said. And turned on my heel (as well as I could
anyway) and crutched off. I was relieved to get out of
there. It was hard to breathe in there. There was just way
too much "cute" going on. I gagged.

"Hideous," I said, to no one in particular.

"What's hideous?" said a voice near my ear.

I jumped about a mile. Which would have been fine if I hadn't been standing right beside some sort of goldfish pond. Which, naturally, I fell into.

"I'm sorry," said the voice. And a hand reached down to help me up.

"Hi," she said. "Are you okay? I'm so sorry."

I don't want to get too hysterical here when I'm telling this story, but let me just say two words:

Molly. Ringwald.

"Molly Ringwald!" I gasped.

"You know who I am?" she laughed. "I would have thought you were too young. Are you okay?"

"Room," I said. "Clothes, is okay." (Since when did English become my second language?)

"Okay," she said. "If you're sure you're okay. Nice to meet you."

And then she disappeared.

Molly Ringwald!

Ha. Who would believe it? I couldn't wait to get upstairs and call Dad and tell him. I mean, I figured he'd be excited.

But when I called, there was no answer. I sat down on the edge of the bed. Our room was a mess. Clothes were everywhere. Jules' bed was marginally less messy than mine, so I sat on hers. I swear, I had no idea that Jules even KEPT a diary. I thought she was reading some sort of book.

So when I accidentally happened to catch sight of the pink book in her suitcase, I can't be blamed for taking a look.

How was I to know?

Oh God, I'm a terrible friend. Jules is secretly v. nervous and afraid. Gosh, when you read her diary, you'd never know that she was a terrible cow.

Note to Self: Stop being so mean to Jules.

Note to Self2: Also, find out what this entry "cnt stnd JT, is stpd/rude, but lks gd! Lk nice pr pnts. Keep 4 prm."

Note to Self3: Obviously, it means that Jules is only with JT because he will look good on her arm for prom. Really, have no respect for Jules. She's very shallow.
But it also means that she doesn't really like him.
Which means ...
Am terrible friend for even thinking such things. Also, am girlfriend of Brad.
Delete previous entry. Except the part about Molly Ringwald. THAT part was cool.

"Molly Ringwald said I was AVERAGE," said Jules when she got back to our room. Finally. Her eyes were spitting fire. Seriously, you wouldn't want to get in the way of that.
"But it was Molly Ringwald," I said. "I mean, that's cool. Who knew she was one of the judges?"
"She said AVERAGE," cried Jules. She even worked up a tear. Hmmm. Perhaps she was really upset.
"Are you really upset?" I said.
"YES," she said. "Where's JT?"

"I don't know," I said. "I mean, I thought he was with you."

"He wasn't," she said shortly. "He got bored with waiting and disappeared. It's SO great that I have such SUPPORT-IVE friends."

"Well, it WAS boring," I pointed out. "You wouldn't have stood there with me for four hours."

"Yes, I would," she said stubbornly.

"Fine," I sighed. "Want to get some dinner or find your mom or something?"

"No," she said. "I'm never eating again. Did you see how thin some of those girls were?"

"Uh, yes," I said. "They looked hungry."

"Ha ha," she said. "Very funny. You go ahead. I'm going to wait for JT. Or my mom. Or someone who actually cares about me."

"Jerk," I said.

She glared at me.

"Look," I said. "I don't want to fight. Can't we just have fun? I'm sorry your audition was horrible. I don't know what you want me to say."

"Nothing," she said. She lit a cigarette and lay down on the carpet. (Gross. Who knows what's been down there? There is something inherently disgusting about carpets. They are just, well, gross.)

"So JT's dad and my mom are out to dinner. How lame is THAT?"

"They are?" I said, surprised. I mean, it hadn't occurred to me to wonder how JT had got here. He's rich. I just figured he'd ... I don't know, actually. I hadn't thought about it.

"I'm sure JT's dad is just being, um, nice," I said.

"Right," said Jules, rolling her eyes. "Like my mom is the kind of person who goes out for dinner with a rich, good-looking guy and doesn't try to get her claws into him."

"Hmm," I said. "She's never flirted with MY dad."

"Come ON, Haley," she said crossly. "Look at your DAD."

"Oh," I said. "Anyway, JT's dad is hardly going to cheat on JT's mum."

"Right," she said. "Haley, one day you're going to figure out that all men are cheaters. Look at BRAD."

"Ouch," I said.

"Sorry," she said.

I shook my head. I mean, what did I know? She was probably right. At least, in her world, where you dated a guy just so you'd have a good-looking date for prom.

"Let's order dinner," I said. "And just hang out here until they all come back or whatever."

"Okay," she said.

And just like that we were (sort of) friends again.

▶ ▶ ▶

Sunday, May 3

MOOD	Okay, at least it's sunny
HAIR	Okay
HEALTH	Okay
HOROSCOPE	Don't know, as don't have newspaper.
~~JT SIGHTINGS~~	~~irrelevant~~

9:17 a.m.

Think JT's dad and Jules' mom not only are NOT having an affair but possibly hate each other. V. weird atmosphere over breakfast.

"Disneyland was so cool," said JT. "You guys totally missed it."

"I know," I said, raising my eyebrow at him and looking significantly at Jules, who hadn't spoken a word since finding out that she hadn't made the cut.

In a weird sort of way, I was glad she hadn't. I mean, if she had, she would have been TOTALLY UNBEARABLE for the rest of time. But this sort of sucked, too. Now she was scarily quiet. Which could mean that she was about to tear a big piece out of one of us.

I just hoped it wasn't me.

"Disneyland," she said witheringly, "is for CHILDREN."

"Uh," he said.

"But," she continued, her eyes steel-cold, "that WOULD suit you, wouldn't it? Because you are a CHILD. A sad, stupid CHILD."

"Um," I said.

"What?" she said, flashing her eyes onto me.

"Nothing!" I said.

"Jules," said her mother. "Be nice."

"Be NICE?" she said. "Like YOU? I don't have a chance to be nice, Mom. Because *you're* a nasty snob. You've taught *me* how to be a nasty snob. So now *I'm* a nasty snob. I'm an AVERAGE-LOOKING nasty snob with," she read slowly from the piece of paper she was clutching, "a plain nose."

I giggled. I mean, it wasn't funny. I swear, I don't know why I laughed.

"OH SHUT UP!" she yelled. And then she ran out of the room crying. I would have followed her if I could have. I swear. I mean, I might have. But there was too much going on at the table, and besides, having a broken leg makes fast movement impossible.

"Wow," said JT. "That was …"

"Yeah," I said.

And we bonded for a second. Sort of. I mean, he looked at me. He actually looked kind of upset.

"Are you okay?" Jules' mom was saying to him worriedly. I suddenly had this weird flashback to when she stole Jules' LAST boyfriend. So you could say I was just looking out for Jules (who is my b. friend, after all) when I jumped up and dumped the orange juice all over Jules' mom's lap.

It was the least I could do.

"Supportive friend," I said.

"Haley, what are you DOING?" Jules' mom yelled.

"Sorry?" I said.

JT laughed.

His dad stood up. "You people are crazy and we have a flight to catch." He grabbed JT's chair and pulled it out. JT stood up.

"See you," he said amiably.

Hmm. Maybe Jules was right. There was something a bit … vacant about JT.

Really, don't think I even HAVE a crush on him anymore.

Weirdly enough, I want to go home.

Things I Miss about Home:
1. Normal people.
2. My bed.
3. Brad (i.e., a normal, intelligent, nice, cute-ish boy).
4. Kiki.
5. Everything.

5:45 p.m.
The flight back was the longest of my life. I won't bore you with it. It's enough to say that there were babies on the laps of people on both sides of me.

Babies who BARFED.

Seriously.

Gross.

Note to Self: Look up on internet to see if anything contagious can be passed on from having to inhale the repulsive smell of baby barf for several hours.

Number of times Jules glowered at me: 8

Total number of words Jules spoke to me: 4 ("Why are you staring?")

Total number of words Jules and her mom spoke to each other: 0

Weird factor of trip: 10,000

Likelihood of ever travelling with Jules again: 1 in 10,000,987,891

▶ ▶ ▶

Tuesday, May 6

MOOD	Good!
HAIR	Good!
HEALTH	Good! also, itchy under cast
HOROSCOPE	Always keep your eyes open for obstacles to your plans. Try to have an open mind!
~~JT SIGHTINGS~~	~~irrelevant~~

8:10 a.m.
You'd think I'd been gone for a month-and-a-half, and not just a few days. There were no less than 10 messages on the phone from Bruce Bartelson this weekend, which my dad reminded me over a thousand times. (Since when did he like Bruce Bartelson? Since when did he KNOW Bruce Bartelson?)

"He kept saying something about the prom," Dad said. "I didn't really pay attention."

"I know," I said. "He has a weird voice. It's hard to listen to."

"Huh," said Dad. He was staring out the window. Seriously, given the choice between Totally Vacant Dad and Dad-with-MYG, I'm going to have to say that Dad-with-MYG (nightmare that she is) was better.

"Have you heard from Melody?" I said.

"Pass me the remote," he said, scratching his head. His hair was all froufy. It was quite frightening — wiry and, well, not terribly clean.

"Gross," I said.

"What?" he said.

"Nothing," I said.

"What's gross?"

"Nothing!" I insisted. "I was just thinking out loud."

"Maybe I should cut it," he mused.

"No, no," I said. "I mean, yes, you should."

Really, he should. I just didn't want him to think that I thought he was gross. "But I wasn't saying your hair was gross, there's just some bird crap in it, that's all."

He slumped forward. "I think I'll cut it," he said, starting to flick the channels up and down aimlessly.

"Okay," I said. "Look, I'm late for school. Are you going to be okay?"

"I'm fine, sweetie," he said, kissing me on the forehead. "I'm just sad, but I'll be fine. Okay?"

"Okay," I said, patting him on the arm. "Call her," I said. He waved his hand half-heartedly.

Honestly, he's getting v. pathetic in his old age.

9:18 a.m.

As soon as I crutched into the school, BB was on me like green on grass.

"Haley!" he blurted.

"Yes," I said, leaning back as far as possible. (He had cereal caught between his teeth and a gross milk-flavour to his breath.)

"Thank GOD you're BACK!" he said. "We've got to get the plan ready for the PROM."

"Bruce," I said. "I'm not on the prom committee anymore, remember? I quit."

"You did?" he said. His brow furrowed. "No, you didn't."

"Yes, I did," I lied. "Remember?"

"No!" he said.

"It's okay," I said and ducked into the girls' room.

Really, BB is v. hard to shake. I inspected myself in the mirror. Not bad, considering. Well, just considering. I was looking at a tiny blossoming zit on my left nostril, when I noticed a sort of crying, snuffling sound.

I coughed, so that whoever it was wouldn't be embarrassed.

"Are you okay?" I said.

"No!" said the voice. "Haley, is that you?"

"Yes," I said. "Kiki?"

"YES," she wailed.

"What's wrong?" I said. I bent down so I could see which stall she was in. I found her shoes (red Sketchers, v. cute) and went into the next stall. "What is it?"

"It's ..." she started crying again. "I'm ..."

"What?" I said. I have to say, I was getting very nervous. Kiki isn't one for crying. She NEVER cries. "Is it Stephano?" I said.

"No!" she said. "I mean, yes!"

She shoved something under the wall at me. At first I couldn't tell what it was. It was this white plastic thing. And it was wet, which was kind of gross, and had a bunch of coloured stripes on it.

"Ew," I said. "What is THAT? It smells like pee." I thought it was some kind of mint dispenser or something. She cried harder. I held it up to the light.

"Kiki," I said. "I have no idea what this is."

"I ..."

"What?" I said. I threw the thing away. I'm sure she'd peed on it. Maybe it was one of those things that you peed on so that you …

I stopped cold.

"Oh my god," I said. "Kiki, are you pregnant?"

There was a long pause. Was she crying? I could hear sniffling. I got down on my knees and prepared to go under the door.

"You can't be!" I said, trying to manipulate my leg. I was horrified.

"I'm not!" she said.

"You are!" I said. Because I was suddenly sure.

"Haley!" she said. And that's when I realized she was giggling, not crying. Giggling? "I've got …"

"What?" I said.

"I've got a bladder infection!" she howled. "It hurts SO MUCH!"

"Oh!" I said. Then I started to laugh. I laughed so hard that I almost peed my pants. I mean, seriously.

I thought she was PREGNANT. I thought it was going to be like one of those teen after-school specials. I was so relieved that it's possible I got a bit hysterical. I can't actually laugh without getting the hiccups. And I got them so badly that I couldn't breathe.

Luckily, Kiki had a paper bag handy.

When she finally came out of the stall, she was looking at me really funny. "I'm just going to go to the clinic to get antibiotics," she said. "Are you okay? You wouldn't believe how much this hurts."

I nodded. "I'm fine," I said. "I'm totally fine."

"You're so weird," she said, hugging me.

"I know," I said.

"See you later," she said.

"Bye," I said.

Pregnant! Ha ha ha. Ha ha. Ha. I mean, that just didn't HAPPEN to people like us. Not at Sacred Heart High. Not to people who have been taking Sex Ed since, like Grade Eight. I laughed a bit more. I was feeling a little crazy, to be honest.

I stayed in the bathroom for the whole first period. Weird, I know. But I'd suddenly got this inspiration for making my art self-portrait and I wanted to make it while I had it in my head.

2:03 p.m.

"This is ... interesting," said Mrs. Stinson, squinting at my model. "What is it?"

"It's me," I said proudly. And it was. It was all the contents of my purse, arranged to look like me. I mean, what is more "me" than all the stuff I carry around with me?

"Very good," she said finally. "Very ... creative."

Things I've Accomplished that I Can Check Off My List:

1. Finish Art Project.
2. Get boyfriend back.

Things Still to Do:

3. Decide what to do with rest of life.
4. Make up with Jules.
5. Find prom dress.

5:45 p.m.

I was watching *Pretty in Pink* for the ten thousandth time (and brushing The Cat) when Dad walked in. I didn't really look up at first.

But when I did, I almost fell out of my chair.

"OH my GOD," I said. "What happened?"

His hair was …

Well, it was GONE. Completely.

"Well," he said sheepishly. "I cut it myself. And then it looked really weird, so I went to my friend and he cut it for me. It's a little shorter than I wanted."

"You're not kidding!" I said. I hopped over and felt it. It was all bristly. And silver! He looked so dignified.

And so OLD.

"Wow," I said. "You look … wow."

"It feels weird," he said, scratching it. "My head feels light."

"Huh," I said. "It's nice."

"I look like a real dad now, huh," he said.

"Yup," I said. "All grown up."

He settled into the couch next to me. "Oh!" he said. "*Pretty in Pink*! I love this one."

"I met Molly Ringwald," I said. I don't know why I said it, because obviously I'd told him a million times already.

"Really?" he said.

I looked at him. "Just kidding," he said. "I know you met Molly Ringwald."

"I know that you know," I said. "I was just saying."

"I know," he said.

So we watched it together. I love my dad, sometimes, you know. I really really do.

► ► ►

Wednesday, May 14

MOOD	Fine
HAIR	Fine and enh
HEALTH	Enh
HOROSCOPE	Confusion is apparent today. Don't make any rash decisions! Someone will give you an ultimatum.
~~JT SIGHTINGS~~	~~irrelevant~~

4:56 p.m.

"So Haley," Steven said, leaning over the desk. "I'm afraid I have some bad news."

I looked up at him warily. Last time he had "bad news" it meant that we'd run out of UnBurger patties and I had to spend time in the kitchen chopping mushrooms for three hours.

"Uh," I said.

"I'm afraid," he coughed. I felt spittle on my face, which I wiped off as subtly as possible. V. disgusting. Think of all the airborne viruses! I stood up and glanced at my watch. I had to go because I had to get to the clinic to get my cast removed. My cast was finally coming off! Just in time for prom.

"I have to go," I said.

"Okay," he said. And he stood aside to let me pass. "Oh, by the way? I have to fire you."

"Oh!" I said. I stopped for a second. "Okay," I said. I mean, I figured that sooner or later they'd realize that a) I had no idea what I was doing, and b) never did anything. I was a little disappointed, but also relieved. I hated The UnBurger.

I didn't care if I never saw another UnBurger again.

"Bye," I said. I wish I'd said something like "You spit when you talk!" But I didn't think of it then.

I always think of good comebacks when it's too late. Not that it was a good comeback, but you know what I mean.

The clinic was really busy by the time I got there. I sat down in the waiting room and made myself comfortable. They had a v. good selection of magazines there.

6:49 p.m.
This clinic is boring. V. outdated and dull selection of magazines.

8:49 p.m.
Honestly, I could take this cast of myself. What do I need them for?

9:00 p.m.
Where is Brad? When I called him, he said he'd be right here. Oh good, there he is.

9:21 p.m.
"Brad," I said. "Don't be goofy. Just CUT it."

He was standing over me in his parents' garage with a hand-saw looking frightened and/or frightening.

"Are you sure?"

"Look," I said. "I had this thing changed a few times and all they do is hack it off with a saw-thing. Really, it's no different than that. You won't hurt me. Just do it."

"It just seems like a weird thing to do," he said. "Maybe we should go to your place and get your dad to do it."

"Seriously," I said, "my dad should be kept away from all tools in general. Even hand tools. Let ME do it."

I grabbed the saw out of his hand. He cringed. It was surprisingly easy to cut through the plaster. What I was NOT prepared for, was what my leg looked like underneath. I mean, when I'd finally hacked and chopped the cast off, I was horrified.

Brad just about fainted.

Surprising Qualities about My Leg:
1. Is tiny. And … withered.
2. Is v. white.
3. Or WOULD be v. white if it was not covered with inch long blackish hairs.
4. Strongly resembles some sort of man-eating worm.

"Wow," said Brad. "Your leg looks weird."

"What are you doing, son?" his dad said, popping his head around the door of the garage. "Oh!"

"Nothing!" said Brad. (Question: why do people always say "nothing" when they are clearly doing "something"?)

"What the HELL are you doing with that saw?" his dad said, grabbing it out of my hand. He seemed to barely register the pieces of cast all over the ground. I mean, I can't say that I blame him. Perhaps it was a slightly unusual thing to be doing, after all.

"We had to take off my cast," I said helpfully.

"Oh," he said. He looked at my leg and flinched (I swear). "Oh," he repeated. He kind of stepped back and put the saw down. "Okay," he said. He looked completely perplexed. "Well," he said. And then he left.

Brad looked at me.

He sort of laughed.

"What?" I said. And that did it. We looked at each other and just burst out laughing. If you thought about it, it was hilarious. I was just lying there half-dressed with one normal leg and one leg that resembled an earth-dwelling insect. And he was holding a saw in his hand.

"Your poor dad," I gasped.

"I know," he said.

Brad is so much fun. We just laughed for, like, half an hour. Sometimes, I love being with Brad.

► ► ►

Monday, May 19

Summary of Problems:

1. Formerly broken leg is weak and wobbly and does not want to be walked on.
2. Brad cannot always be with me to piggyback me home

and/or to school and/or to the movies and/or to dinner
and/or to his games, even though I have seen all of
them over the weekend (some sort of tournament)
(which his team won).

3. Jules is still not talking to me.

4. Dad is still moping around the house (although now
that I'm used to his hair, is a bit like living with Richard
Gere) (he is bizarrely good-looking without his gross
hippie hair) (is very unnerving)

5. Still have no prom dress. (Perhaps will cut down living-
room curtains in style of *Pretty in Pink*) (unfortunately,
living room curtains are beige and have some sort of
plaid pattern on them that is just Not Pretty)

I need a plan.

I have exactly 65 dollars and 18 cents, which seems unlikely
to buy me a dress. And I don't want to ask Dad for money.
(Question: did Melody fire him?) He's been around the
house a LOT lately. I don't want to depress him by pointing out his parental shortcomings, i.e., his inability to
afford a prom dress for his only daughter.

Still, I don't know how I'm going to conjure up a prom
dress out of thin air.

I wish that I had taken sewing instead of Drahma. Or
art. (Have nothing to show for either class except ability
to mimic trees and weird self-sculpture thing.*)

---

* Which I had to dismantle as needed bus pass, bank card and chapstick,
not to mention pen and zit-cover-up stick.)

Friday, May 23

MOOD	Creative
HAIR	Medium okay
HEALTH	Medium okay
HOROSCOPE	Effervescent is your middle name today! Get out there and show the world who you are.
~~JT SIGHTINGS~~	~~irrelevant~~

3:45 p.m.

"Oh, NO," I moaned.

"What is it?" said Jules, spinning around in the dressing room. She was wearing Vera Wang. It was actually a bridesmaid's dress, but naturally (!) it was perfect for graduation. It was silk and ... well, it was beautiful. "Does it make my ass look huge?"

"No," I said. "It does NOT."

"Then what's your problem?" she said, flicking her hair. Honestly, have no idea what the girl eats because judging by her body it's NOTHING, but her hair grows like a weed. I scratched my head self-consciously. My hair was now just scraping my chin and cut into choppy layers (long story involving a straightening iron and hairspray and a strange burning smell).

"I don't have a problem," I said.

"Oh," she said. "Do you think they'll have a tux that matches this?"

"Jules," I said, carefully, "It's black. Most tuxes ARE black. I think you'll be fine."

"Oh, good," she said.

I moaned again.

"Are you in pain?" she sighed.

"No!" I said. "I'm just ... I don't have a dress," I admitted.

"Well, you better hurry up," she said. "I thought you said you had one."

"Uh, I thought I did," I said. "But, uh, well, I didn't."

"Oh," she said. "Most of the stores are sold out of good ones. Maybe you can find something in the thrift shop."

"Maybe," I said through gritted teeth. Like watching her try on a thousand dollar dress wasn't torture enough. "Anyway, forget it."

"Forget what?" she said.

I Iuh.

Can always count on Jules to make me feel a) stupid, and b) invisible.

Nice.

6:49 p.m.

"I don't miss hockey sometimes," said Brad, nuzzling into my shoulder. I squirmed a bit and may have moved out of the way. I mean, I'm so happy that we're back together, but he's always TOUCHING me.

"Shhh," I said. "You'll miss the movie."

"It's the PREVIEWS," he said loudly.

"I LIKE the previews," I hissed, chomping on a mouthful of popcorn. I looked over at him. But then I stopped being mad, because he was looking so cute. So cute-ish, anyway.

"Sorry," I whispered. I put my hand on his leg. He grinned.

"Shh," I said.

"I didn't say anything," he said.

"I know," I said.

"Shhh," he said.

Really, Brad can be v. funny sometimes. SOMETIMES.

Afterwards, we drove home. Okay, we drove around and then we made out in the car. It was kind of embarrassing, especially when the police came and tapped on the window and then burst out laughing when they saw what we were doing. And then when I got out of the car, I tripped and they thought I was drunk. So they gave Brad a breathalyzer test because they figured maybe we were both drunk and on top of having nowhere else to KISS, we had nowhere else to drink.

But, of course, his blood alcohol was zero.

Duh.

After that, he drove me straight home.

"Have you thought much about prom?" I asked, trying not to sound like I was ASKING, but just casually. Like I was talking about the weather.

"Uh," he said. "Not really. You want to go to yours or mine?"

Naturally, I'd forgotten that he went to a different school. It hadn't even occurred to me that I might go to his. But if they were on different dates, then that might be okay.

"Let's go to both," I said.

"Okay," he said. "Hey, I love this song." Then he turned up the radio, which meant no more talking.

11:41 p.m.
Immediate problem: Now need not only ONE dress, but
TWO dresses.

Note to Self: Learn how to sew.
   And/or how to steal.
Stealing might be more efficient than sewing. But v.
embarrassing if caught.
   Learn how to sew.

► ► ►

Monday, May 26

MOOD	Undecided
HAIR	Not long enough for updo so pointless
HEALTH	Nothing broken
HOROSCOPE	Watch out for people who may be watching you for surprising reasons. Walk carefully.
~~JT SIGHTINGS~~	~~irrelevant~~

10:45 a.m.
Normally, I love holiday weekends. But this one is just
about over, and apart from accomplishing nothing, I've
eaten an entire bag of Oreos.
   Because I'm stressed.
   On Saturday, I bought a bunch of fabric. It's really pretty
— pink (naturally) and sort of goes from dark to light.
What I was picturing was some kind of strapless dress
with a dark bottom, getting lighter at the top. What I've got
is, well, something that resembles a long throw cushion.

And I can't even put it on.

Obviously, I thought of zippers, but the truth is that it's not as easy as it looks on TV or in the movies. Damn Molly Ringwald, anyway.

Now my immediate problems include not only NOT having a dress, but having no money left to buy a dress. Or any more Oreos, for that matter.

Also, have a pounding headache.

I don't even have to look it up to know what THAT means. I mean, it's worse when I bend my head forwards and stare into the light. It's a subarachnoid hemorrhage.

(From MDAdvice.com):

Symptoms:
- Severe headache that worsens when bending head forward.
- Eyes sensitive to light.
- Lethargy.
- Confusion.
- No recent head injury.

Possible Problems:

Bleeding in membrane around brain.

What to Do:

Call doctor now.

See Subarachnoid Hemorrhage.

See Brain or Epidural Abscess.

See?

I suppose that if I DO have a hemorrhage of some sort, what my prom dress looks like really doesn't matter v. much.

Must go lie down and envision dramatic scene of JT, I mean BRAD, sobbing on my coffin and shouting, "SHE WAS TOO YOUNG TO DIE! I LOVED HER SO MUCH AND NOW SHE WILL NEVER KNOW!" Or the like.

► ► ►

Wednesday, May 28

MOOD	Frantic
HAIR	Quirky
HEALTH	Amazing, considering hemorrhaging brain issues
HOROSCOPE	If everyone else jumped off a cliff, would you? Make all your own choices today. Following the pack might lead to an unpleasant surprise.
~~JT SIGHTINGS~~	~~irrelevant~~

Hmmf.

Is it just me, or is my horoscope getting more and more ridiculous?

I crumpled up the paper in disgust and chucked it in the overflowing recycling bucket. Since Melody left, the house has really fallen into a shamble. I don't know why, really. I mean, I used to clean it but then she came along and did it all and now I just can't be bothered. I stuffed down the contents with my foot, jumping about a mile in the air when The Bird came flapping out of the bucket, squawking like the house was on fire.

"Sheesh," I said. "I mean, sorry."

The house was weirdly quiet. Like it was empty.

I went upstairs to see if Dad was sleeping. His bed was made (!)* and he wasn't there.

"Dad?" I yelled.

"Dad?"

Great. Have been abandoned by my father to live in squalor.

4:50 p.m.

Dear Junior:

Great news! Dad and Melody have got back together. I never thought that I'd think that was great news, but I do. I mean, she's still Much Younger than him and totally inappropriate, but he's almost back to his normal self now. When I got home from school, they were giggling away in front of *Dr. Phil.*

It seemed ... well, it seemed almost normal.

Still have not solved problem of prom dress and multiple proms to attend.

New problem: Apparently I agreed at some point — when? — to go to the prom with BRUCE BARTELSON. This is a problem which now takes paramount importance over ALL OTHER PROBLEMS.

Must call Kiki.

Love,

Stressed-Out Girl

7:41 p.m.

Phone Call with Kiki:

Kiki: So I hear you're going to the prom with Bruce Bartelson. How does Brad feel about that?

---

* Dad never makes his bed. V. SUSPICIOUS.

Me: I'm NOT going to the prom with Bruce Bartelson.
        I'm not! You have to help me get out of it.

Kiki: I can't help you.

Me: You HAVE to help me.

Kiki: I can't help you. I'm totally swamped with study-
        ing for finals. I can't blow them, they're important.

Me: I have finals, too! This is more important!

Kiki: Finals in WHAT? Art?

Me: YES.

Kiki: Hmmm.

Me: Fine, so it's not as hard as Advanced Trig, but it's
        still studying. Anyway, you have to help me. Please.

Kiki: You know what, Haley? You got yourself into it ...

Me: Fine. Thanks a lot.

Have been deserted by best friend in hour of need. Great.
THIS never happened to Molly Ringwald. No, sir. Come
to think of it, Molly Ringwald usually had a string of
male friends. Like Duckie, for example. She didn't have
female friends. Suspect this is because female friends will let
you down at every opportunity. There is NO LOYALTY!

"What am I going to do?" I asked The Bird.

"Stupid stupid stupid," he said.

"No KIDDING," I said. "But that's not helping."

"What's not helping?" chirped Melody, sticking her head
around the door.

"Nothing," I scowled. I mean, I'm glad she's back and
everything, but that doesn't mean that I want her in my
ROOM. When I'm having an important conversation with

someone. Okay, so it was with The Bird, but still. It's private.

"Are you okay, hon?" she said. She's v. persistent.

"Fine," I growled. "I have two proms to go to at two schools. At one prom, I have two dates. I have zero dresses. My friends have deserted me. I have a pile of fabric. I have no money. And … and … and …" At this point, I was crying. Apparently the AND is that I have no dignity.

I hiccupped.

"And?" she said.

"And I'm probably going to fail my art final!" I wailed.

"Aw, honey," she said. She came over and sat beside me on my (unmade) bed and sort of patted me on the back. "Maybe I can help."

"How?" I sobbed. I felt like an idiot, but I couldn't stop crying. (See: Brain Tumour). "And I probably have a BRAIN TUMOUR?"

She regarded me gravely. "Look at me," she said. She stared into my eyes for a minute. You know, when you look at her, she's not actually as homely as she first appears. Maybe if she, like, wore some eye makeup or something.

"You don't have a brain tumour," she said gently. "Now I don't know if you know this, but I make a lot of my own clothes."

"Really?" I said. "You'd never know." Which is true, almost. I mean, granted she wears the ugliest clothes on the planet, but they do look like they were made properly. I mean, they have zippers. And buttons. And everything else.

"So maybe I can help," she said, with a glint in her eye.

"Uh," I said. I know I was desperate. But not desperate enough to wear a MYG styled gown. I don't think. Well, maybe I was.

Okay, I totally was.

"Okay," I said.

Hmmm. Maybe if she could help solve the problem of Not Having a Dress, she could also help solve the multiple-dates-multiple-proms problem.

Maybe.

JUNE

Monday, June 2

MOOD	—
HAIR	Green
HEALTH	—
HOROSCOPE	You are entering a rare cycle that will occur only once again — in 2009 — enjoy it while you can!
~~JT SIGHTINGS~~	~~irrelevant~~ 12

Days Until Prom: 18
Dresses: 2!!!!! (Thank you, Melody!) (They aren't even ugly.)
Prom Dates: 2 (Help!)
Days Left of School: 15

9:09 a.m.
*List of Reasons-to-Be-Anxious, Made in Lieu of Listening
to Izzy Archibaud Perform Her Final Drama Monologue:*

1. Have NO IDEA what I'm doing after grad, unlike EVERYONE ELSE, who seem to have v. elaborate plans. WHEN did they make these plans? What was I doing?

2. Have EVEN LESS of an idea how I'm going to tell Brad that I'm accidentally going to prom with Bruce Bartelson. Or how I'm going to tell Bruce Bartelson that I don't remember saying that I'd go with him. I mean, I hate him and everything, but don't want to hurt his feelings as I know what it's like to have a crush.

3. Am slightly worried about failing PE as have taken up "bowling" to meet requirements and cannot do it to save my life, and will likely fail PE "final" and have to repeat it in summer school, which would be v. embarrassing.

4. Don't know whether I have to invite my actual mother to grad ceremony as have seen her exactly once and she hasn't returned my phone calls (I leave messages for her at the church office), although the nunnery doesn't have a phone and she'd have to go down to the corner to call back from a payphone. I don't think she actually cares about me.

12:45 p.m.

"Oh, Haley," sighed Jules. "Stop MOANING. You aren't the only person in the world with problems, you know."

"Oh?" I said politely. "And are you having some sort of problem I can help you with?"

"Me?" she said. "No, no problems."

"Thought not," I said. "But I should have known better than to ask you for help with getting out of this stupid prom situation."

"Just TELL Bruce the truth," said Jules. "That would probably work."

"I don't want to hurt his feelings," I said. "I kind of, well, feel sorry for him."

"Why?" she said. "He's a loser. It hardly matters."

"It TOTALLY matters," I said incredulously. I mean, I know she's a bit of a cold fish, but that's v. insensitive.

"I doubt he cares, Haley," she said.

Wow.

Jules is v. mean. Don't know why I ever considered her a friend.

"Sorry!" she yelled after me. I kind of stopped and looked back at her. Jules never apologizes. Hmm.

Very suspicious.

I wonder what she wants.

▶ ▶ ▶

Thursday, June 12
AKA
My Birthday

Dear Junior:

It's my birthday. I'm 17. I guess I never thought I'd live to be 17, mostly because weird things kept happening. I figured I'd die young. Anyway, I didn't die. I'm still alive.

And 17.

I haven't written for a few days because things around here have been, well, madness.

I don't even know where to start.

Oooh, I could start with the fact that for my birthday,

Brad gave me a ring. It's not, like, a RING. We're not engaged. That would be stupid. I mean, I'm only 17. It's a pretty pearl ring. I love it. He said it was a birthday and grad present.

He used the L-word.

I know, it's weird. I mean we WEREN'T seeing each other as much as we WERE this year, but he was busy with hockey and I was busy, well, being neurotic and crazy. But I tried to put "crazy" on the shelf for a while and in the last two weeks things have been … great. Really great. Not just "great" because I think it's the right thing to feel. I do feel "great."

Like, Brad took me bowling every night for a week to help me practise for my stupid PE final. Who would do that? He's totally thoughtful. And you know, bowling shoes are actually kind of cool.

Anyway, I'll get back to the L-word in a minute. There's a lot more that's been going on. For one thing, Dad and Melody are definitely up to something. It's a "surprise." But I think it has something to do with a car. For me? For graduation? I don't want to get excited in case it isn't. But I picked up some clues.

For example, the name of three car dealers on the Call Display.

I guess I kind of suck for not getting around to taking my driver's test this term, but I had a broken leg! I was busy!

Oh, in other news, I told Bruce Bartelson that I couldn't go to prom with him after all because I actually, suddenly, have a Real Boyfriend™, and I hoped he would under-stand. And he cried. He did. I felt so evil. Actually, I've never seen a boy cry before. Not like that. Come to think of it, it was v. embarrassing. For both of us.

I hear he's going with Izzy Archibaud now. HA.

Anyway, Brad and I still have two proms to go to. We haven't really worked it out yet. But I have two dresses, so it's okay. I think. I mean, it will work out. I'm sure of it.

I can't believe he used the L-word.

It seems so surreal.

Love,

Haley

PS — Jules and JT broke up. I thought I'd care, but actually I don't. I don't even really have anything to say about it. It's weird. Now that he's available, he just looks so *gross* to me.

PS again — which doesn't meant that Jules was right when she said I always liked unavailable boys. It just means that the cure for a lifelong crush is to fall in love (sort of) with someone else.

Not that I'm in love with Brad.

But he does have the nicest blue eyes you've ever seen. Well, the nicest ones I've ever seen anyway.

Oops!

Got to run. I'm late for my prom committee meeting. Oh, yeah. I had to join it again. I know I quit. But I felt guilty so I rejoined. I know I'm lame. Please don't hate me.

PSSS — Not that I care about prom committee or anything. It's just that some of the committee geeks are actually okay and they'll probably sing happy birthday or something and it would suck not to be there.

PS4 — Wonder who Jules is going to end up going to prom with?

▶ ▶ ▶

Sunday, June 22

The Big Finale!

Well, I did it. I can't believe it. I graduated from high school. Haley Andromeda Harmony. I didn't actually do WELL, but I passed. And that counts for something, right?

I cried during the ceremony. For a couple of reasons. I mean, Kiki's speech was so great. It made me realize that even though I hadn't really felt like I was having fun during TGYML, I actually was. I had my first job, my first boyfriend, my first leg-break. I ran my first marathon, or the first part of my first marathon. I did a lot of stuff for the first time.

The second reason that I cried was The Bee. See, the ceremony was outside. It was hot and summery. I was sitting in the crowd and looking around for my dad and Melody so I could wave. We had a big grad class and it kind of went on and on. And I was tired! I couldn't sleep the night before because I was nervous that I'd trip on the stage or fall over or inappropriately get the hiccups, or, well, any number of things. I saw Melody, or I thought I did, and I started waving. But when I put my arm up, I guess a bee landed on it, and so I tried to flick it off, and in doing so, somehow flicked it into my eye and it STUNG ME.

And I'm allergic to bee stings.

And of course my eye started swelling up like crazy and I felt like I couldn't breathe and was a little worried about anaphylactic shock. I mean, it could happen. Let's face it, I haven't nearly died yet this term and I'm overdue for a near-death experience. At first, I just sat there, but I couldn't stand it. I could feel my cheek swelling up. Jules was sitting next to me, laughing (naturally). And I could see Kiki noticing from the podium. And, well, I didn't want to mess up her speech. So I got up to sneak out, and it's possible that I may have hyperventilated from panicking, so when I got up, I got light-headed and, well, I fainted.

Which naturally interrupted everything and everyone got up to see what had happened, so the video of my graduation mostly involves the first-aid people trying to get through the sea of black robes to where I was lying on the grass. I had come around by then, and it struck me as a tiny bit funny and I got the giggles. So I was lying there in my grad robe, laughing hysterically with half my face swollen up (naturally!) and thinking I might die from shock at any moment, when I got the hiccups.

So there it was, the thing I was worried about: getting the hiccups during grad. But I forgot to worry about the possibilities of insects and unconsciousness. Which just does go to show that the thing you worry about is never the thing that actually happens, not exactly, so to ward off all the bad things from happening, you must completely entertain all strange ideas, such as wild African cats jumping out of the stands and gnawing off your arms. Like tigers.

Not that it would happen, but that's what I was thinking. I was a little overwrought, maybe.

So they loaded me up with antihistamines and Dad and Melody took me home. They were all grave and serious at first but when they realized that I was actually okay, they laughed their asses off. You'd think they'd never seen someone with half a swollen face before.

When we got home, there was a bunch of flowers at the front door. From my mom. It's weird. I mean, a few months ago that would have meant a lot to me, but now it just looked sad. The thing is, she doesn't need me in her life and somehow I managed to get through without her, so I guess I don't need her as much as I used to think.

La la la.

You learn something new every day.

Having two proms was … great. Okay, it wasn't great, it was crazy. For one thing, Melody made me the exact dress from *Pretty in Pink*. Okay, so it's an ugly dress, but it meant something to me. And Brad even wore an '80s tuxedo and he looked exactly — but exactly! — like Andrew McCarthy.

I'm totally serious when I say THAT was my dream come true.

I'm a dork, what can I tell you?

The pictures are all weird because I had to turn my face so only the unswollen part was showing. Not that the pictures really matter. I mean, they do. I'm sure I'll have them forever. In one of them, JT is behind us (drunk) waving his hands in the air.

He looks like an idiot.

He IS an idiot.

I guess I should backtrack and tell you about prom night (which wasn't the same night as grad because we couldn't book the hall for that night for complicated reasons). First of all, I was freaking out because my face was all swollen (still) and I couldn't get my makeup to look right. I looked like the kid from that movie *Mask*, with Cher. So why I was bothering with makeup was anyone's guess. Kiki had come over to get ready at my house. And Jules?

Well, that's a whole OTHER story, but Jules had gone to New York. With her mom. On some kind of modelling audition. I have no idea how these things repeatedly happen to Jules, but they do. That's just the way it goes. She left on the morning of prom. Actually, I thought she'd be sad about missing prom, but when I asked her, she rolled her eyes and said, "Like PROM matters more than an audition that could change, like, my whole life."

So I guess she didn't care. A little part of me thinks that maybe she wanted to miss it because she didn't have a date, anyway, but maybe that's just mean.

I kind of feel sorry for Jules. I do. I mean, her mom's impossible and Jules thinks that everyone likes her because she's pretty, but the truth is that people are freaked out by her looks and then she pushes them away by being mean. But enough psychoanalysis of Jules. Sometimes I'm all-Juled out.

Kiki's dress was gorgeous. Flat-out lovely. She looked

like a princess. And standing next to me, she looked better because I was wearing a weird '80s dress and my face was swollen. It occurred to me that probably no one I know had even seen *Pretty in Pink*, so they just would think I was wearing an '80s dress for no reason.

Oh well. I guess it pays to have a quirky reputation. Would they really be surprised?

I was totally self-conscious, to tell you the truth. But then when Brad and Stephano arrived (limo!), it was okay. Because Brad was in an '80s tux. I'm glad that he has a sense of humour. I mean, a lot of guys wouldn't have done it.

And Stephano, of course, looked totally perfect. But not as crushable as I used to think. His shoes were weird, for one thing. And he had a chunk of green food stuck on his top right tooth. But no one seemed to notice, and I was hardly going to point it out. Anyway, as soon as the limo pulled out of the driveway, he pulled out a bottle of who-knows-what and started pounding it back.

"Drink!" he said.

"Uh, no thanks," said Kiki. She really doesn't drink. She looked kind of nervous.

"Aw," he cajoled. "Come on, gorgeous. Drinky drinky drinky." He put his hand on my leg.

Ew.

I picked it up and dropped it again, glaring at him as well as I could out of my swollen eye. "I can't," I said. "I'm on antihistamines."

Stephano got kind of mad. I'd never seen this side of him before. "Come ON," he said. "Don't be such stiffs. It's your little prom!" (I'd forgotten that he'd already graduated. "Little" prom? He was now officially not only uncrushable, but getting awfully annoying.)

"Little?" said Brad. He had a weird gleam in his eye. Frankly, I was worried.

"Uh," I said. "I'll drink!" I was just trying to keep the peace.

"No," said Kiki. "Don't. You know what you're like. You can't drink."

"Oh, like you CAN?" I said. I wasn't being nasty, I just honestly have never really seen her drink. I took a sip and just about threw up. And immediately got dizzy. I put my head between my knees. V. dignified, I'm sure. Brad patted my back. (Really, Brad is v. nice.)

"We're not drinking," he said calmly.

"Give it here," Kiki said, calmly, and swilled back a bunch of whatever it was.

Brad looked at me and shrugged. "Whatever," he said. "Get drunk. Throw up."

"I won't throw up," said Kiki. But to be honest, she was kind of slurring. Already.

"Uh," I said. "Maybe you shouldn't."

"Yes, you should," said Stephano with a gleam in his eye. "Tonight is going to be a wild time at your little school with your little friends."

"Wild," I said. "Huh." I was kind of hoping it would be fun. Romantic. Not necessarily "wild." Me + Wild Parties usually = disaster, anyway.

Kiki took another big slug. "You should 'ave some," she said.

"Why are you doing this?" I said. I wanted to grab it away from her.

"Cutting loose," she said. Her head was kind of … droopy … at this point.

"Oh," I said.

We pulled up at the school. It was all decorated up, which was no surprise to me having done half of it myself. Okay, I didn't actually DO it, but I did think of some of the ideas and then got Izzy to do them. I guess she felt stupid about being a Brad stalker and willingly did all the weird things I made her do. Such as string fake flowers up from one building to another so it was like walking through, well, a flowery corridor.

It had started to rain a little bit when we got there. We all piled out of the car. Brad was looking around for JT. He was a little TOO worried about him. I mean, I know he's family and everything but I wanted the prom to be about US. I had this stupid idea of, I don't know, maybe Kevin Bacon's prom from *Footloose* or something. Where there would be dancing, and singing.

But that's not EXACTLY what happened. Because as soon as we started walking to the school, Kiki lit a cigarette. She was a little … um, well, drunk, I guess. And she accidentally lit her hair-do on fire. It didn't catch fire. But it … smoked.

So there she was with a big smoking head, looking all confused. And Stephano saved her by pouring whatever gross thing he was drinking on her smoking hair. Which ignited. So Brad threw his polyester '80s jacket over her head and the fire on her hair went out, but the jacket melted onto her dress.

Kiki was totally hysterical. Obviously. Who wouldn't have been? I was mostly just shocked that it wasn't happening to me. I just stood there, watching, with my big swollen face. By this time, it was pouring with rain and I was drenched, but I didn't really notice because it was all just so bizarre.

What I didn't notice was that the rain was causing the colours on the paper flowers to run. So while I thought I was just getting wet, what was really happening was that I was getting … well, DYED. But wait, it gets more ridiculous. Because by then, a bunch of teachers had come running out of the school, including Mr. Pork Butt, and he was all, "HALEY HARMONY, WHY DO YOU ALWAYS DO THINGS LIKE THIS?"

I couldn't point out that I hadn't really done anything, because there was so much chaos and I was laughing a bit. I made sure Kiki was all right first, and she was. Until she threw up on my shoes, that is. So there I was, trying to look pretty, covered with dye from the flowers and vomit, and Brad was standing there in a white shirt that was completely drenched and we were laughing hysterically, or as hysterically as we *could* laugh. If by "we," I mean "me." (It's hard to laugh out of half a face.)

In any event, Mr. Dorky Butt wouldn't let us into the prom. He said we had to go somewhere else. Someone came out and took pictures (my prom pictures!) and I tried to look pretty and turn my face to the side so it wasn't swollen. But as I saw later in the pictures, I looked monstrous anyway. Those paper flowers were really colourful, believe me.

Anyway, somehow in the confusion, JT showed up and said, "I'll take you home to clean up." Which was nice of him. But he meant "home" to his house. When all of us got there, his parents were like, "Uh, no, you aren't coming in here." Which I thought was weird. But his parents are pretty snobby, so whatever.

"Where can we go?" I moaned. My teeth were chattering.

It was JT's idea, really.

I swear, I don't even know what possessed me to agree. I blame the antihistamines.

He said, "Jules is away."

And as it happens, I know where the key is to Jules' house. Of course, I do. We've been hanging out at each other's houses since the first grade.

And it did seem sort of like a good idea. I figured I could wash up and borrow something of Jules' to wear and we'd just go. What I didn't think of was that while I was changing and showering, Brad and JT (well, mostly JT) would get into Jules' mom's liquor supply and start playing some kind of drinking game that involved a weird sort of hockey in the kitchen (and several loud crashes).

When I came down (I borrowed Jules' dress) (it was BEAUTIFUL) (and it almost sort of fit) (I know it's wrong and I'll probably go to hell for it, but she wasn't there to wear it and I'm sure she would have wanted me to) (well, not "wanted" me to, but…) (Anyway). I think I looked okay.

Brad stopped playing with JT as soon as he saw me. He was wearing a white shirt that he must have got from Jules' mom's closet (she always has a supply of men's clothes from her many boyfriends, I guess) over his wet tux pants. He looked really … well, great.

Like a movie star.

And he was all, "You look so beautiful."

And for a few seconds, it was the most romantic moment of my life.

Then JT threw up on the Persian rug.

Note to Self: The surest cure for a crush is to watch your former crush vomit on someone else's rug. And know that you'll have to clean it up. Because, after all, you are the person who is constantly cleaning up what other people (and cats) cough up.

"Argh!" I screamed. "What are you doing? You IDIOT!"

I mean, we'd all but broken in, I'd borrowed (okay, stolen) Jules' prom dress. And now we'd RUINED THE RUG.

At which point, JT started balling.

Really, some people just shouldn't drink. I swear.

Brad looked at me and rolled his eyes. And winked. And suddenly, I started to laugh. Because, you know, I had never thought to worry that on prom night, we'd be in Jules' house with JT vomiting on the rug, my hair stained (!) from running paper flowers, Kiki and Stephano who knows where, and NOT dancing to romantic music in the school gym.

I laughed so hard, I got the hiccups. Badly.

I was still hiccupping wildly when we finally cleaned up, dumped JT on his front lawn, and got to Brad's prom.

Which was exactly — but exactly! — what I had wanted. It was picture perfect. Well, except for my Technicolor hair and swollen face and slightly too tight (but beautiful!) dress.

And afterwards. Well, ha.

Like I'm going to write THAT down.

Let's just say, it was a night that I'll remember forever.

EPILOGUE

I guess. I mean, this is the end, right?

Dear Junior:

I still don't know what's next. And I'm kind of, totally, scared. I mean, Brad is going to hockey camp. It's not really camp. It's where you play hockey on a farm team for some big NHL league for years until they "call you up."

I've learned a lot about hockey this year. Ask me anything. I could probably tell you.

As for me, I don't know what I'm doing in September. I mean, Kiki is obviously going to Harvard, where she will become brilliant and successful. And Jules will be in New York, modelling for some catalogue I've never heard of (that was her big "audition" that she deked out of prom for), and also successful (though not brilliant). (I mean, how smart can walking around in designer clothes make you?) (Please.) (I should add that she still isn't talking to me due to accidental Prom Party at her house, without her there.) And JT … well, who cares what JT is going to be doing?

I sure don't.

But why worry about September? It's months away. I don't even know what I'm doing in *July*.

But I'll be okay. I think.

Oh, damn. The Bird's just crapped on my head. Be right back.

11:05 p.m.

Dear Junior (cont'd!):

Okay, I didn't come right back. Because Dad and Melody gave me my surprise. It's so …

Well, I don't even know what to say.

First, I was just running to the bathroom to rinse the crap out of my (green) (it's a long story about a small incident with chlorine in the water and too much bleaching, which isn't as funny as it sounds) hair when Melody called, "Haley! Come here!"

So I went downstairs, half-expecting her to want to teach me how to tie-dye or something. (Ever since the whole sewing incident, she's been wanting to "teach" me everything.) (If you ever need a potholder macraméd, you know who to ask.) I stomped down the stairs as well as I could (my leg is still a little weak and wonky, to tell you the truth) (probably, I'm slow to heal because my body is busy staving off more deadly plagues such as cancer or mono or the chicken flu).

"What?" I said. (Ever since she and Dad got back together, they've been nauseatingly touchy-feely. Literally. Like, he's always rubbing her back and she's always running to the bathroom to puke.) (Which, come to think of it, is pretty weird. I hope she's not actually sick.) (Although she's a doctor, she could cure herself.)

They were sitting side by side on the couch, like kids who were in trouble. They both looked totally guilty. Dad had grown a gross little moustache to make up for the fact his hair was so "conservative." It made him look furtive, to tell the truth. But I told him it looked good, because I hate hurting his feelings. I was thinking of trying to shave it off while he's sleeping, but that would be hard because he sleeps with Melody now and I'm sure one of them would be woken up by the sound of the moustache trimmer.

"What?" I said. I was kind of wondering if maybe they were about to deliver The Lecture. You know, the one where they tell me to get on with my life, etc. etc. Or, horror of horrors, say that I had to start paying rent now that I'm out of high school.

"We have an announcement," they said. They said it together. Yes, I know this is unspeakably lame. Next thing you know, they'll start dressing alike.

"What is it?" I said uncomfortably, kicking a passing ball of cat hair with my bare toe. (The hair immediately stuck to the freshly applied nail polish.) (Gross.)

"Well," said Dad. "You're going to be a Sister."

For a second, I thought that he meant that he'd sold me to the nunnery. Or that because my mom was a nun, I was going to be forced to follow her footsteps.

"But I'm not religious," I said.

Melody burst out laughing (I may be getting used to her, but her donkey laugh still grates on my last nerve).

"No," she said. "A big sister."

"I'm not big," I said. But then I figured it out. I'm a little slow, but I'm not stupid.

Oh my God.

My dad had made her pregnant.

"Uh," I said.

"Is that all you're going to say?" said Dad.

"Uh," I said. I swear, I wanted to say something else, but I couldn't. I mean, nothing else came out of my mouth.

"Uh," I said again.

"I think she's in shock," said Melody. "Maybe she needs some ginger tea."

"Uh," I said again.

"Well, seeing as she's in shock anyway," said Dad. "Let's give her her present."

He kind of steered me to the front door, which is harder than you might think because my leg is so stiff and weird and there is so much crap piled in the front hall. I tripped over the newspaper pile and hit my forehead on the bookshelf.

"OUCH!" I yelled. I think it was bleeding a bit, to tell you the truth. It totally hurt. I almost started crying.

But I didn't.

Because he opened the door and I saw my graduation present.

It

was

a

Volkswagen van.

"Aw," I said. "I LOVE those things."

"I know you do, kiddo," said Dad. And he handed me the key.

Really, the story would have been much better if I'd been able to leap into it and drive off, maybe pick up Brad and go to the beach and then we could do something romantic and cool.

But I can't drive.

So what actually happened was that we all jumped into the van and my dad drove and we wove around the city until Melody got queasy and we had to stop in the middle of traffic so she could jump out and throw up behind a bush on the side of the highway.

You know, I like Melody better all the time.

Love,

Haley

PS — I've written a list to help us get through the next little bit. Just to put it all in perspective, you know? Here it is:

Goals for the Summer:

1. Pass Driver's Test.

2. Take fun hippie van on tour of North America. With boyfriend? With best friends? With someone? Or by myself?

3. Oooh, could maybe write book about experience and earn huge advance and great fame for being youngest

writer of book-about-travels-across-North America. Could have mad-cap escapades and bungee jump in different states. Or other "adventures."

4. Maybe should take writing class before leaving.
5. Think about what to do when I grow up.
6. Learn a bit about babies, in case Melody's comes when I'm still living at home, though this is unlikely as by then I will be well on the road to Fun Adventurous Adult Life.
7. Just take one step at a time.

Oh, and in case you're wondering, all those medical sites don't just list symptoms. Some of them list cures. There are cures for a lot of things. Even for crushes. You just have to stop believing in them, and eventually they go away.

The weird thing is, that's also true for Brain Tumours. Or at least it's true for the sort of Brain Tumours that come and go.

Peace out, Junior. More later, I promise.

Love,
Haley Andromeda Harmony

ACKNOWLEDGEMENTS

I began this book with the acknowledgements, even if they turn up at the end, because I wrote them before I wrote the book. (Don't worry, this is a normal part of the process. The title and acknowledgements can take years — YEARS — of careful consideration. Believe me. Would I lie to you?)

Let me explain: What you, my lovely reader, need to understand is that the process of writing is highly complex. Do not try this at home! Okay, do it if you want. Really, it's quite fun, if you use the word "fun" loosely to describe something that may not have been that much fun at the beginning but became more fun after you saw your book perched on a shelf in the bookstore and then witnessed someone actually PURCHASING said book. I highly recommend it. It's a lot more fun than, say, "working at the phone company." But I digress. I was explaining the process of book-writing, and far be it from me to wander off topic. After months of careful thought, during which time I did little else, I've deduced that the six stages of book writing are the following:

1. Procrastination
2. Self-loathing re: period of time spent procrastinating
3. Panic
4. Hypochondria — triggered by extra adrenalin formed during Stage 3 Panic and aided by hours spent on the internet analyzing "forgetfulness" and "fatigue"
5. Fatigue
6. Burst of creative energy so overwhelming it occasionally requires years of recovery but has the fringe benefit of producing a voluminous pile of paper that can be turned into a book by a clever publisher, editor, and printer.

Obviously, the most important thing to do to trigger Step 6, the All-Important Step during which actual writing takes place is to:

1. Eat so much you feel sick
2. Complain and moan to everyone who will listen
3. Thank those people in the acknowledgements of your book

So naturally, I have an essay-length thank you letter to write. First of all, I have to thank Clayton Rhodes Stark. See, just as I was typing that sentence, he phoned and said "Go, team, go!" and then hung up. That's what I'm talking about. That's it, exactly. It also helps that he's the Love of My Life (LOML), and I'm wearing a ring the size of your head to prove it. Okay, not the size of your head. (Not that size matters. It really doesn't. Or does it? I'll let you think about that.) In any event, he saved my life and saves it again every single day. Thank you. I love you more than I love my spleen, baby. I swear.

In second place, I clearly have to thank Michelle and Lynn for buying the book WITHOUT EVEN SEEING IT and thus forcing me to turn a random sequence of events that existed only in my own head into something print-worthy. Their blind faith is dizzying. And besides, if they didn't want to print it, there'd be very little point in writing it, would there? It's entirely their fault.

Carolyn, for selling it, natch. And for being the Superagent to the Stars, hand-holder and nurturer who keeps us all going even when we've secretly already given up.

My family, for loving me. And for saying nice things and asking supportive questions that do not always trigger panic attacks, such as "How many pages have you written?" "Isn't that book due soon?" And "How much longer do you think that will take?" I love you all, even though you're all nuts.

You, for buying it. And especially all the people who actually wrote to me and told me that they thought *The Healing Time of Hickeys* was funny and ASKED for a sequel. You asked! Ask and ye shall receive, my loyal friends. (Please ask again, I'd like to write a third.)

The list of loyal listeners (as per usual, you know who you are but I like listing your names because it makes it seem as though I'm an astoundingly popular and well-liked person, with millions of friends scattered about the globe) (when in actuality, I sometimes go weeks on end without leaving the house): Ali, Lisa, Pamela, Melissa,

Melissa, Dani, Heather, Deirdre, Kandi, Nancy, KB, Jennifer, Heather, Karri, Jill, LynnDenise, Meghan, Rebecca, Lyndsey, Marnie, Lela, Carolyn, Aileen, Kim, Tina, Adrien, Jacquelyn and Cate. If I've missed anyone, feel free to punch me in the throat. Well, not literally. (I'd like to actually give Dani a special honorable mention for brazenly sweeping into bookstores and rearranging the shelves at will such that *The Healing Time of Hickeys* is well-placed at eye-level. Now THAT'S friendship.) (And everyone else who has ever rearranged a shelf on my behalf.) (Feel free to do this yourself. If approached by book-store staff, your best bet is to pretend to be an employee. If this doesn't work, I'd recommend running. It's easier than trying to explain.)

Kate and Khen — for the e-mails that got me writing and helped during the endless months of Step 1 (Procrastination). Also, I apologize for not writing lately. I've been busy! Writing this book!

The ghost in my beautiful (albeit temporary) house, for fixing the printer.

Everyone who ever got into one of those tiny boats with me and rowed around the Inner Harbour at 6:00 a.m. in the freezing cold darkness. I loved it, I really did. It's just that I kept getting pneumonia from all those early mornings and cold rains. I'm a wimp. I confess.

The extravaganza of medical websites which contain a plethora of information that has, in turn, saved many a doctor from actually having to talk to me. (This is especially true now that I'm pregnant and having to investigate an array of frightening and bizarre happenstances that I won't tell you about for fear of frightening you.) Let me add that, should you use these sites, it's important to use *credible* sites. For example, look for the words "Harvard" in the credits. Do NOT take medical advice from someone's blog. This is never a good idea. The following sites are, hands down, my favourite, and I owe them a debt of gratitude for the information they provided me in the writing of this book: www.webmd.com; www.mdadvice.com; medline plus; www.adam.com; and www.mayoclinic.com. Thank you, thank you and thank you.

The producers of all TLC programming. Let me explain: procrastination is really no fun if you're just sitting staring at the wall. But sitting and staring at the TV while watching *Makeover Story* and *Trading Spaces*? THAT'S TIME WELL WASTED. I mean, think about it: TWO NEIGHBOURS TRADE HOUSES AND MAKE OVER A ROOM IN EACH OTHER'S HOUSE! It's crazy, great TV. Oh, and while I'm talking about TV, I'd just like to give a shout out to Fox because, damn, that's just good entertainment. UPN! ABC! NBC! CBS! I love you all. Keep making Reality TV and I'll just keep doing what I do best, which is think about writing books while watching Reality TV. And eating Cheetos. You know what's really good? Those snack mixes that contain Cheetos PLUS OTHER FOOD. Eating THAT while watching *America's Next Top Model* can make an otherwise bleak Tuesday into something altogether more amusing.

You know, it's impossible to be unhappy in a world where Munchie Mix is available at the corner store and TV is so outlandishly horrendously fabulous. Think about it. Be happy. Read more books. Watch crappy TV. Laugh more.

Jump off high places, but make sure your feet are attached to that elastic cord. It's not as scary as it looks.

Or so I've heard. I mean, I wouldn't honestly do that myself. That's just crazy.

Try rowing. It's fun. You'll like it, I promise. Just don't forget to bring a change of clothes.

And always, ALWAYS try to keep Steps 2-5 to the least amount of time as possible. Life's too short to hate yourself while imagining your own death from the Bird Flu. Trust me. I mean, that Bird Flu is really rare, right? It's not like I've ever visited a market in Southeast Asia where they sell live chickens. So, logically, my odds of actually contracting such a thing are 1-in- ... well, probably billions really. Just because I happen to have fever, sore throat, and muscle aches. It's just a coincidence. I'm sure of it.

Really.

ABOUT THE AUTHOR

Karen Rivers has published seven previous YA books, including two for teens: the first Halcy Harmony book, *The Healing Time of Hickeys* (Polestar/Raincoast, 2003), shortlisted for the 2003 Canadian Library Association "Young Adult Book of the Year" prize and a Canadian Children's Book Centre selection; and *Surviving Sam* (Polestar/Raincoast, 1998), a finalist for the White Pine Award. She lives in Victoria, British Columbia.